Phonetics

A problem-based introduction to phonetics, with 300+ exercises integrated into the text to help the student discover and practise the subject interactively. It assumes no previous knowledge of the subject and highlights and explains new terms and concepts when they are first introduced. Graded review questions and exercises at the end of every unit help the student monitor their own progress and further practise new skills, and there is frequent cross-referencing for the student to see how the subject fits together, and how later concepts build on earlier ones. The book highlights the differences between speech and writing in Unit 1 and covers all the essential topics of a phonetics course. An accompanying website (www.cambridge.org/knight) features audio samples and answers to selected exercises.

RACHAEL-ANNE KNIGHT is Senior Lecturer in Phonetics in the Department of Language and Communication Science at City University London.

Phonetics:
A coursebook

RACHAEL-ANNE KNIGHT
City University London

CAMBRIDGE UNIVERSITY PRESS
Cambridge, New York, Melbourne, Madrid, Cape Town,
Singapore, São Paulo, Delhi, Tokyo, Mexico City

Cambridge University Press
The Edinburgh Building, Cambridge CB2 8RU, UK

Published in the United States of America by Cambridge University Press, New York

www.cambridge.org
Information on this title: www.cambridge.org/9780521732444

First published 2012

Printed in the United Kingdom at the University Press, Cambridge

A catalogue record for this publication is available from the British Library

ISBN 978-0-521-73244-4 Paperback

Additional resources for this publication at www.cambridge.org/knight

CONTENTS

FIGURES

PREFACE

This book details a fairly traditional view of articulatory phonetics, and some related aspects of phonology. Our focus throughout is on English phonetics, as English is the language of instruction, and the one with which all readers will therefore be familiar. Aspects of general phonetic theory are illustrated using examples from English, and supported by other languages where appropriate. We begin in Section 1 with a concentration on individual speech sounds, think about how sounds combine into words in Section 2, and finish in Section 3 with phenomena that occur when words are combined into longer stretches of speech.

The book is aimed at students with no prior knowledge of phonetics or linguistics; therefore, new terminology is emboldened and explained when it is first introduced. The book is suitable for first-year undergraduates studying subjects such as linguistics or speech and language therapy, and may also be used for revision by more advanced students. It would certainly be possible for students to teach themselves a good deal of phonetics using this coursebook. However, as phonetics is the study of speech, discussion with a tutor, who can demonstrate particular sounds and clarify any variant aspects of pronunciation, is sometimes recommended in the text. The book may also be used in class, with students working through the exercises either before or during contact hours. Whether used alone, with a tutor or in a class, the units should be attempted in order. Each unit builds on the last, and it is assumed that all previous units have been completed at each stage.

The aim of this book is to encourage students to think for themselves in order to discover facts about phonetics. One of my favourite textbooks as a student was Rowntree's *Statistics without Tears: An Introduction for Non-mathematicians*, so I was very happy to be asked to produce something along similar lines for phonetics. The book is formed of a large number of exercises which involve saying words and phrases, transcribing written material or simply thinking about particular issues. Exercises are there for students to discover particular aspects of phonetic content, and not simply to practise what has gone before in the text. This means that all the exercises within a unit should be considered compulsory. Students should attempt each exercise in full before reading the comment section that follows. And, as the comment sections not only give answers to the exercises, but introduce new concepts and terminology, they should also be read in full. At the end of each unit there are review questions and review exercises. These are optional, but allow students to measure their own progress. Answers to the review exercises are found at the back of the book, while answers to the review questions can be checked by looking back through the relevant unit.

As in any textbook, there are a number of aspects that cannot be covered due to space limitations. In particular, this book is confined largely to articulatory rather than acoustic phonetics, because I have found that students seem better able to grasp articulatory aspects first, and then to apply these to acoustics. Likewise, decisions have to be made about how to present certain elements, such as when to introduce slash and square brackets, and whether to use terms such as 'phonemic' or 'broad' transcription. In every such case, I have relied on my teaching experience, and on the advice of my friends and colleagues, in order to present things in the clearest way for beginning students. I hope that this book will stimulate students to enjoy phonetics and go on to further study in this exciting area. To this end, some ideas for further study are suggested in the resources section.

ACKNOWLEDGEMENTS

Any textbook is a synthesis and amalgamation of ideas, and not just the work of the person named on the cover. As such, I am indebted to many previous teachers of phonetics (some of whom are named below), and I would like to make a general acknowledgement of teaching materials and lecture handouts at University College London (UCL) and City University London, which have no doubt influenced several sections of this book. I would also like to acknowledge the resources that I have consulted most frequently while preparing the manuscript. They are Patricia Ashby's *Speech Sounds*, Alan Cruttenden's *Gimson's Pronunciation of English*, David Abercrombie's *Elements of General Phonetics*, John Wells's *Longman Pronunciation Dictionary*, and Trask's *Dictionary of Phonetics and Phonology*. I have also relied on the *Handbook of the International Phonetic Association*, and, in particular, have borrowed examples from the illustrations of Thai, Chinese, Hungarian, Catalan, Hebrew, German, French, Hindi and Swedish. In addition, the *Speech Internet Dictionary* at UCL has been extremely useful.

I would also like to thank the following individuals for helping directly and indirectly over the course of this project.

My teachers at Roehampton University, UCL and Cambridge, for teaching me not only what to present, but how to deliver it so that students feel nurtured, encouraged and inspired to know more. In particular, Judith Broadbent, Ishtla Singh, Sarah Barrett Jones, Jill House, Sarah Hawkins and Francis Nolan.

My colleagues in the phonetics world, particularly those on the Summer Course in English Phonetics in 2004 and 2005, for showing me new ways to teach and explain things. In particular, Jane Setter, Michael and Patricia Ashby, John Maidment, Phil Harrison and John Wells. I suspect you will see echoes of your teaching here, and hope you think I have done it justice.

My colleagues at City University London, for giving me time, space and encouragement to finish this book, even when the going got tough. In particular, Susanna Martin, Madeline Cruice, Lucy Dipper, Chloë Marshall, Lucy Myers and Lia Litosseliti.

My good friend Deborah Anderson, for an amazingly thorough proofreading job, with no complaint, as well as lots of long, encouraging phone calls. And my colleagues Susanna Martin, Rachel Smith and Mark J. Jones, for comments and suggestions. Jill House went beyond the call of duty by commenting on the entire manuscript at quite a late stage, which corrected many of my errors and greatly improved the text. Apologies to you all if I ignored your advice; I am sure I will regret it.

My lovely students, past and present, for all your suggestions, and your openness to trying new things in new ways, even though you did not always feel like it. This book has been written for my future students, taking into account all the things you have taught me along the way.

Richard and the doggies (Poppy, Gonzo, Tyler and Nina), my mum, and my nan, for everything else.

The author gratefully acknowledges the inclusion of excerpts from The One Where Underdog Gets Away in season one of Friends, headlines from the BBC, and the following sources accessed from Project Gutenberg:

Bronte, E. (1850). Wuthering Heights. Project Gutenberg. Retrieved 24 June 2011: www.gutenberg.org/files/768/768-h/768-h.htm

Austen, J. (1813). Pride and Prejudice. Project Gutenberg. Retrieved 24 June 2011: www.gutenberg.org/files/1342/1342-h/1342-h.htm

Conan Doyle, A. (1901–2). The Hound of the Baskervilles. Project Gutenberg, Retrieved 24 June 2011: www.gutenberg.org/files/2852/2852-h/2852-h.htm

1 Sounds and symbols

UNIT 1 THE DIFFERENCE BETWEEN SPEECH AND WRITING

1.1 Key learning areas

In this unit we will:

- discover what phonetics is all about
- explore the relationship between sound and spelling
- find out how to count the number of sounds in a word
- learn how to divide sounds up into vowels and consonants.

1.2 Introduction

When most of us think about language and speech, we tend to think about the way words are written. Because we spend so much time learning to read and spell, and are constantly told how important spelling is, we often focus on spelling rather than on speech or sound.

However, this book is about **phonetics**, the study of speech sounds. This means that throughout this book we will be thinking about the way humans produce speech, and what speech sounds like, rather than the written form of language. We are going to start in this section of the book by thinking about individual sounds, build up to see how sounds vary in words, and, in the final section, look at the things that can happen when words are put together in sentences.

In fact, one of the most important things to do in the study of phonetics is to realise that sound and spelling are very different things. As we will see in this unit, spelling is often a poor guide to a word's pronunciation.

1.3 Writing systems and pronunciation

Different languages use different types of writing. The system of Egyptian hieroglyphics was based on using a picture or symbol (known as an ideogram, pictogram or **logogram**) to represent most words. Logograms look like the object represented, so possible logograms for the words 'book' and 'leg' could be those shown in Figure 1.1. However, logograms *do not* give any clues to the way the word is pronounced (although in the hieroglyphic system other

Figure 1.1 Example logograms for 'book' and 'leg'

symbols did help with pronunciation). Therefore, this type of system (known as a meaning-based or **logographic** system) requires thousands of symbols in order to represent all the words in a language. Most purely logographic systems have now died out, but many Chinese characters are logograms, modified over the years to look quite different now to the objects they represent.

In contrast, sound-based or **alphabetic** writing systems *do* try to represent the pronunciation of each word. However, some languages represent sounds more consistently in their spelling systems than others. In some languages, like Italian, a word's spelling corresponds more or less exactly to its pronunciation. In Italian, the word for book is *libro*, and leg is *gamba*, where all the letters are pronounced with a fairly consistent value (although even here there is not a strict, one-to-one correspondence of sound and letter).

However, this letter-to-sound consistency is less the case in English, as we can see just by looking at the two words we have used above. The <b> in 'book' can be silent in other words like 'debt'; the <oo> makes a different sound in 'food' in most accents; and the <k> can be silent in words like 'knight'. Similarly for 'leg', the <l> can be silent in words like 'calf'; the <e> can make a different sound in words like 'pretty'; and the <g> can make a different sound in words like 'George'. Because the English language has been influenced by many other languages throughout its history, and because all languages change over time, the English spelling system is not always a good guide to pronunciation. Of course, English words usually give a fair indication of at least part of a word's pronunciation, which is why we can read aloud words that are new to us, but there are also many inconsistencies, which we will now investigate.

Note that angled brackets < > surround letters; we will look at more types of brackets as we work through the book.

1.3.1 Many sounds to one letter

Exercise 1.1 Let us have a look at the following list of words. Focus on the letter <c> in each one. What sound does the <c> represent in each word?

face cherub control duck much city

Remember not to read on to the 'comment' section below until you have completed the exercise in full.

Comment In 'face' and 'city' the <c> represents a sound like that at the start of 'sun'. In 'duck' and 'control' it represents a different sound, like that at the start of 'kitchen'. In 'cherub' and 'much' it is joined by <h> to make yet a third sound, like that at the start and end of 'church'. The same letter can therefore represent different sounds in different words.

1.3.2 Many letters to one sound

Exercise 1.2 Now let us think about the opposite situation: how one sound can be represented by several different letters or combinations of letters.

a) Think about the sound made by the word 'I' (the pronoun referring to 'me').
b) Now think of several other words containing the same sound as the word 'I', and see how that sound is spelt in each case.

Tip You may want to think first about words that rhyme with 'I' to get you started.

Comment Words might include 'pie', 'cry', 'nine', 'high', 'buy', 'Tyne'. Note that they are all spelt differently from 'I', even though they contain the same sound. In particular, the word 'eye' sounds identical to 'I', but is spelt differently.

So, we have seen that one complication of English spelling is that sounds and letters do not have a one-to-one correspondence. The same letter can represent different sounds, and the same sound can be represented by many different letters, and letter combinations, in different words.

1.3.3 Silent and double letters

Many English words also include silent letters in their spelling, as we suggested above. Words like 'knight' have a silent <k> and start with the same sound as 'Nan', rather than with the same sound as 'king'. Words like 'psychology' and 'pterodactyl' have a silent <p> at the start, and many other letters can be silent. In addition, many English words contain double letters, and we will now think about how these are pronounced.

Exercise 1.3 Let us think about the following words that contain double letters. Say each of the words below. When you come to the part of each word represented by the double letters, listen carefully and work out if you hear two of the same sound. You may like to practise this with someone else and try to work out what you hear.

letter summer winner apple rubber offer

Comment In each case, the double letter only corresponds to one sound within the word (double letters can actually affect the way the previous vowel is pronounced, but this is not important to the current point). Again, we can see that there is no direct match between spelling and sound.

1.4 Letters and sounds

One of the key skills for a **phonetician** (a person who knows about and uses phonetics) is to divide a word into its individual sounds, which are also referred to as **segments**. Speech is a continuous and dynamic process, but, for convenience, we can think about splitting it up into smaller sections consisting of individual sounds. This is rather similar to dividing up a movie into a number of still images or snapshots.

Think about the words 'dog' and 'cat'. Each of these contains three letters and also three sounds or segments.

The sounds into which each word can be divided are as follows:

'dog': d as in 'doughnut', o as in 'off', and g as in 'goat'.
'cat': c as in 'camel', a as in 'and', and t as in 'table'.

As we have just seen in the previous section, however, spelling can be misleading, as there is not always a simple match between sounds and letters.

Exercise 1.4 Each of the words below contains three letters, but how many *sounds* are there in each word?

Take each word and try to break it down into the smallest parts possible, then count how many parts there are. Remember that we are thinking about the way the word sounds, not how it is spelt.

lie the eye owe emu fox pit try

Tip It may help to cover up each word as you work on it, so that you are not distracted by the spelling.

Comment 'Owe' and 'eye' both have only one sound. You may disagree, as you can feel your mouth moving somewhat, but these words do only contain one sound, as we will discuss in Unit 6. 'Lie' and 'the' both have two sounds; 'pit' and 'try' have three. 'Emu' has four for some speakers, but three if you do not pronounce a sound like that at the start of 'yogurt' after the 'm' sound. 'Fox' also has four sounds, as the <x> letter represents two sounds: a sound like that at the start of 'kite', followed by one like that at the start of 'socks'. In fact, if we think about the sounds at the *end* of 'fox' and 'socks', we can hear they are the same, even though the spelling is different.

Exercise 1.5 Now let us look at these words. First of all, count the letters, and then try to work out how many sounds each word contains.

tough bud ex- beige cup love ox buff

Comment Hopefully, you have found that all these words contain three sounds, despite containing between two and five letters. For example, the <gh> at the end of 'tough' represents only a single sound, as does <ff> at the end of 'buff'. <e> at the end of 'love' does not represent a sound at all, as demonstrated by the popular spelling <luv> that we use all the time in texts and emails.

As we can see, the number of written letters in a word does not always tell us how many sounds a word contains. Therefore, when thinking about phonetics, it will be very important not to think about the spelling of a word when we want to think about its sounds.

We have seen in the previous exercises that spelling and sound are separate. In fact, we can think of them as two separate levels for analysis. The technical term for the level of spelling is the **orthographic** level. The technical name for the sound level is the **phonetic** or **phonemic** level. We will discuss the difference between phonetic and phonemic much later on in this book.

1.4.1 Homographs and homophones

Another example of how the orthographic (spelling) and sound levels are separate comes from the existence of homographs and homophones.

Homographs are words that sound different but are spelt the same. For example, 'polish' may mean 'furniture polish' or refer to a person or thing that comes from Poland. These homographs are used to great effect in an episode of *One Foot in the Grave*, a BBC sitcom from the 1990s: Victor spends a long time looking for sherry from Poland because Margaret has not left enough space between 'polish' (meaning furniture polish) and 'sherry' on the shopping list. Of course, this could not have happened if she had read the list out, as the two meanings of 'polish' sound different.

Homophones, on the other hand, are words that sound the same but are spelt differently. For example 'dough' and 'doe', and 'cue' and 'queue' are homophones for all English speakers. There are other cases, however, where a person's accent will determine whether a pair of words are homophones or not, as we will see in Exercise 1.6.

It can sometimes be difficult to remember the meanings of homophone and homograph, and sometimes students get them confused, but knowing the origins of these words can help. Homo- comes from the Greek, meaning 'the same' (as in homogeneous), and we will use it for another term later on in this book. 'graph' is also from the Greek, meaning 'writing' (as in autograph), as is 'phone', which means 'sound' (as in telephone and phonetics). So words that are homographs have the same writing (spelling), and words that are homophones have the same sound.

Exercise 1.6 As we have said above, some words may not be homophones in all accents. Let us see if the following pairs of words are homophones for you (that is, do you pronounce them the same?). It would also be useful for you to ask a friend from a different part of the country or the world for their opinion.

1	luck	look
2	witch	which
3	Shaw	shore
4	cot	caught
5	sun	son

Comment

1. For most speakers of Southern English, the first pair does not sound the same. 'Luck' is pronounced with the same vowel as 'strut', while 'look' has the same vowel as 'foot'. For most speakers of Northern English, both will be pronounced with the same vowel as 'foot', so they are homophones. However, speakers from certain parts of the north, such as Lancashire, may pronounce 'look' with the same vowel as 'goose', and 'luck' with the same vowel as 'foot' so they are not homophones.
2. The second pair will be homophones for most speakers, although Scottish and Irish speakers may produce the first sounds differently, with the first sound of 'which' having a more whistling or hissing quality.
3. The third pair will be the same for many speakers, but many North American speakers, as well as those from Scotland, Ireland or the West Country, will produce an 'r' sound at the end of the second word.
4. The fourth pair will sound different for most speakers of British English, but may be homophones for speakers of Scottish English or some varieties of North American English.
5. The fifth pair will be pronounced the same for the majority of speakers, regardless of their accent.

1.5 Accents

Later on in this book, in Unit 14, we will be discussing regional accents in a bit more detail. However, it is important to say at this point that the way a person pronounces a word will vary according to where they were born, grew up and live, as well as their 'social class'. Their age may also be an important factor, as might the situation in which they are speaking. This book will work most often with an accent of English known as **Standard Southern British English** (SSBE). This is the pronunciation used by many people on television and radio, and by many university lecturers and teachers. It is basically the pronunciation of fairly educated speakers in the South East of England. It is not quite the pronunciation used by the British royal family, or by those who have attended a public school. We will refer to that pronunciation, which is used by around 3 per cent of the population of England, as **Received Pronunciation** (RP).

Many people will find that their pronunciation is similar to SSBE in many respects. However, we must also recognise that not everyone speaks SSBE, so exercises and examples will try to comment on accent variation where possible.

It is also crucial to point out that this book does not recommend any particular pronunciation or accent. The aim of this book, and of phonetics in general, is to describe what occurs in any accent, rather than to prescribe what *should* occur. SSBE is used as a convenient reference, as it is the accent with which the majority of the English-speaking population are familiar (at least through television and radio), and the accent to which many non-native learners aspire.

1.6 Introduction to transcription – consonants and vowels

One of the key skills of a phonetician is **transcription**. As we have seen, spelling cannot tell us unambiguously how a word should be pronounced. Transcription, therefore, provides us with a shared system of symbols that only ever refer to one sound and that allow us to write down pronunciation clearly and consistently. We will begin to look at these symbols in the next unit. For now, let us start to do some transcription by thinking about a major division in speech sounds: vowels versus consonants. Again, it is important not to think about spelling, as the terms 'consonant' and 'vowel' mean something different when we are discussing spoken language. In spelling, for example, we use twenty-one consonants, but in spoken English we use around twenty-four depending on our accent. Likewise, in spelling we use five vowels, but in spoken English we use around twenty.

We will consider the differences between consonants and vowels in detail in later units. In brief, though, spoken **consonants** are sounds made with a lot of constriction in the mouth, so that the air coming up from the lungs gets squashed. Consonant sounds also tend to occur at the start and end of syllables – for example, like those at the beginning and end of the words 'dog', 'cat', 'pen' and 'tub'. **Vowels**, on the other hand, are sounds made with the mouth quite open, and they occur in the middle of syllables. For example, the sounds in the middle of the words in the previous list are all vowels. Vowels can also occur in isolation: the words 'eye', 'are' (for SSBE speakers) and 'owe' all consist of single vowel sounds, without any consonants surrounding them.

1.7 CV structures

We can begin to think about transcription by noting down the sounds in a word as either C for consonant or V for vowel. For example, 'dog', 'cat', 'pen' and 'tub' can all be represented as CVC, since they start and end with a consonant and have a vowel in the middle. Words like 'eye', 'are' and 'owe', in contrast, are all represented as V, since they only contain one vowel sound.

Exercise 1.7 What are the CV structures of the following words? It may help you to try to count the sounds in each word first, and to remember not to think about the spelling.

glass think hatch flute robber ring

Comment 'Glass' is CCVC, as the double letter <s> represents only one sound. 'Think' is CVCC, as the <th> letters represent a single sound. 'Flute' is CCVC, as the <e> at the end is silent (and tells us only to make the <u> a long sound). 'Hatch' is CVC, as <tch> at the end of the word represents only a single sound. 'Ring' is either CVC or CVCC, depending on your regional accent. Most English accents do not pronounce the <g> at the end of 'ring', but accents of Birmingham and surrounding areas may do. Finally, 'robber' is either CVCV or CVCVC. The double <b> only represents one sound, but accents vary as to whether they pronounce the final <r>, as we will explore now.

1.8 Rhotic and non-rhotic accents

Some speakers pronounce an 'r' sound at the end of words like 'robber' (as in the previous exercise), and some speakers do not. This is largely down to the speaker's regional accent. Speakers who do pronounce an 'r' in this position are called **rhotic** speakers, and will always pronounce an <r> whenever it occurs in the spelling of a word. Others will only pronounce an 'r' sound when the letter <r> occurs at the beginning or in the middle of a word, that is, in front of a vowel. These speakers are referred to as **non-rhotic** speakers. People who come from the West Country in England, Ireland, Scotland and parts of the United States are likely to be rhotic, whereas those from Australia, London and the South East, and northern parts of England are likely to be non-rhotic – thus SSBE is non-rhotic.

Exercise 1.8 It would be useful to take some time now to think about whether you pronounce an 'r' sound in words like 'car'. This can be confusing, as the spelling suggests that there *must* be an 'r' sound. However, consider if your tongue stays still after the vowel. If it does, then you speak with a non-rhotic accent; if it does not, and you raise the tip or middle of your tongue, then you speak with a rhotic accent.

Comment Rhoticity will be mentioned at several points in the book, as it is one of the major divisions between accents of English. If you are unsure about whether you speak with a rhotic accent or not, it would be useful to ask a phonetics teacher to help you decide.

1.8.1 The history and status of 'r'

In past times, all speakers in England would have been rhotic and would have pronounced an 'r' at the end of words like 'robber' and 'car', and it is this pronunciation that was taken to America on the *Mayflower*. However, the rhotic pronunciation was subsequently lost in most of England, and therefore did not travel to Australia with the colonists.

Now the pronunciation of 'r' at the end of words is sometimes a matter for social comment. People in the UK often focus on this feature in West Country speech, and associate rhotic pronunciations with people who have traditional country professions, such as farming. The situation in North America is rather different, as it can be seen as prestigious to speak with a rhotic accent, the opposite situation to that in the UK. This disparity demonstrates that there is nothing inherently prestigious or otherwise about a particular pronunciation; it is the views of the speech community that give a sound or accent its status. The 'r' sound, in particular, has a very interesting history in English (and in other languages) that we will touch on at various points throughout this book.

1.9 More CV structures

Exercise 1.9 The following words are longer than those in Exercise 1.7. Try to produce CV structures for them.

Jupiter haricot television elephant necessary

Comment 'Jupiter' is CVCVCV for non-rhotic speakers or CVCVCVC for rhotic speakers. 'Haricot' is CVCVCV, as the final <t> is silent. 'Television' is CVCVCVCVC, as the two vowels <io> represent a single sound. An alternative pronunciation for 'television' is or CVCVCVCC. Speakers vary as to whether they produce a vowel before the final sound in words such as 'television' and 'puddle'. If there is no vowel, then the final sound is referred to as syllabic. We will return to this idea later, when we think about syllabic consonants (in Unit 8), but for now either answer is fine. 'Elephant' is VCVCVCC, as the <ph> represents only one sound. However, as for 'television', some speakers may not produce a vowel between the <ph> and the <n>, making the structure VCVCCC. 'Necessary' is CVCVCVCV, as the double <s> only represents one sound.

You may have noticed that often C and V sounds alternate, and this is a common pattern in most of the world's languages. In fact, nearly all languages have words that are either CV or CVCV in structure. In addition, CV is often the pattern that young children (in most languages) produce first, as we see if we look at a child's typical first words (mummy, daddy, doggy, and so on). However, (adult) English is relatively unusual in the languages of the world because it allows several consonants to occur together in a cluster, so we can have structures like CCVCC, as we will explore further in Unit 8.

Exercise 1.10 Let us decide which of the following words start with a spoken vowel and which with a consonant. We need to remember that just because a word starts with a *written* consonant or vowel, this does not necessarily mean it starts with a *spoken* consonant or vowel.

honour unicorn horse yellow ewe umbrella weather

Comment 'Honour' and 'umbrella' start with vowels; the rest begin with consonants. Sounds like those at the start of 'yellow' and 'weather' may feel a bit like vowels because the mouth is quite open. As we will see later, they are pronounced very much like vowels, but we will continue to call them consonants because they occur at the same place in the syllable as other consonants (at the start and end), as we will explore later in Unit 8. It may be hard to feel any restriction in airflow for the first sound in 'horse', because the restriction occurs in the throat, rather than in the mouth, as we will see in Unit 3.

1.10 Summary

In this unit we have looked at the differences between spoken and written languages, and seen that the English writing system does not have a one-to-one relationship between spelling and sound. We have learnt to count the sounds in words, and seen a basic distinction between spoken vowels and consonants, based on the openness of the mouth.

1.11 Looking forward

Next we can move on to describing consonants and learning some symbols for the transcription of Standard Southern British English.

1.12 Review questions

Have a look at these questions to see if you have understood the main points to learn from this unit. If you cannot answer them, please read back through this unit, where you will be able to find the answers.

- What is phonetics?
- Why do we say that sound and spelling are different levels of analysis?
- How do we define spoken consonants and vowels?

1.13 Review exercises

If you would like more practice in counting sounds and deciding if they are vowels or consonants, then have a go at the following exercises. The answers to these can be found at the back of the book (page 261).

1 Divide the following list of words into those containing two, three and four sounds.

hand case door gold list four mail loan hay ball high disk

2 Compare the words on the left to the CV structures on the right and find the mistakes in each, assuming a non-rhotic accent.

think	CCVCC
union	VCVVC
finch	CVCCC
summit	CVCCVC
five	CVCV
metre	CVCCV
knave	CCVC

3 Match the CV structures on the left to the words on the right, assuming a non-rhotic pronunciation. There should be only one match for each.

CVC	eulogy
CVCC	music
CCVCVC	trumpet
CVCV	catches
CCCVCC	cover
CCVCCVC	thought
CVCVC	stripes
CVCVCV	bank

UNIT 2 CONSONANT VOICING

2.1 Key learning areas

In this unit we will:

- see that voicing (or the lack of voicing) is one of the key features referring to consonants
- explore how the vocal folds are relevant for voicing
- learn the symbols used for the transcription of Standard Southern British English consonants.

2.2 Introduction

In the last unit we discussed the division of speech sounds into vowels and consonants. We decided that vowels are sounds produced with the mouth quite open and that consonants are produced with a more closed mouth. We also saw that vowels occur in the middle of syllables, while consonants occur around the edges. Our aim in this unit, as well as in the next two units, is to think about three principal components of consonants. We will describe their voicing in this unit and then look at their place and manner of articulation in the following two units, before moving on to vowels.

2.3 Speech production

Exercise 2.1 To start with, let us have a think about how humans produce speech.

a) Which parts of our body do you think are involved in the process of making speech sounds?
b) How can we make different sounds?

Comment
a) You have probably mentioned parts of the mouth (tongue, lips and teeth) and possibly internal organs, such as the lungs and the brain.
b) You may also have noted that different sounds are produced by altering the position of the mouth, ideas that we will now explore in detail.

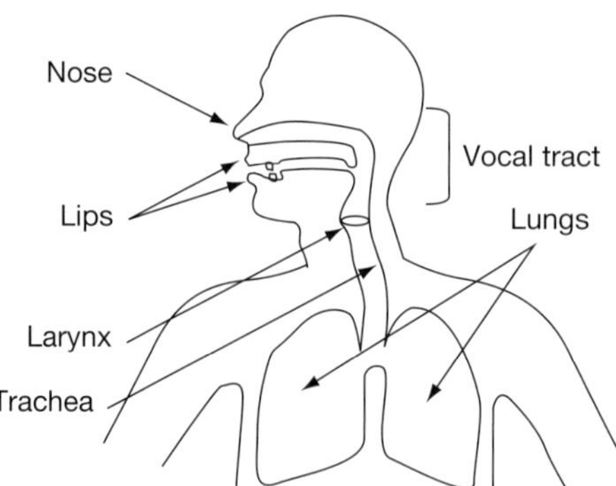

Figure 2.1 Some parts of the body used to produce speech

There are a large number of body parts involved in speaking. Aside from anything else, we need our brain to plan words and sentences and to send appropriate signals to the rest of our body. However, the activity of the brain is beyond the scope of this book and we will not consider it further here. Instead, we will focus on the parts of the body between the lips and nose and the lungs. These body parts are labelled in Figure 2.1, and we will look at the other, non-labelled, structures in more detail shortly.

2.3.1 The necessity of air

It will become clear as we work through this book that air is required in order to produce any speech sound. We hear sound when some medium (usually air) is set into vibration. Even the sounds of ringing crystal glasses or music played through an MP3 player involve air set into vibration. Sound then travels as waves through the air until it reaches our eardrums, where the vibrations are passed to the inner ear and are eventually turned into electronic signals, which are sent to our brains.

Sound can travel through other media too, but will travel at different speeds than if it is travelling though air. This is why things sound different when you put your head under water, where sound can travel more quickly than in air. It is also why, in westerns, you sometimes see people listen for horses' hooves by putting their ears to the ground. As sound travels more quickly through solids, the sound of hooves will be heard in the earth before it is heard in the air. Thus, sound needs a material to travel through and for that material to be set into vibration. In speech, we usually set air into vibration.

In producing most speech sounds, including all the sounds used regularly in English, the air we use comes from the lungs. This air travels up from the lungs, passing through the **trachea** (windpipe), until it reaches the larynx, where it might be set into vibration. The **larynx** is commonly known as the voice box, and the front of the larynx is the protrusion that can be felt in the front of the neck, which is called the Adam's apple in men. The air passes through the larynx into the **vocal tract**, which is the air passages of the head and neck.

What happens in the vocal tract will be the focus of the following three units. Our major concern in this unit is with what happens at the level of the **vocal folds**, which lie inside the larynx. In order to imagine where the vocal folds are, it is helpful to imagine that a person has had their head chopped off and you are looking down into their neck. From above, you might then be able to see the vocal folds as two strings of tissue arranged in a V-shape, with the point of the V at the front.

2.3.2 Vibration of the vocal folds

The vocal folds do not stay in the same position all the time. A person can either keep the vocal folds wide apart (known as keeping them **abducted**), as happens during normal breathing, or shut them completely (known as keeping them **adducted**), as happens when coughing. When they are shut, they block the flow of air from the lungs, as happens when we hold our breath. During speech, the folds can either be kept far apart, as in Figure 2.2, or they can be narrowed, as shown in Figure 2.3, so that they vibrate when air from the lungs passes through them. As we said above, sound is produced when air is made to vibrate, and the

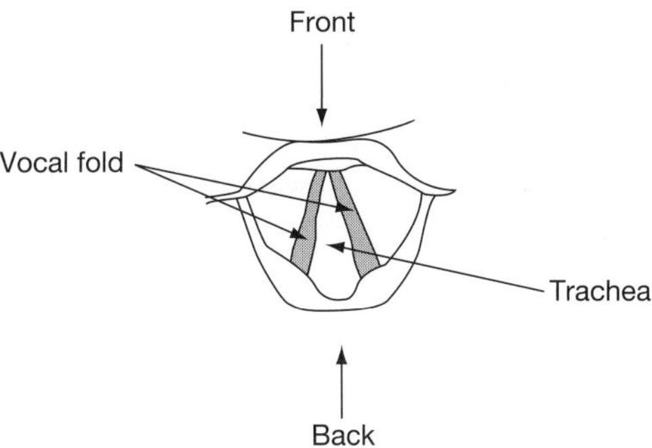

Figure 2.2 The vocal folds abducted

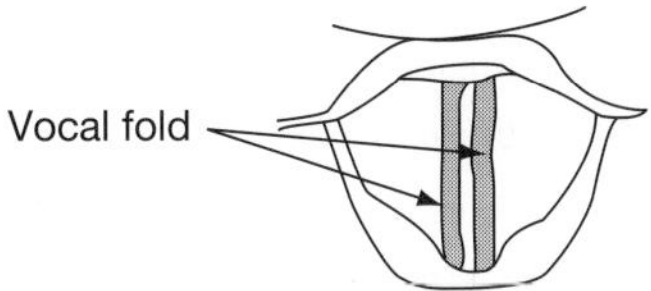

Figure 2.3 The vocal folds narrowed

vibration of the vocal folds is one of the major ways in which we make our speech audible.

It is important to understand that the speaker does not use muscles to open and close the folds for every cycle of the vibration. Instead, muscles are used to narrow them by just the right amount, so that aerodynamic constraints take over and they vibrate in the airstream from the lungs (if you are interested in acoustic phonetics, you may be familiar with the term 'Bernoulli effect', which describes how this happens).

2.4 Voiced and voiceless sounds

In the most basic terms, a sound produced while the vocal folds are vibrating is called a **voiced** sound. A sound produced while the folds are not vibrating is called a **voiceless** sound. All vowels are voiced, as we will see later in this book, but consonants can be either voiced or voiceless. Voiceless sounds usually have the vocal folds wide apart, or, for a few sounds, they may be tightly closed.

There are various ways to tell if sounds are voiced or voiceless. The first is to feel the larynx with the fingers while producing a sound. Vibrations can be felt quite easily for some voiced sounds. A second way is to cover your ears while producing a sound and see if you can hear a buzz, which indicates that vocal fold vibration (voicing) is present.

Exercise 2.2

a) In the pairs below, one word starts with a voiced consonant and the other with a voiceless consonant. Think about the initial consonants of each word. Say them out loud and try to work out if they are voiced (with vocal fold vibration) or voiceless (with no vibration).
zip / sip
fault / vault
coven / govern
dense / tense

Tip

Remember to isolate the consonant rather than trying to say the whole word, and remember to say the sounds out loud. If you whisper, this will not work, as whispering never produces vocal fold vibration.

b) Were some of these pairs easier to work out than others? Why do you think that might be?

Comment

a) The words beginning with voiced consonants are 'zip', 'vault', 'govern' and 'dense'.
b) The first two pairs tend to be easier to work out, partly because the consonant sounds are longer, giving you more time to focus on whether or

not you feel vibrations. We will talk more about this in Unit 4; we will also see other reasons why some sounds are harder to categorise than others when we start to think about allophones of voicing in Unit 9.

2.5 Symbols for English consonants

As we mentioned in the last unit, phoneticians have an array of special symbols with which they can write down, or transcribe, the pronunciation of words and sounds.

These are the symbols for the voiceless consonants of SSBE, with an example word to show where each sound occurs.

- /p/ as in pig
- /f/ as in fun
- /θ/ as in theory
- /s/ as in soon
- /ʃ/ as in ship
- /t/ as in tank
- /k/ as in kind
- /h/ as in home
- /tʃ/ as in cherub

And these are the symbols for the voiced consonants.

- /b/ as in bent
- /v/ as in vole
- /ð/ as in they
- /z/ as in Zen
- /ʒ/ as in pleasure
- /d/ as in dale
- /g/ as in grind
- /m/ as in mail
- /n/ as in nail
- /ŋ/ as in sang
- /dʒ/ as in June
- /l/ as in lull
- /r/ as in red
- /j/ as in yogurt
- /w/ as in went

Exercise 2.3 Let us have a look at the symbols above for voiced and voiceless consonants. Try to work out:

a) which ones look familiar and seem to represent the right sound
b) which ones look like they should represent a different sound
c) which ones look unfamiliar – that is, not like letters of the English alphabet
d) which letters of the alphabet are missing
e) why they all have / / round them.

Comment a) These symbols are all part of the **International Phonetic Alphabet (IPA)**, which aims to provide a separate symbol for every meaningful sound in every language of the world. The alphabet has been through many incarnations since the nineteenth century. Many of the symbols will be familiar to you (probably /p f s t k h b v z d g m n l r w/), and seem to represent the same sound as in English spelling. This is because many of the authors of the alphabet were European and drew on symbols used in the spelling of their native languages. Other symbols, however, were added when needed.

b) The most confusing consonant symbol for English speakers is probably /j/. We are used to this symbol being used in spelling to represent the sound at the start of 'July' and 'Judy'. However, in many other languages 'j' is used to represent a sound like that at the start of 'young', which is also its IPA usage.

c) The unfamiliar symbols are probably /θ ʃ tʃ ð ʒ ŋ tʃ/ and /dʒ/. /ð/ was an Old English character call 'eth'. /ʒ/ was a character called yogh, and represents a different sound to /z/, even though some people write the *letter* <z> using this symbol. /θ/ is Greek, known as theta. /ŋ/, sometimes known as 'eng', and /ʃ/, known as 'esh' were used by Pitman in an alphabet that was a precursor to the IPA. /tʃ/ and /dʒ/ are both combinations of other symbols, for reasons that will become clear in Unit 4.

d) You might expect to see symbols like /c/ and /q/. These symbols do not represent any English sounds, but we will meet them later when we talk about other languages. As we saw in the previous unit, the *letter* <c> can represent a number of sounds. Sounds normally written as <c> can be transcribed with /k/ in words like 'can' and /s/ in words like 'ice'. <qu>, as in 'queen', is transcribed as /kw/.

e) Slash brackets round the symbols are used to tell us that the symbols represent sounds, just as <> is used to indicate letters. It is important, therefore, that we always include brackets to indicate whether we are notating sounds or spelling.

Exercise 2.4 Look at the bold consonants in each word below.

many fea**th**er **ch**eck ba**t** nee**d**

a) Work out whether they are voiced or voiceless.
b) Work out which symbol is used to represent them in transcription.

Tip To complete the exercises, remember to isolate the consonants from the rest of the word that is, just say the consonant on its own.

Comment a) and b) 'Many' starts with /m/, which is voiced. 'Feather' has a voiced /ð/ in the middle. 'Check' starts with /tʃ/, which is voiceless. 'Bat' ends with voiceless /t/, and 'need' ends with voiced /d/.

Exercise 2.5 You are now ready to begin transcribing! Of course, we have only introduced the symbols for the consonants, so just use V in place of any vowel sounds for now. All the following are breeds of dog, and the words get longer and harder as you go along.

pug afghan terrier rottweiler chihuahua

Tip You may want to work out a CV structure first, and, as always, do not be fooled by the spelling.

Comment 'pug' is /pVg/, an easy one to start with. 'Afghan' is /VfgVn/. 'Terrier' is /tVrVVr/ for rhotic speakers and without the final /r/ for non-rhotic speakers. Do not be thrown by the double <r> in the spelling. 'Rottweiler' is a tricky one. Firstly, the double <t> only represents one /t/ sound. Secondly, some people pronounce the <w> as /w/ and some as /v/ (because this word is a German place name). Also, there is the issue of rhoticity. Rhotic speakers will produce a final /r/, whereas non-rhotic speakers will not. Any of the following are acceptable: /rVtvVlV/, /rVtwVlV/, /rVtvVlVr/, /rVtwVlVr/. 'Chihuahua' is a great illustration of the contrast between sound and spelling. Because this dog breed is named after a Mexican state, it is rather different to most English words. /tʃVwVwV/ would probably be a good transcription for most speakers.

2.6 The importance of the voicing parameter

As we go through the book, we will see that we need to understand voicing for a variety of reasons. To begin with, we will look at some typical examples of child speech that illustrate the importance of voicing.

Exercise 2.6 The transcriptions below are an example of how a young child learning SSBE might produce words.

Orthography	Adult target	Child's version
'dog'	/dVg/	/dVk/
'bird'	/bVd/	/bVt/
'cat'	/kVt/	/kVt/

Have a look at the words above.

a) Which sounds does the child produce correctly and which are incorrect?
b) Can the child produce both voiced and voiceless sounds?
c) Is the child more accurate at the start or end of words?
d) How might we describe the patterns present in the child's speech?

Comment a) /b/, /k/ and /t/ are always produced correctly. /g/ is pronounced incorrectly. /d/ is correct on one occasion, but not on the other.
b) The child shows evidence of producing both voiced (/d b/) and voiceless (/k t/) sounds.
c) The child only makes mistakes at the ends of words.
d) At the end of words, the child can only produce voiceless sounds. This is a process known as **word final devoicing.** It is common in young children as their language develops. Interestingly, some languages never allow word-final voiced consonants. Dutch, for example, has identical production for pairs such as *hard* ('hard') and *hart* ('heart'), both with a final /t/.

Exercise 2.7 Knowledge of voicing can also help us when we are learning to transcribe. In written language we add an <s> to most nouns when we want to pluralise them. Therefore, 'rat' becomes 'rats' and 'ram' becomes 'rams'. However, things are not quite so simple in spoken language.

Think about 'rats' and 'rams'. If you make the final sound really long in each case, you should be able to hear that they are different. Listen to the sound and feel your larynx. What do you notice?

Comment You should be able to hear and feel that the two sounds are different. If you feel your larynx, you will feel that the sound at the end of 'rats' is a voiceless /s/, whereas the one at the end of 'rams' is a voiced /z/. In fact, when a noun ends in a voiceless sound, like the /t/ in 'rat', we pluralise it with voiceless /s/; and when it ends in a voiced sound, like the /m/ in 'ram', we pluralise it with voiced /z/. (However, you will find this does not quite work for words ending in sounds like /ʃ/, for reasons we will discover in Unit 4.) A similar thing happens with possessives too, as you will see if you compare the sound made by the <s> in 'Jack's' and 'John's'. Do take care, though, to remember that this rule only works for **suffixes** (endings that we add to words, such as plurals and possessives). It is perfectly possible to have /s/ following a voiced sound when such endings are not involved, such as in the word 'false' /fVls/.

2.7 Summary

In this unit we have see that some consonants are voiced, with vocal fold vibration, and that some are voiceless, without such vibration. We have also learnt the symbols for transcribing SSBE consonants.

2.8 Looking forward

In the next unit we can move on to another feature of consonants (place of articulation) and begin to introduce sounds from other languages.

2.9 Review questions

Have a look at the following questions to see if you have understood the main points to be learnt from this unit.

- How do humans produce speech sounds?
- Where are the vocal folds found?
- What is the difference between voiced and voiceless sounds?
- Copy the flash cards at the back of the book. Find an example word for each symbol and then add this and 'voiced' or 'voiceless' to the back of each card.

2.10 Review exercises

If you would like to do more work with voicing and transcription, have a go at the exercises below.

1 The following are all English names for places. Divide the list into words that start with voiceless or voiced sounds.

London Glasgow Cardiff Dublin Belfast

2 Divide the following words into those pluralised with an /s/ and those pluralised with /z/. You might find it useful to transcribe them first.

hat cap fad bag back cliff heath sieve

3 Match the transcription on the right to the words on the left. SSBE pronunciation is used, and there should only be one match for each.

hid	/bVθ/
kitty	/bVðə/
hit	/kVtV/
foal	/kVtVn/
vole	/hVt/
both	/hVd/
kitten	/fVl/
bother	/vVl/

UNIT 3 CONSONANT PLACE OF ARTICULATION

3.1 Key learning areas

In this unit we will:

- see how place of articulation (POA) is an important feature of consonants
- learn the names of the articulators
- investigate the role of passive and active articulators.

3.2 Introduction

So far we have focussed our attention on consonants and have decided that these sounds are produced with more restriction to airflow than vowels. We have also learnt that one of the main ways in which consonants differ from one another is in terms of their voicing – that is, in terms of whether the vocal folds are vibrating or not. In this unit we are going to think about another feature of consonants: place of articulation (POA).

3.3 Articulators

Exercise 3.1 Produce the words 'May' and 'December' and focus on the initial sound in each word. Think about which parts of your mouth move when you make each sound. Be careful to focus only on the /m/ and the /d/. You will just make it hard for yourself if you try to focus on the whole word at this stage.

Which parts of the mouth can you feel moving? Are the parts of the mouth that are moving the same for /m/ and /d/, or different?

Tip For this exercise it may help you to use a mirror, or to work with a friend, so that you can look at each other while you produce sounds.

Comment You will probably have noticed that the lips move for /m/ and that the tip of the tongue moves for /d/.

In the previous unit we saw that the vocal tract refers to all the passageways above the larynx through which air can flow when we produce speech. An **articulator** is the name given to a part of the vocal tract that can be used to form a constriction. When we describe consonant production and **place of**

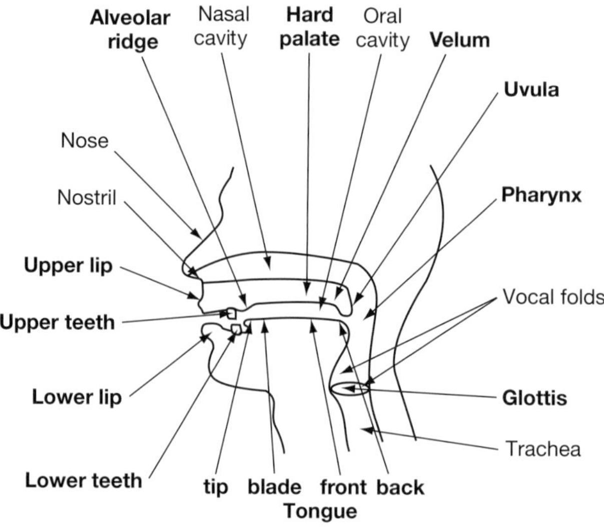

Figure 3.1 The vocal tract

articulation in phonetics, we think about the place in the vocal tract where there is maximum constriction to airflow. There are always two articulators involved in making this maximum constriction. For /m/, the articulators are the two lips; for /d/, the articulators are the tip of the tongue and the roof of the mouth.

The articulators themselves are named using a special set of terminology. As in most disciplines, we use special names for things that we need to talk about often and with a high degree of precision.

Figure 3.1 shows the vocal tract in more detail. The names of the articulators are shown in bold.

Many of the articulators will be familiar to you. For example, the lips and teeth are parts of our anatomy that we are all familiar with. Some of the other names may be less familiar. The alveolar ridge, for example, is not a term most people come across before they study phonetics. However, the **alveolar ridge** can be identified easily as the prominent ridge of hard bone behind the upper teeth, which you can feel with your tongue. The **palate** is the hard, bony surface further back than the alveolar ridge, and the **velum** is the soft palate, which is even further back in the mouth. The **uvula** is the piece of flesh that hangs down from the back of the velum and can be seen if you open your mouth and look in the mirror. We have already met the vocal folds in the previous unit. They can vibrate to produce voicing, as we have seen, or they can be used to restrict the airflow and act as a place of articulation. The space between the vocal folds is called the **glottis**.

The **tongue** is also an articulator and is involved in the production of the majority of the sounds present in English and other languages. However, in order to be precise when we talk about articulation, we need to label parts of the tongue separately. The tip, blade, front and back of the tongue can all be labelled individually.

You will note that there are also names for the cavities of the vocal tract, namely the **oral cavity** and the **nasal cavity**. These two are joined together, and joined to the space above the larynx by another space called the **pharynx**, at the back of the mouth.

Exercise 3.2
a) Look in the mirror and try to identify the articulators shown in Figure 3.1. Which can and can not be seen in the mirror?
b) Use your tongue to feel the articulators along the upper surface of the mouth. Start with the upper lip and run your tongue back along the roof of the mouth. How far back can you go?

Comment
a) The uvula is probably as far back as can be seen in the mirror. The larynx and vocal folds are inside the body and cannot be seen or felt with the tongue.
b) The articulators that can be felt with the tongue vary from person to person. Most people will be able to use the tongue tip to feel the lips, teeth, alveolar ridge and hard palate. Depending on the flexibility of the tongue, you may also be able to feel the velum. The uvula cannot usually be reached by the tongue, and is responsible for our gag reflex – for example, if it is touched by a toothbrush.

3.3.1 Active and passive articulators

As we have said previously, when we produce consonants we constrict air, which is usually flowing up from the lungs. To form a constriction we use two articulators. In the majority of cases, only one articulator moves and this is called the **active articulator**. The articulator that it moves towards is called the **passive articulator**.

In the examples that we have looked at already, we can identify active and passive articulators. In /m/ the active articulator is the bottom lip, because it moves, whereas the passive articulator is the top lip, which the bottom lip moves towards. For /d/ the active articulator is the tip of the tongue; the passive articulator is the alveolar ridge.

Exercise 3.3 Think about the sounds at the start of the words below. Remember to isolate them from the rest of the word. Say them slowly and try to work out which is the active and passive articulator for each one. As with the previous exercise, it may help to look in a mirror.

car tank van lorry bike

Comment It is worth noting that this is quite a difficult exercise to do. We are not used to thinking about how we speak or introspecting about our own vocal organs. However, this will get easier with practice. Have a look at the answers below and then go back to the exercise to see if you can relate the answers to your own articulation.

The /k/ in 'car' is formed by the back of the tongue (active) moving towards the velum (passive). /t/ in 'tank' and /l/ in 'lorry' are both formed in the same place as /d/, with an active tongue tip and a passive alveolar ridge. /v/ in 'van' is formed when the bottom lip approaches the top teeth. /b/ in 'bike' is formed in the same place as /m/, when the bottom lip approaches the top one.

3.4 Places of articulation

Now that we know which articulators are involved in producing sounds, we have another set of labels to learn. As mentioned above, when we refer to the place of articulation of consonants, we are describing the place in the vocal tract where there is the most constriction of airflow. The place of articulation is normally named after the passive articulator. So, a sound formed with the tip of the tongue approaching the alveolar ridge is said to have an alveolar place of articulation. /t/, /d/ and /l/, for example, all have the alveolar ridge as the passive articulator, so are said to have an alveolar place of articulation.

Below are the names of the places of articulation that are used for consonants in SSBE. They are ordered from the front of the vocal tract towards the back.

POA	Active articulator	Passive articulator
Bilabial	Bottom lip	Top lip
Labiodental	Bottom lip	Top teeth
Dental	Tongue tip	Upper front teeth
Alveolar	Tongue tip	Alveolar ridge
Postalveolar	Tongue tip or blade	Region behind the alveolar ridge
Palatal	Tongue front	Hard palate
Velar	Tongue back	Velum
Glottal	Vocal folds	None (the vocal folds move towards each other)

Exercise 3.4 The sounds below are all formed at different places of articulation.

a) First of all, identify each sound from its symbol and produce it between vowel sounds (e.g. 'ah' /f/ 'ah').
b) Then try to work out which sound is produced at which place of articulation.

/h/ /p/ /v/ /ʃ/ /j/ /g/ /θ/ /n/

Comment a) Again, this is quite a difficult exercise to complete as we are not used to thinking about the position of our articulators. Look at the answers below and then return to the exercise to see if you can understand why the answers are as they are.
b) /h/ is glottal, which is why you cannot feel any constriction in the vocal tract above the larynx. /p/ and /v/ are fairly easily identified as bilabial and labiodental, respectively, especially if you use a mirror. /ʃ/ is postalveolar, /j/ is palatal, /g/ is velar, /θ/ is dental and /n/ is alveolar.

Below is a list of all the consonants of SSBE (with one exception), ordered by their POA, extending from the front to the back of the vocal tract.

Bilabial	/p/ /b/ /m/
Labiodental	/f/ /v/
Dental	/θ/ /ð/
Alveolar	/t/ /d/ /n/ /s/ /z/ /l/
Postalveolar	/ʃ/ /ʒ/ /tʃ/ /dʒ/ /r/
Palatal	/j/
Velar	/k/ /g/ /ŋ/
Glottal	/h/

3.4.1 /w/: a special case

You might have noticed that /w/ does not appear in the list above. This is because, unlike the other consonants listed, /w/ has two equally important places of articulation. If you look in the mirror, or at someone else saying /w/, you will definitely see some lip movement, which you might think would make the place of articulation bilabial. However, we know from techniques like ultrasound, which allow us to see inside the mouth during speech, that the tongue also moves when we produce /w/. The tongue moves in such a way that air is constricted between the back of the tongue and the velum. Importantly, the constrictions at the lips and at the velum are equal in degree. If we took one away, the sound would no longer be /w/. So we say that /w/ has a **labial-velar** place of articulation. /w/ is an example of a **double articulation** because it is produced with equal constriction of airflow at two places in the vocal tract.

Exercise 3.5 Work your way through the list of SSBE sounds above, putting each consonant between 'ah' vowels. Concentrate on your articulators and see if you are convinced that the POA is as given above.

Comment In general, consonants do not vary a great deal between speakers, or even different accents, of English. We will return to accents in later units, but for now you should check any difficulties with a teacher, if possible.

There are also a couple of other English sounds you need to know about that we have not yet covered.

3.4.2 Other English consonants

These sounds have not yet been covered for two reasons. Firstly, neither sound makes a meaning difference in the English language – that is, it occurs as a version of other sounds without affecting a word's meaning. Secondly, especially for the second sound, they are not used by all speakers. We will return to these sounds in future units too, where these ideas will become clearer.

The first sound we need to think about is often referred to as a **glottal stop**, which is symbolised as [ʔ] in the IPA. This sound is very common in English, and tends to occur as a version of /t/ in certain environments, depending on a person's accent. In some accents of English, [ʔ] can occur as a version of /t/ only at the ends of words – for example, many speakers of SSBE might pronounce 'cat' as [kVʔ]. For other accents of English, [ʔ] can also occur in the middle of words. Speakers of Cockney and Glaswegian English, for example, might pronounce 'water' as [wVʔV] (with a final /r/ for Glaswegian, as it is a rhotic accent), but this pronunciation would be unlikely for an RP speaker. When a speaker uses [ʔ], it is sometimes said that they are they are 'dropping their 't's'. In reality, they are just using another version of /t/; /t/ has not been deleted, but pronounced in a different way, as a glottal stop. Thus, a term for this phenomenon is **glottal replacement**, or glottalling.

The place of articulation for [ʔ] is glottal, as the name glottal stop suggests, so the major constriction of air when this sound is produced is made by the vocal folds. The second part of the name, stop, means that the air is restricted completely. We will return to this idea in the next unit, on manner of articulation. As the vocal folds are pressed tightly together for the glottal stop, they are not able to vibrate at the same time, so this sound is voiceless.

Another sound that it is important to know about is [ʋ]. This sound has a labiodental place of articulation as the air is constricted most by the bottom lip approaching the top teeth. [ʋ] is often referred to as a labiodental /r/, because some speakers of English use [ʋ] as a version of /r/ – for example, at the start of words like 'rabbit' and 'rhubarb'. Most speakers produce /r/ by constricting the air between the tip of the tongue and the postalveolar region, which is why we have described /r/ as postalveolar above. If we want to symbolise this precise articulation we can use [ɹ]. But an increasing number of speakers are starting to use [ʋ] in places where other speakers use [ɹ].

[ʋ] may well be familiar to you. People quite often notice if speakers use this sound as a version of /r/, and might describe the phenomenon as 'not being able to say your 'r's'. For example, some celebrities, such as Jonathan Ross, Paul Merton and Bill Oddie, use [ʋ] for /r/. However, note that [ʋ] is not the same as /w/, which has a labial-velar POA. This is a confusion that has been perpetuated in the media (for example, Jonathan Ross calls himself 'wossy' on Twitter), presumably because <w> is the closest way to represent the sound of a labiodental /r/ using spelling.

Labiodental /r/ has been in the English language for hundreds of years. However, over the last thirty years or so, more and more speakers have started to use it. Its use does not seem to be related to any particular accent, but does tend to be related to age, with more younger speakers favouring it. I use a labiodental /r/ when I speak, and generally find that about 10 to 15 per cent of my students do too.

Exercise 3.6 In this exercise you will concentrate on your own speech to work out what type of /r/ you use and when you use glottal stops.

a) First of all, try this familiar tongue-twister: 'Round and round the rugged rock the ragged rascal ran'. As you can see, there are lots of /r/s in this sentence. Your job is to think about which articulators you are using to constrict the air when you produce your /r/ sounds. Are you using your bottom lip to approach your top teeth and therefore using [ʋ], or is the tip or back of your tongue approaching the roof of your mouth behind your alveolar ridge to produce [ɹ]? You can look in a mirror if this helps. You can also make a very long extended /r/ sound at the start of these words.

b) Now, think about where you would use a glottal stop. It is extremely unlikely that you do not use any at all! Does it sound okay for you to use a glottal stop at the end of words like 'hit' and 'met' in phrases such as 'she hit Sarah' and 'she met Sarah'? What about in the middle of words like 'butter' or 'little'?

Comment a) For the /r/ sounds, be careful not to confuse lip-rounding with labiodental place of articulation. Many speakers who produce /r/ as [ɹ], using their tongue and a postalveolar place of articulation, also protrude their lips slightly during this sound. For speakers who use labiodental [ʋ], the lip shape looks rather different (and more like that for /v/ and /f/), as only the bottom lip moves and it approaches the top teeth rather than protruding.

b) The likelihood is that you will use glottal stops at least some of the time. When you use them can depend on your accent and age, who you are talking to and even the situation you are in. So, it is possible that you might use glottal stops in the middle of words on some occasions and not others. Keep this in mind and listen to yourself and others for the next few days, to see how many you hear.

One final comment is that it is absolutely fine to use any of the variants we have just discussed. Variation is one of the most interesting aspects of the study of phonetics, and it is certainly not the case that some variants are correct and others are wrong. Have a listen to the speech of people around you, on TV and on the radio, and think about the types of variation you observe. We will return to types of variation and reasons for variation in Unit 14.

3.5 Brackets

You know by now that spelling is enclosed in angled brackets <> and that speech sounds are shown in slash brackets, such as /p/ or /t/. However, you will also have noticed that [ʔ], [ɹ] and [ʋ] are shown in square brackets. Both slash and square brackets mean that we are referring to sounds rather than letters, and that we are giving a transcription rather than using spelling. The difference between slash and square brackets also gives us some extra information, however. We will cover this in more detail in later units, but will address it briefly now.

When we put a sound in slash brackets we are indicating that the sound makes a meaningful difference in the language. We can determine that it makes a meaningful difference by swapping it for another sound. For example, if we take the word 'lit' and change the /t/ for a /p/, we get the word 'lip'. This word means something different and indicates that /p/ and /t/ make a meaning difference in English. However, if we swap /t/ in 'lit' for [ʔ], we can hear the difference in sound, but there is no meaning difference. Likewise, swapping [ɹ] for [ʋ] – for example, in the word 'rose' – will not make a meaning difference, even though you can hear a difference in articulation and sound. So, if we are only transcribing meaningful sounds, we use slash brackets. However, if we want to be more precise about the way those sounds are produced, we can use square brackets. For example, we can say that /r/ can be produced as either [ɹ] for [ʋ].

So, in simple terms, meaningful sounds go in slash brackets and variants of sounds go in square brackets. Do not worry if this distinction is confusing at the moment, as we will go into much more detail later on, particularly in Units 9 and 13.

3.6 The importance of place of articulation

The terms for place of articulation are important, as they let us describe and compare different types of sound. That is partly what we did above when we talked about whether people use a postalveolar or labiodental place of articulation when they produce /r/, for example. We can make the same kind of comparison when we talk about the speech of children, or the speech that speech and language therapists hear in the clinic.

Exercise 3.7 Here are some transcriptions of speech produced by 'Katy', who is three years old.

Orthography	Adult	Katy
cap		/tVp/
Meg		/mVd/
ring		/rVn/

a) First of all, write in the transcription of the adult pronunciation (assuming SSBE and using V for the vowels).
b) Then compare the adult pronunciation to Katy's pronunciation.
c) Can you find a pattern that describes the difference between Katy's pronunciations and those of an adult?
d) Thinking about the pattern you have identified, how would Katy pronounce 'king'?

Comment a) For SSBE adults, 'cap' is /kVp/, 'Meg' is /mVg/ and 'ring' is /rVŋ/.
b) and c) Where the adult uses a velar, Katy uses an alveolar. This is a pattern called **fronting**, in which sounds are replaced with ones that have a place of articulation further towards the front of the mouth. It is common in young children until the age of around three and a half years.
d) Katy would likely produce 'king' as /tVn/, fronting both the velars to an alveolar place of articulation. Thus, she may be difficult to understand, as 'king' and 'tin' will be pronounced in the same way.

3.7 Non-SSBE places of articulation

So far we have concentrated on the place of articulation of consonant sounds in SSBE. This is not because SSBE is particularly exciting or special, but because it is the variety that all readers of this book will probably be familiar with. Although English has consonants produced at quite a range of places of articulation, there are some other places of articulation that are not represented in Standard Southern British English. Below are some examples of sounds taken from the *Handbook of the International Phonetic Association*, which gives phonetic illustrations for many languages. If you know a speaker of the language referred to, you could ask them to produce these words for you.

3.7.1 Alveolo-palatal

These sounds are produced with a constriction between the blade of the tongue and the alveolar ridge and the palatal region. Such sounds occur in Swedish (at the start of the word *kjol*, meaning 'skirt'), for example. They are symbolised as [ɕ] and [ʑ].

3.7.2 Retroflex

Retroflex sounds are produced with a constriction between the tongue tip and the portion of the roof of the mouth where the alveolar ridge meets the hard palate. Retroflex sounds are different to alveolars, or postalveolars, however, in that the tip of the tongue is curled back so that the underneath of the tongue forms the constriction. These sounds are common in languages of South Asia, and are also one of the most noticeable features of Indian accented English. In Hindi, for example, the first sounds in the words for 'postpone' (/ʈɑl/) and 'branch' (/ɖɑl/) are both retroflexes. We have not yet introduced vowels, but the /ɑ/ sound in these words is rather like the English vowel in 'car'.

3.7.3 Uvular

Uvular sounds are produced by forming a constriction between the back of the tongue and the uvula. You may be familiar with the r-like sounds in French (starting the word *roue* meaning 'wheel') and some varieties of German (starting the word *Rasse*, meaning 'race'), which are produced with a uvular place of articulation. There are lots of different uvular sounds, symbolised, for example, [q ɢ ʀ ʁ χ].

3.7.4 Pharyngeal

Pharyngeal sounds are produced by constricting air, either between the walls of the pharynx or between the back of the tongue and the back wall of the pharynx. These sounds are found, for example, in 'Oriental' Hebrew, such as in the middle of the word /maˈħar/, meaning 'tomorrow', where /a/ is somewhat like the vowel sound in the English word 'cat'.

3.8 Summary

In this unit we have seen that consonants differ in place of articulation, which relates to the place of maximum constriction in the vocal tract. We have also learnt the names for the articulators.

3.9 Looking forward

In the next unit we will see that the degree of airflow constriction is important for our third and final consonant feature: manner of articulation.

3.10 Review questions

Have a look at these questions to see if you have understood the main points to be learnt from this unit.

- How would you define place of articulation?
- What are all the places of articulation used in SSBE?
- What is the difference between a passive and an active articulator?
- Add POA to each of the flash cards that you copied and started to fill in at the end of the last unit.

3.11 Review exercises

1 Match the symbols on the left with the places of articulation on the right. There will only be one match for each one.

/p/ postalveolar
/z/ labiodental
/f/ palatal
/ð/ velar
/tʃ/ alveolar
[ʔ] dental
/j/ bilabial
/ŋ/ glottal

2 For each set of sounds below, please find the odd one out. Note that you will need to be careful, as the odd one out may be different from the others in terms of either voicing or place of articulation.

a) /t/ /d/ /p/ /n/

b) /s/ /z/ /θ/ /k/

c) /b/ /v/ /dʒ/ /f/

d) /p/ /tʃ/ /r/ /dʒ/

3 For each section below, find appropriate words according to the instructions you are given.

a) Find words that rhyme with 'can', but which start with bilabials. There should be three.

b) Find words that are like 'make', except that they finish with an alveolar sound in place of /k/. There should be six. Remember to keep the vowel the same and not to think about spelling.

c) Find words where the first two sounds are exactly like those in 'tut', but which end with a velar sound instead of the final /t/. There should be three.

UNIT 4 CONSONANT MANNER OF ARTICULATION

4.1 Key learning areas

In this unit we will:

- see how manner of articulation (MOA) is another key feature of consonants
- investigate how MOA refers to the way air flows in the vocal tract
- identify the different manners of articulation that occur in English and other languages.

4.2 Introduction

We have seen that consonants can be described and distinguished by their voicing and by their place of articulation. In this unit we will look at the third feature of consonants, manner of articulation (MOA).

4.3 A third feature of articulation

Exercise 4.1 Think about the following sets of consonants. First of all, label them according to their voicing and place of articulation. Secondly, decide if the consonants in each set sound the same or different.

a) /d/ /n/ /l/
b) /ʒ/ /dʒ/ /r/
c) /g/ /ŋ/
d) /b/ /m/

Comment You should have labelled all the consonants as voiced. In set (a) they are all alveolar; in set (b) they are all postalveolar; in set (c) they are both velar; and in set (d) they are bilabial. If this exercise was difficult, you should return to the previous units in order to learn the labels more thoroughly. You will also have realised that the sounds in each set do not sound the same.

Because the consonants in each set share the same voicing and POA, but sound different, this indicates that there must be at least one more feature of consonants that distinguishes these sounds. This third important feature of consonants is **manner of articulation**. This feature refers to how the air flows in the vocal tract. As we know, different sounds are produced by moving different articulators. We learnt in the last unit that place of articulation (POA) refers to the place in the vocal tract where there is the greatest constriction to airflow. However, the *degree* to which the air is constricted is not the same for all consonants. So POA refers to the place of maximum constriction, but that maximum constriction may be more or less, depending on the consonant in question. Manner of articulation is, in part therefore, concerned with the **degree of stricture** in the vocal tract, which refers to how close the articulators get when a sound is formed. For example, they may touch and form a firm seal, or approach each other with a small gap for air to escape.

4.4 Manner diagrams

One of the ways we can represent how the articulators move, and different degrees of structure, is through manner diagrams, like the one in Figure 4.1. In these diagrams, a line is drawn to represent each articulator, and time is shown from left to right. In Figure 4.1, the lines indicate that one of the articulators stays still, while the other one approaches it, touches it for some time, and then moves away again.

Exercise 4.2 In Figure 4.1, which line do you think represents the active articulator and which represents the passive articulator?

Comment As you will hopefully remember from the previous unit, the active articulator is the one that moves, while the passive articulator is the one the active articulator moves towards. So, in Figure 4.1, the top line is the passive articulator and the bottom line is the active articulator. For example, the diagram might represent the sound /t/, where the tongue approaches the alveolar ridge, touches it briefly and then moves away again. In all the manner diagrams in this unit, the top line represents the static passive articulator, while the bottom line shows the movement of the active articulator.

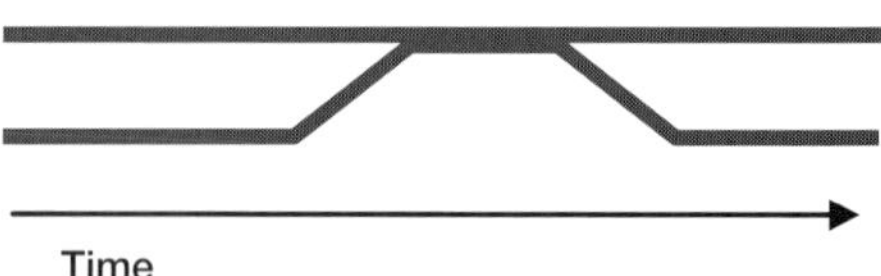

Figure 4.1 An example manner diagram

Figure 4.2 Manner diagram for a plosive

4.5 Manners of articulation used in English

As in previous units, we will start by thinking about the different manners of articulation used in SSBE. For each one, we will describe the way the articulators interact, look at a diagram, and think about which sounds in English are produced with this manner of articulation.

It is important, for each class of manner of articulation, to experiment with producing the sounds and establish if you can relate your own articulation to that described.

4.5.1 Plosive

Plosive sounds in English are /p b t d k g/ and [ʔ]. These are actually the sounds that are represented by the example manner diagram in Figure 4.1, shown again in Figure 4.2.

Three stages are represented. To begin with, the articulators are in their resting position, as if a person were breathing normally. Then, if we imagine the articulation for /p/, for example, the bottom lip approaches the top lip. This is called the **approach** phase of a plosive. The bottom lip continues to approach the top lip until they touch. While they are touching, the air from the lungs cannot escape and pressure builds up behind the closed lips. This part of the sequence is termed the **hold** phase. You may also hear plosives called **oral stops**, as the air in the oral cavity is stopped completely. Then the bottom lip moves away from the top lip, and air escapes rapidly, with the slight popping sound characteristic of plosives. This is called the **release** phase. If produced between vowels, for example, we can say that the plosive has **wide oral release**, as the active articulator moves far away from the passive articulator in the release phase. The same sequence occurs for all the other plosives, but, of course, different active and passive articulators are involved. You may wish to try to describe the articulation of an alveolar or velar plosive.

4.5.2 Fricative

Fricative sounds in English are /f v θ ð s z ʃ ʒ/.

Exercise 4.3 Try producing the English fricative sounds listed above. Hold each one for a while, and concentrate on what you can hear. Do the sounds have anything in common?

Comment Fricatives are characterised by the hissing sound that can be heard when they are produced, and this is hopefully what you will have heard when practising with the sounds above.

The hissing heard in fricatives comes about because the air from the lungs is escaping through a small gap. The air becomes choppy and turbulent, and hissing is heard. So, when a fricative is produced, the articulators come close together, but not so close that they touch (see Figure 4.3). We call this **narrow approximation**. The small gap through which the air escapes causes the hissing noise, just as a small gap in a window can let in a draught, which you might hear as a whistling noise. It is important to note that the articulators may be touching at the sides of the mouth, and you can probably feel this if you practise with a fricative such as /s/ or /f/. There is, however, enough of a gap for air to escape in the centre of your mouth, and this is where the turbulence occurs.

4.5.3 Approximant and lateral approximant

Approximant sounds in English are /w j l/ and /r/, including both [ɹ] and [ʋ]. Approximant sounds are rather like vowels in some ways. They are produced with little constriction in the vocal tract, so that air passage is not restricted, as shown in Figure 4.4. They are formed when the articulators are positioned in **wide approximation**, so that the gap between them is not narrow enough to cause friction. If you go back to our gap in the window example, it might help you to think about the difference between fricatives and approximants. When a window is wide open, air can pass in and out freely and does not make a noise. We only hear the air when it is squeezed through a small gap and becomes turbulent. So the open window is like an approximant, and the window letting in a draught is like a fricative. Obviously the analogy is not perfect, because approximants are audible. However, they are audible because of the vibration of the vocal folds (as if someone were playing a banjo outside the window), and not because noise is produced in the mouth.

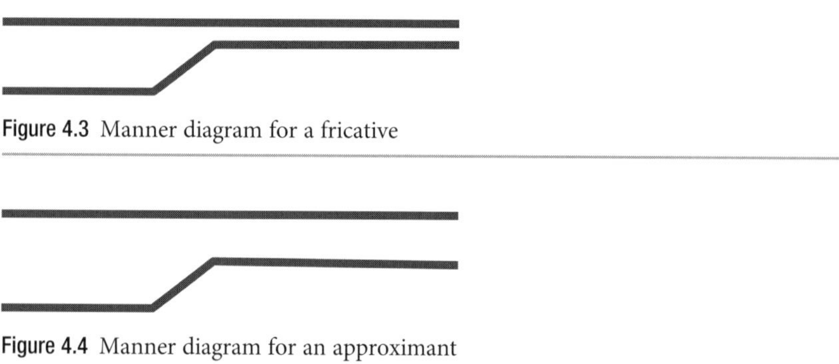

Figure 4.3 Manner diagram for a fricative

Figure 4.4 Manner diagram for an approximant

Exercise 4.4 In this exercise we will be trying to demonstrate the different types of airflow for approximants in English.

First of all, put your articulators in the position for /w/. Try to hold them in this position, but do not try to speak or add any voicing. Now, keeping your articulators in the same place, breathe in strongly for a few seconds and try to concentrate on where you feel cold air in your mouth. Do the same for /j/ and /r/, and finally for /l/.

Where do you feel cold air in your mouth? Is it on the sides of your tongue or in the middle? Is it the same for all four sounds?

Comment For /l/, it is likely that you felt cold air on the sides of your tongue, while you would have felt it in the middle of your tongue for the other sounds. If you are a labiodental /r/ user, you will probably have felt air in the middle of your lower lip, as well as in the middle of your tongue.

This experiment demonstrates that /l/ is produced a little differently to the other approximants. For /w j r / (including both [ɹ] and [ʋ] versions of /r/), there is an obstruction at the sides of the mouth, which you can feel if you produce these sounds and hold them for a time. Recall that the articulators are in wide approximation, and here this refers to what is happening in the **midline** of the mouth. To identify the midline, it can help to imagine a line going from between your top front teeth back to the uvula, dividing the mouth into the left and right sides. For /l/, the *obstruction* is in the midline, and when you produce this sound you can feel the tip of your tongue resting on the alveolar ridge. The *sides* of the tongue, however, are lowered and in wide approximation to the palate. So this type of sound is called a **lateral approximant**. Lateral means 'side', and the label indicates that the airflow is around the sides of the tongue. All other approximants in English have airflow down the midline of the tongue and are called median approximants, or simply approximants.

4.5.4 Affricate

Exercise 4.5 To understand how an affricate is formed, try the following. Produce a /t/ sound, followed very quickly by a /ʃ/ sound. What English sound do you hear? It will not be identical to an English sound, but will sound very close to one. Try the same with /d/ followed by /ʒ/. The symbols will give you a clue too.

Comment The first sounds like /tʃ/, the sound at the start and end of 'church', while the second sounds like /dʒ/, the sound at the start and end of 'judge'. These are the only two affricates in English.

Figure 4.5 Manner diagram for an affricate

From Exercise 4.5 you will have identified that affricate sounds have elements of plosives and elements of fricatives. In fact, the approach and hold phase of an affricate is very similar to that of a plosive, in that the articulators approach and touch, blocking the flow of air completely. It is in the release phase that there is a difference between plosives and affricates. As you will remember, for a plosive, the articulators part rapidly and air bursts out from between them as they move into wide approximation. For an affricate, the articulators only part narrowly, so that air escapes slowly, becoming turbulent and making a hissing sound like a fricative.

4.5.5 Nasal

Exercise 4.6 Finally, we will investigate the nasal manner of articulation. Try producing the following nasal sounds, with and without holding your nose: /ŋ/ /m/ /n/. Do they sound different when you are holding your nose? Does this make them sound like any other English sounds? Which ones?

Comment The nasal sounds will have sounded a bit like the voiced plosives at the same place of articulation. So /ŋ/ sounds somewhat like /g/, /m/ like /b/ and /n/ like /d/. This is because the articulation of nasals and plosives is similar in many respects.

When producing a nasal sound, the actions in the oral cavity are the same as for a plosive at the same place of articulation. So, to produce an /n/ sound, the tongue tip approaches the alveolar ridge, touches it, and then moves away again, as it does for /d/. The vocal folds vibrate throughout. However, we know that /d/ and /n/ do not sound identical. The reason for this is the position of the velum.

We have already met the velum as a passive articulator, and the place of articulation for /k g ŋ/. However, the velum can also move up and down. When it is raised, it seals off the nasal cavity so that air cannot escape through the nose, as shown in part 1 of Figure 4.6. This is known as **velic closure**. When the velum is lowered, air *can* escape through the nose, as shown in part 2 of Figure 4.6. The effect of a lowered velum when producing a nasal is that the air does not build up behind the closed articulators. It cannot pass them, but, as the velum is lowered, the air can and does escape through the nose. As we will see shortly, the position of the velum is also a crucial factor when describing other sounds.

The crucial difference between a nasal and a plosive is that the velum is lowered for a nasal, as shown in part 3 of Figure 4.6, and raised for a plosive, yet

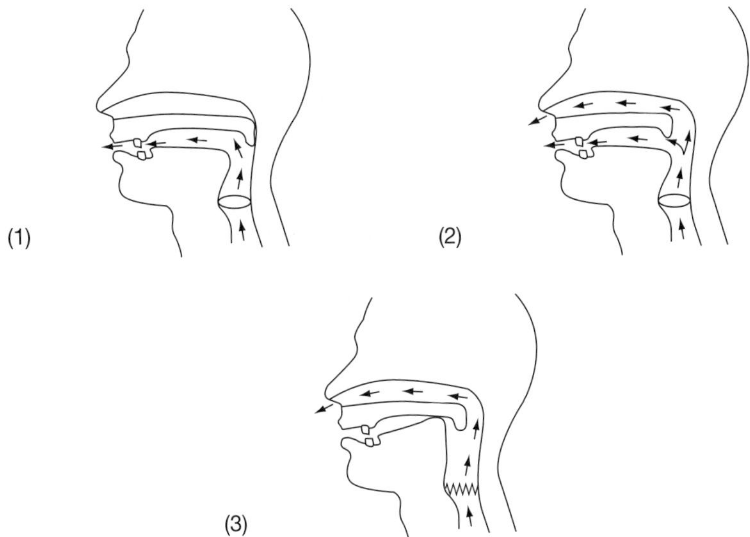

Figure 4.6 Mid-sagittal sections showing (1) oral airflow, (2) oral and nasal airflow, (3) nasal airflow

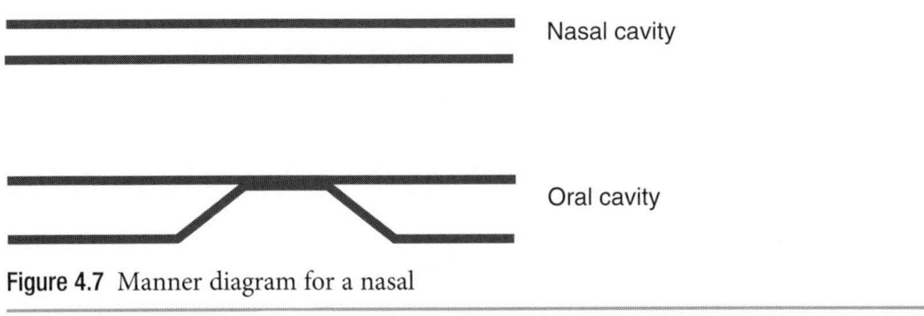

Figure 4.7 Manner diagram for a nasal

they both have a complete blockage to air in the oral cavity. This means that, in nasal sounds, air can make its way to the nasal cavity, where it vibrates with a characteristic sound. You may also hear nasals called **nasal stops**, as the air in the oral cavity is stopped completely, even though it can escape through the nose. Thus, manner of articulation is not just about degree of stricture, but also about whether air flows into the nasal cavity.

Exercise 4.7 We are generally not aware of the movement of our velum. However, it is possible to make it easier to feel this movement. If you put your tongue on your alveolar ridge and keep it there and then silently and rapidly switch back and forth between /d/ and /n/, you may be able to feel your velum moving.

Comment It can be quite difficult to feel the movement of the velum, but keep practising this exercise, making sure that everything else in the vocal tract, such as the position of the tongue, stays the same. You can then move on to /g/ and /ŋ/, and /b/ and /m/, and try the same thing with these pairs.

It is important to learn what each MOA label means in terms of articulation. It is also important to learn which sounds are produced with which manner of articulation. This will make life much easier for you as you learn more phonetics, as later on we will use these labels freely, without further explanation, and it will be easier for you to follow if you have learnt them already.

Exercise 4.8 For each of the sounds below, you should now be in a position to give all three labels: voice, place and manner.

Symbol	Voice	Place	Manner
/j/			
/m/			
/f/			
/tʃ/			
/ð/			
/k/			
/l/			
/w/			

Comment

Symbol	Voice	Place	Manner
/j/	+	palatal	approximant
/m/	+	bilabial	nasal
/f/	–	labiodental	fricative
/tʃ/	–	postalveolar	affricate
/ð/	+	dental	fricative
/k/	–	velar	plosive
/l/	+	alveolar	lateral approximant
/w/	+	labial-velar	approximant

In the table above, '+' indicates that a sound is voiced, and '–' that it is voiceless. A full list of labels for SSBE consonants in given in Appendix 2 (page 282), for easy reference.

4.6 Larger manner classes

We have now learnt the manner labels for the consonants of SSBE. However, there are also two larger manner classes into which we can group sounds and the labels we have learnt. **Obstruent** sounds are those sounds that involve some kind of pressure change and noise in their production. They include plosives, affricates and fricatives. For these sounds, the velum must be raised – that is, there must be velic closure – since otherwise pressure cannot build up because air simply escapes through the nasal cavity. Obstruents can be voiced or voiceless. We said in Unit 2 that vocal fold vibration is one way that we can make sound audible. Another way is to create noise within the oral cavity, and all obstruents contain some such noise, either from the release of plosives or from the friction present in fricatives and affricates. Because of the pressure build-up, voiceless sounds will be audible due to the noise created, whereas voiced obstruents contain both noise due to pressure and audible vocal fold vibrations.

Sonorant sounds, on the other hand, do not involve changes in pressure or the production of noise. They can be produced with either a raised or lowered velum, and are always voiced or they would not be audible (recall that no noise is produced in the oral cavity, as we saw in the case of approximants). For nasals, the velum is always lowered. For median and lateral approximants, the velum can be raised or lowered, and in English this is dependent on the surrounding sounds, a fact we will revisit in Unit 11. Note that we can also classify vowels as sonorants.

Exercise 4.9 For each set, decide whether the consonants are obstruents or sonorants.

a) /t ʒ tʃ/
b) /r w j l/
c) /m ŋ n/

Tip It is best to do this by identifying the MOA first, and then remembering which sounds fall into which class.

Comment The sounds in (a) are obstruents, as they are plosives, fricatives and affricates. Those in (b) are sonorants, as they are median and lateral approximants. Those in (c) are also sonorants, as they are all nasals.

4.7 The importance of the manner feature

As for the other consonant features we have identified, MOA allows us to think about the similarities and differences between sounds. This can be helpful when comparing different languages or accents, the same language at different stages of development (a two-year-old, and a four-year-old, for example), or the speech produced by a person with a speech disorder.

Exercise 4.10 a) Look at the following transcriptions, which are representative of the speech of a young child. Transcribe the adult target (assuming SSBE) and then compare the adult and child versions. What do you notice about the child's pronunciation?

Word	**Child**	**Adult**
fish	/fVt/	
juice	/dVt/	

b) How do you think the child will pronounce 'shoe' and 'Sue'? Is the child's pronunciation of these words likely to cause any confusion?

Comment a) The adult pronunciations are /fVʃ/ and /dʒVs/. In common with many young children, this child is replacing fricative and affricate sounds with a plosive at the nearest POA. This is likely to be because less precise control over the articulators is required for plosives than for these other sounds. This process is often called **stopping**, as sounds are replaced with oral stops.

b) Stopping can lead to ambiguity when the child speaks, as many different words might be pronounced in the same way. For example, the child in the exercise above will probably pronounce both 'shoe' and 'Sue' as /tV/. Of course context will usually help listeners understand the child's meaning, and stopping typically ceases after the age of around 4 years.

In Unit 2 we discovered that the voicing of plurals depends on the voicing of the final sound of a noun. We looked at examples like 'ram', where the voiced final sound triggers the plural to be /z/, and other examples like 'rat', where the voiceless final sound triggers the plural to be /s/. We also noted that there was an additional complication for some sounds like /ʃ/, which is the focus of our next exercise.

Exercise 4.11 Look at the following words. How are they pluralised? Can you see any common features between these words that might explain why these plurals work differently to the ones we have already investigated?

watch brush bus fez wedge

Comment All these words would be pluralised with a vowel and /z/ – that is, /Vz/. You may have noticed that the sounds at the end of these words are all fricatives and affricates. However, it is only *certain* fricatives and affricates that trigger these particular plurals, namely /s z ʃ ʒ tʃ dʒ/. These sounds have very high-frequency energy, and are sometimes known as **sibilants**. In contrast, nouns ending with the (non-sibilant) fricatives /f v θ ð/ simply take /s/ or /z/ as a plural, depending on whether the final sound is voiced or voiceless (as in 'myths', for example).

4.8 Manners of articulation not found in SSBE

The manners we have dealt with so far are those found in SSBE. And, in fact, English has a large number of all possible manners represented. There are a few manners, however, that are not represented in SSBE, but are found in other languages throughout the world.

4.8.1 Trill

Trills are probably familiar to many people, even though they are not found in SSBE. One type of trill is the sound people make when they are 'rolling their 'r's', or when they are imitating a cat purring. This type of trill is found in languages like Spanish (in the word *perro*, meaning 'dog'). For a trill, one articulator taps rapidly against another. In the case of the trill described above, the tongue tip makes brief contact three or four times with the alveolar ridge (see Figure 4.8). This type of trill is symbolised as [r]. This may be a little confusing, as it looks rather like the symbol /r/ that we have been using for English. Note, however, that the brackets are different, a point we will return to in the next unit.

4.8.2 Tap

A tap can be thought of as a very brief plosive. The articulators come together completely, but only very briefly (as shown in Figure 4.9), so there is not enough time for pressure to build up, and the characteristic popping noise of a plosive is not heard. Taps may also be thought of as one cycle of a trill. Taps occur in Catalan, for example, in words such as *cera*, meaning 'wax', and in Spanish, where a tap makes a meaning difference in contrast to a trill (in words such as *pero*, meaning 'but'). The symbol for an alveolar tap is [ɾ].

Figure 4.8 Manner diagram for a trill

Figure 4.9 Manner diagram for a tap

4.8.3 Lateral fricative

Exercise 4.12 Think about, or reread, the descriptions of approximants and lateral approximants above. How do you think a lateral fricative will be different to the fricatives we have already met?

Comment The fricatives we have discussed so far (such as [s] and [ʃ]) could also be termed median fricatives, as air flows down the midline. A lateral fricative is one where the major *blockage* to air is in the midline of the vocal tract. Air passes around the sides of the tongue, as for a lateral approximant, but this time the tongue edges are in narrow, rather than wide, approximation to the sides of the roof of the mouth. This means that the air becomes turbulent as it escapes, and friction is heard. The manner diagrams will look the same for median and lateral fricatives. You may be familiar with the Welsh 'l' sounds in place names like *Llangollen*. This sound is a voiceless alveolar lateral fricative. You can try to produce one by making a voiceless /l/ and bringing the sides of the tongue into closer approximation with the roof of the mouth, so that friction occurs. The symbol for this sound is [ɬ].

4.9 Summary

Here we have seen that manner of articulation relates to how air flows in the vocal tract. This is related, in part, to the degree of stricture, and, in part, to whether or not air flows into the nasal cavity. We have also learnt that there are two large manner classes, called obstruents and sonorants, which relate to whether or not pressure builds in the vocal tract.

4.10 Looking forward

In the next unit we will see how all the features we have looked at so far can be incorporated into a single chart, and how we can draw diagrams of the articulators to show how sounds are produced.

4.11 Review questions

Think about the questions below to see if you have fully understood this unit.

- How would you define manner of articulation?
- What is the difference between a nasal and a plosive at the same place of articulation?

- Which manners fall under the class of obstruent, and which are sonorants?
- Add MOA to each of your flash cards.

4.12 Review exercises

1 Think about the sounds at the start of each word below. There will be two examples of each MOA found in English, treating median and lateral approximants as separate manners, so divide them up accordingly.

lentil
fish
mayonnaise
bagel
rice
pasta
cheese
noodles
yogurt
jam
sausage
lemon

2 You now know the three most important features of consonants. Look at the groups of consonants below and work out which is the odd one out in each group. The difference could be in voice, place, manner or one of the larger manner classes.

a) /b p v dʒ n l r/
b) /g l t d n s z/
c) /f ʃ ʒ θ v w ð/
d) /n l r w d j m/

3 Decide whether the statements below are true or false. If they are false, explain why.

a) The velum is lowered for /g/.
b) All nasals are sonorants.
c) All voiced sounds are sonorants.
d) The air is turbulent during the production of a fricative.
e) Air flows over the sides of the tongue for /j/.

UNIT 5 THE IPA CHART AND MID-SAGITTAL SECTIONS FOR CONSONANTS

5.1 Key learning areas

In this unit we will:

- investigate how consonants are represented on the chart of the International Phonetic Alphabet (IPA)
- learn how we can draw diagrams that show the articulation of consonants.

5.2 Introduction

In the last few units we have covered a great deal of ground. We now know how speech is different from writing, understand the main difference between consonants and vowels, appreciate how consonants are produced, and can describe the three principle features of their articulation: voice, place and manner. These three features can be combined to give a single label, known as a **VPM label**, for each consonant. For example, we can say that /t/ is a voiceless alveolar plosive.

5.3 More consonant sounds

So far, however, we have concentrated on consonants that are present in a fairly standard version of English. This is because this is the language and variety that most readers will be familiar with, at least through the media, even if they do not speak it themselves.

There are, however, a large number of sounds that do not occur in this variety of English, or indeed in any variety of English, some of which we have considered briefly in earlier units. The important thing about the VPM features we have concentrated on so far is that they can also describe consonant sounds in any language. Therefore, knowledge of these three features will also enable us to think about and describe sounds in other languages.

Exercise 5.1 Are you aware of any speech sounds other than those we have been describing for SSBE? You might like to think about:

a) the variety of English you or your friends speak
b) the non-SSBE examples in other units

c) other languages that you speak
d) languages that you have heard spoken around you.

Comment At this point it is impossible to say which sounds you might have identified. However, some of the sounds that are often identified when people are asked this question are the trills and taps found in Italian and Spanish, and the 'guttural' sounds found in languages like German and Dutch. The important thing about these sounds, and consonant sounds in any language, is that they can be described in technical terms using the same VPM features that we have been working with for English in the last three units.

5.4 The International Phonetic Alphabet

You may have heard of the phonetic alphabet before you started studying phonetics. It is important, however, not to confuse the NATO phonetic alphabet with the International Phonetic Alphabet. The NATO alphabet provides a standard set of words for letter names, such as Alpha, Bravo and Charlie, for <a>, <b> and <c>, respectively. This alphabet is particularly useful for talking over the telephone or radio, when speech is distorted and certain letter names can sound very similar. In this book, we are not concerned with the NATO alphabet, but rather with the International Phonetic Alphabet, which, as we have seen, is often abbreviated to its initials, IPA.

Like the NATO phonetic alphabet, the International Phonetic Alphabet also provides a type of standardisation, but this time it provides a standard description of all the sounds that can be found in the world's languages. It also provides symbols for these sounds, as we have seen for SSBE, and some sounds in other languages. The IPA thus provides symbols to represent all the sound possibilities found in the languages of the world. However, when it does so, it labels them strictly on the basis of their articulation, and not on their *usage* in any particular language. Therefore, it is appropriate to use square, rather than slash, brackets when referring to symbols from the IPA chart, as we will do throughout this unit.

The IPA uses the features of voice, place and manner to describe and define consonant sounds, and provides a chart for viewing and organising them easily. The full chart is shown in Appendix 1 (page 281). In this unit we will look at the top of the full chart, which shows all the consonants produced using air from the lungs (pulmonic). A version of this part of the chart is shown below, with [p] and [b] in place for illustration purposes.

Exercise 5.2 Look at the chart below and at the example sounds [p] and [b]. How are the features of

a) place
b) manner
c) voice

represented in the chart?

	Bilabial	Labiodental	Dental	Alveolar	Postalveolar	Retroflex	Palatal	Velar	Uvular	Pharyngeal	Glottal
Plosive	p b										
Nasal											
Trill											
Tap											
Fricative											
Lateral Fricative											
Approximant											
Lateral Approximant											

Comment Symbols are placed in the chart according to the voice, place and manner of the sound they represent. The chart is designed as follows:

a) The place of articulation is shown in the columns, which are ordered from POAs at the front (bilabial) to the back (glottal) of the vocal tract.
b) The manner of articulation is shown in the rows, and is ordered roughly by degree of stricture in the vocal tract, from greatest to least.
c) Voicing is shown by the position of a symbol in the individual cell. Symbols for voiceless sounds are on the left of a cell, and voiced sounds are to the right. For example, both [p] and [b] are shown in the cell representing bilabial plosives, but voiceless [p] is on the left, and voiced [b] is on the right.

Exercise 5.3 From the previous units, you know everything you need to fill in the chart with the symbols for SSBE consonants. Try this now, remembering the voice, place and manner label of each, and the layout of the chart.

	Bilabial	Labiodental	Dental	Alveolar	Postalveolar	Retroflex	Palatal	Velar	Uvular	Pharyngeal	Glottal
plosive	p b			t d				k g			ʔ
nasal	m			n				ŋ			
trill											
tap											
fricative		f v	θ ð	s z	ʃ ʒ						h
lateral fricative											
approximant		ʋ			ɹ		j				
lateral approximant				l							

Are there any sounds that you found difficult to place on the chart, or where you have given a different answer to the one above?

Comment /w/ may well be a difficult sound to place on the chart. We have described it as labial-velar, because it has two equally important places of articulation. In effect, that might mean that it needs to go into the chart twice, which clearly would not fit with other sounds and could be confusing. If we look at the entire chart, available in Appendix 1 (page 281), we see that, in fact, /w/ goes in a different place, along with 'other symbols', rather than on the main pulmonic consonant chart.

You may have wondered what to do with dental, alveolar and postalveolar sounds, as there is only a single wide column for them, except in the fricative row. In many languages, there is only one plosive or approximant produced in this region; therefore, separate symbols are not needed to indicate differences in meaning that are produced by a dental versus an alveolar versus a postalveolar sound (although such differences *can* be transcribed, using additional symbols, as we will begin to see in Unit 10). Thus, for most MOAs, there is just one wide column, combining dental, alveolar and postalveolar POAs. The fricatives, by contrast, *do* occur in three distinct columns. We know, just from considering English, that we need symbols for fricatives at all three places to distinguish meaning. For example, the words 'thin', 'sin' and 'shin' all begin with a voiceless fricative sound at a different POA within this region.

In addition, you will see that there is not a row for affricates. As you know, affricates are symbolised by combining the symbols for a plosive and a fricative at the same place of articulation. This means that we can always work out the symbol for an affricate, without this manner needing a separate column.

Finally, you may have been confused over the symbol to use for a post-alveolar approximant. In our earlier units we have used /r/ and [ɹ], so you may have wondered whether the symbol goes the right way up, as in spelling, or not. This is always confusing for beginning students of phonetics. When we are transcribing English using slash brackets, we can use /r/ to refer to the sound at the start of words like 'radish' and 'ruby', however that sound is pronounced. This simply means that it is a meaningful sound in English, and makes a difference in meaning to other sounds, such as /w/ or /p/. When we are talking more precisely about how the sound is articulated, however, we need to use different brackets and different symbols, and these are the ones shown on the IPA chart. For a postalveolar approximant, then, we would use the symbol [ɹ]. You might remember that we said in the last unit that the 'right way up' [r] symbolises a trill, and this can be seen on the IPA chart at the end of this unit. To summarise, /r/ is a very general transcription, which does not tell us in great detail how the sound is articulated. It can be used as a catch-all for [ɹ] and [ʋ], which actually have quite different articulations. In Unit 9 we will begin to see how all our symbols in slash brackets can actually be modified to indicate more precisely the way in which a sound is articulated.

5.4.1 Further features of the chart

The (pulmonic) consonant chart of the IPA has some additional features that we have not yet discussed. An empty cell means that no language has been found in which such a sound exists and makes a meaning difference. This does not mean to say that one will not be found. The labiodental tap was only added to the chart in 2005, after various Central African languages were found to make use of this sound. A shaded cell means that the equivalent sound is considered impossible to produce.

Figure 5.1 is the part of the IPA chart for pulmonic consonants, with all the symbols included.

Exercise 5.4

a) Looking at Figure 5.1, find some symbols that look like letters used to write English, but which are not in fact used to *transcribe* English. What sounds do they represent (give the VPMs)?

b) What symbols are used for the following sounds?

Voiceless bilabial fricative
Voiced palatal plosive
Voiced palatal lateral approximant
Voiced glottal fricative

THE INTERNATIONAL PHONETIC ALPHABET (revised to 2005)

CONSONANTS (PULMONIC) © 2005 IPA

	Bilabial	Labiodental	Dental	Alveolar	Postalveolar	Retroflex	Palatal	Velar	Uvular	Pharyngeal	Glottal
Plosive	p b			t d		ʈ ɖ	c ɟ	k ɡ	q ɢ		ʔ
Nasal	m	ɱ		n		ɳ	ɲ	ŋ	ɴ		
Trill	ʙ			r					ʀ		
Tap or Flap		ⱱ		ɾ		ɽ					
Fricative	ɸ β	f v	θ ð	s z	ʃ ʒ	ʂ ʐ	ç ʝ	x ɣ	χ ʁ	ħ ʕ	h ɦ
Lateral fricative				ɬ ɮ							
Approximant		ʋ		ɹ		ɻ	j	ɰ			
Lateral approximant				l		ɭ	ʎ	ʟ			

Where symbols appear in pairs, the one to the right represents a voiced consonant. Shaded areas denote articulations judged impossible.

Figure 5.1 The (pulmonic) consonants section of the IPA chart

Comment a) The sounds you may have identified that look like letters used to write English are:

[ʙ] voiced bilabial trill
[c] voiceless palatal plosive
[x] voiceless velar fricative
[q] voiceless uvular plosive
[ɢ] voiced uvular plosive
[ɴ] voiced uvular nasal
[ʀ] voiced uvular trill
[ʟ] voiced velar lateral approximant

These symbols show how important it is not to use capitalisation as you would in orthography when you transcribe, as, for example, [ɡ] symbolises a different sound to [ɢ].

b) The symbols are:

Voiceless bilabial fricative [ɸ]
Voiced palatal plosive [ɟ]
Voiced palatal lateral approximant [ʎ]
Voiced glottal fricative [ɦ]

5.4.2 Other parts of the IPA chart

You will have noticed that, so far, we have concentrated only on the part of the chart dealing with *pulmonic* consonants. This implies that there are other types of consonants in a different place on the chart. Indeed this is the case, and we will visit these sounds in Unit 7. The full chart is given in Appendix 1 (page 281), and also contains a place for 'other symbols', as we saw for /w/, which accommodates symbols that do not easily fit elsewhere. In addition, there is a separate section of the chart for vowels, and additional symbols that we will visit in later units.

5.4.3 Using the IPA chart

Because you understand the principles behind the IPA chart, and have an understanding of voice, place and manner labels, you should be able to use the pulmonic consonants chart to find any sound and symbol.

In fact, the symbols act as shorthand for a considerable amount of information. If we write [q], for example, we know that we are referring to a voiceless uvular plosive. But even that label provides a good deal of additional information. We know that the vocal folds are held wide apart, because this is a voiceless sound. We know, because the sound is uvular, that the active articulator will be the back of the tongue. We also know, because the sound is a plosive, that it is an obstruent, and therefore the velum must be raised so that pressure can build up during its production. So, in fact, just transcribing [q] gives us a lot of extra implicit, or hidden, information.

5.5 Mid-sagittal sections

We have learnt that one way to represent sounds is to use a standard symbol from the IPA chart. There is another way to represent sounds, though, that is much less abstract. In this method, we can draw diagrams of the articulators that show how particular sounds are produced. These are known as **mid-sagittal sections**, or, more informally, as **head diagrams**, and show the positions of the articulators in the production of a particular sound. They are useful if you need to show someone else how a sound is produced – for example, if you are working with a client in speech therapy, with a student of English as an additional language, or with a class learning about phonetics.

In mid-sagittal sections, much of the 'hidden' information given by symbols, which we talked about above, is made explicit – that is, the position of the vocal folds, active articulator and velum are all shown in the diagram.

For many people, drawing mid-sagittal sections is a challenge. This is especially the case for people who are not used to drawing, or who think they are not very good at it. However, like most things, a little bit of practice will go a long way. Try to work through the tutorial below, which is a step-by-step guide to drawing mid-sagittal sections.

Figure 5.2 Step 1 for drawing mid-sagittal sections

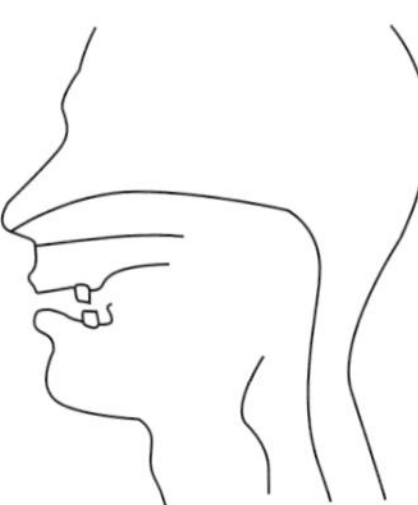

Figure 5.3 Step 2 for drawing mid-sagittal sections

Mid-sagittal sections show the head in profile, as if a person had had their head divided down the midline, and turned their head to their right, so that you are looking at the left side of their face. The facial part of the section will almost always be the same. Try tracing the profile in Figure 5.2 a few times.

When you feel comfortable with that, try drawing it yourself, first of all while looking at the diagram, and then without looking.

Exercise 5.5 Under what circumstances will this profile change – that is for what sounds will it be drawn differently?

Comment The profile will change for sounds with a bilabial or labiodental place of articulation.

Now we need to begin to draw the internal structures of the vocal tract. Again, some of these will be drawn in the same way for the vast majority of mid-sagittal sections.

Exercise 5.6 What structures will be drawn the same way for all head diagrams?

Tip Try to identify which parts of the vocal tract do not move in order to form different sounds.

Comment The structures that do not move are the teeth (upper and lower, apart from a downward movement of the lower teeth if the lower jaw moves), alveolar ridge, hard palate and nasal cavity. These are the parts that are drawn next (see Figure 5.3).

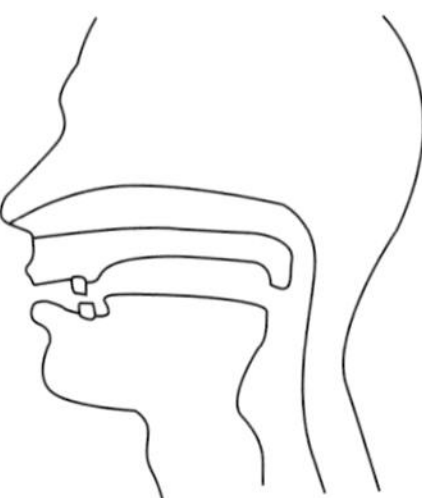

Figure 5.4 Step 3 for drawing mid-sagittal sections

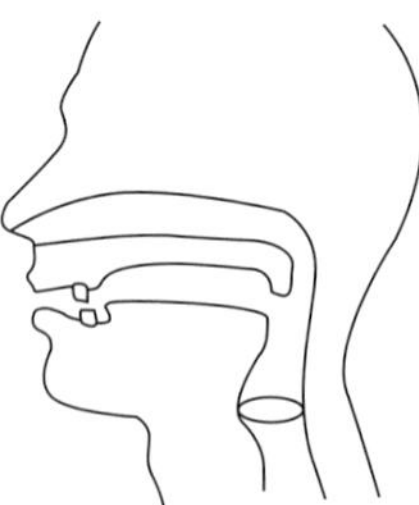

Figure 5.5 Step 4 for drawing mid-sagittal sections

We now come to two parts of the vocal tract that move to form speech sounds: the tongue and the velum. For now, we will draw the tongue in a resting position, as for normal breathing, and the velum open, positioned away from the back wall of the pharynx, allowing the passage of air between the nasal cavity and the lungs (see Figure 5.4).

Finally, we add an indication of the action of the vocal folds, which is also known as the **state of the glottis**. This is represented by a jagged line for voiced sounds to represent vibration, and a circle for voiceless sounds to represent open vocal folds. We can also draw a straight line to represent closed vocal folds, as in [ʔ]. For now, we will draw the larynx open, as for normal breathing. We can also show vertical movement of the larynx for non-pulmonic sounds, as we will see in later units. (see Figure 5.5.)

You have now drawn the basic mid-sagittal section. It is worth practising this basic sketch until you feel comfortable with it and know what all the lines represent. It might help you to shade in the alveolar ridge, hard palate, velum and the tongue, until you can easily see which lines demarcate space, and which demarcate tissue, as in Figure 5.6.

5.5.1 Place and manner of articulation

Obviously, if mid-sagittal sections are to be useful, they need to show more than simply the resting positions of the articulators. As we have seen, much of the drawing will remain the same, but articulators need to be drawn differently

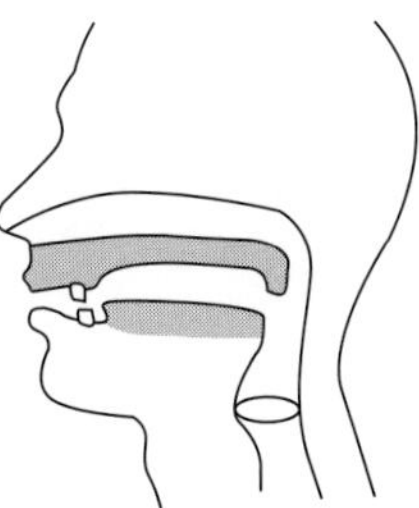

Figure 5.6 A mid-sagittal section with shading

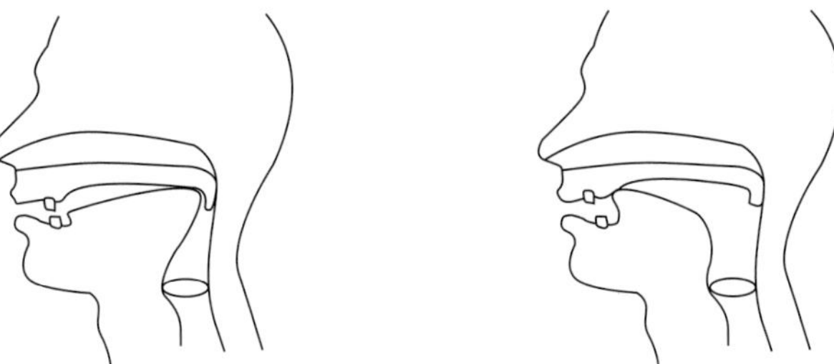

Figure 5.7 Voiceless velar plosive (left) and voiceless alveolar plosive (right)

depending on the place and manner of articulation of the sound that is represented.

Place is shown by altering the position of the active articulator, so that it approaches or touches (depending on the MOA) the passive articulator (see Figure 5.7).

Manner is shown, firstly, by how close the active and passive articulators are (the degree of stricture). They will touch for a plosive or a nasal, be in narrow approximation for a fricative, and be in wide approximation for an approximant, as in Figure 5.8.

For MOA we also need to show how airflow is directed in the vocal tract, and therefore need to show the position of the velum – that is, whether it is lowered to allow air into the nasal cavity or raised (velic closure), directing the air to the oral cavity. Laterals can also be shown by an arrow indicating that air flows around the side of the tongue. Different manners are shown in Figure 5.8.

A question that often arises at this point is which part or phase of an articulation we are drawing. As we know, speech is a dynamic process, and single sounds span a period of time over which the articulators move. The rule of thumb is that we draw the portion of the sound when there is maximum constriction to airflow (such as the hold phase of a plosive). We can add a dynamic aspect to the process by using dotted lines to show an additional position of the articulators. For example, Figure 5.9 shows an affricate, and uses a dotted line to show the position of the tongue after the closure has been released.

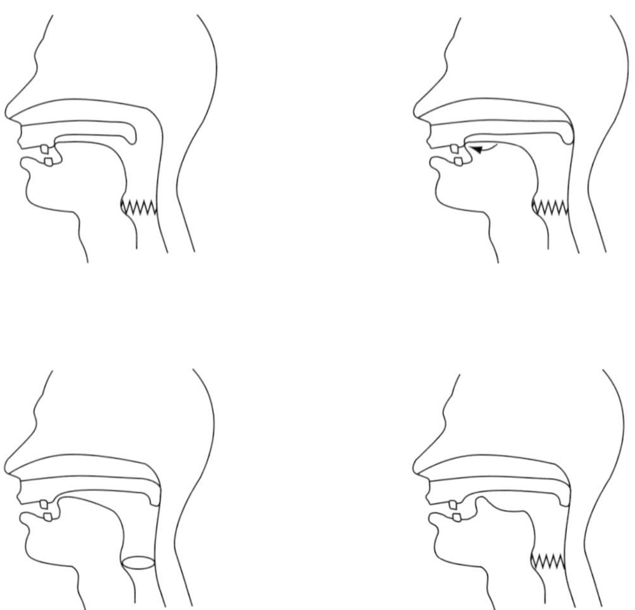

Figure 5.8 Voiced alveolar nasal (upper left), voiced alveolar lateral approximant (upper right), voiceless alveolar fricative (lower left), and voiced postalveolar approximant (lower right)

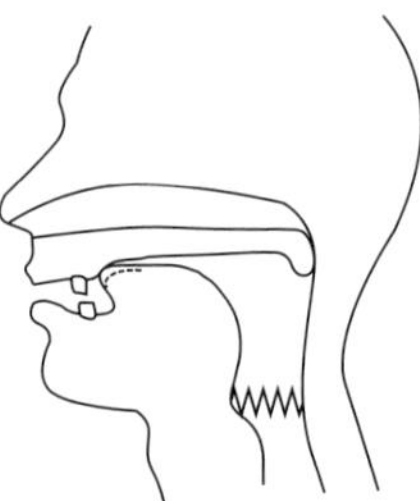

Figure 5.9 Mid-sagittal section of a voiced postalveolar affricate

Exercise 5.7 Complete these diagrams to show the indicated sound.

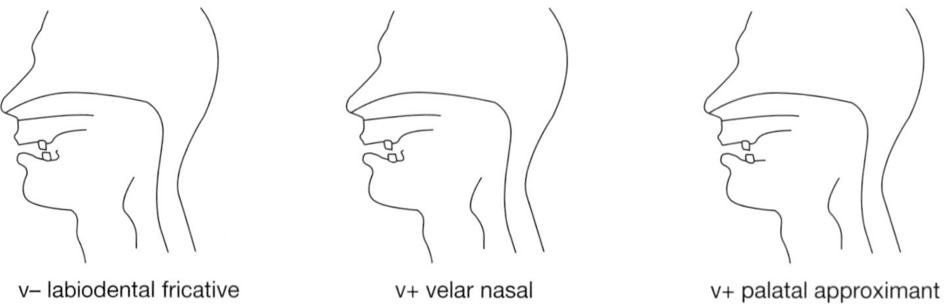

Comment

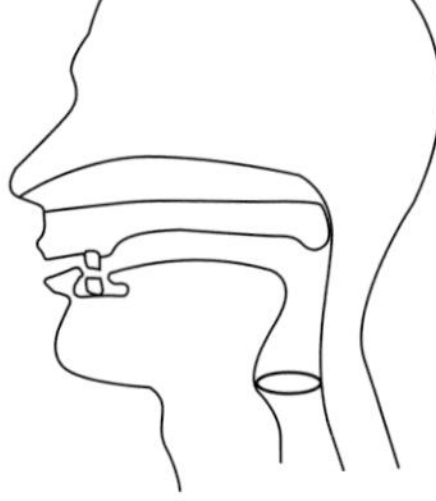

v– labiodental fricative

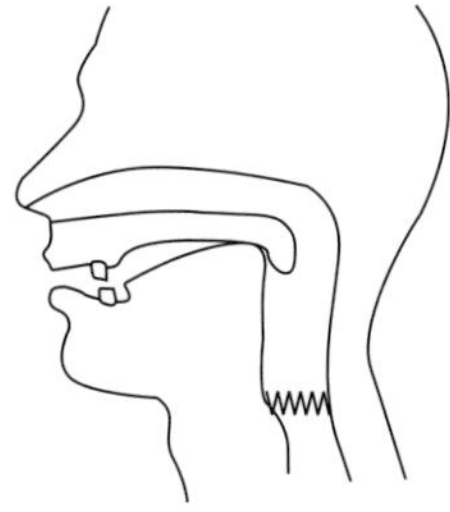
v+ velar nasal

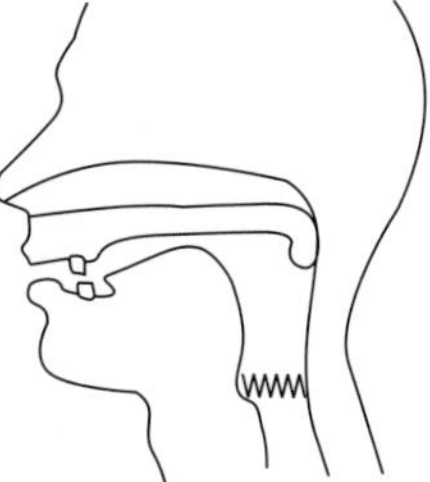
v+ palatal approximant

5.6 Summary

In this unit we have consolidated our knowledge of how pulmonic consonants are produced, and seen how they can be represented on the IPA chart, or by drawing a mid-sagittal section. We will return to consonants in Unit 7, when we consider consonants made on other airstreams.

5.7 Looking forward

In the next unit we turn our attention to vowels.

5.8 Review questions

Have a look at these questions to see if you have understood the main points to be learnt from this unit.

- How is the IPA chart for pulmonic consonants organised?
- List the details that must be included when drawing a mid-sagittal section.
- Draw a mid-sagittal section of the articulators in resting position.

5.9 Review exercises

1 Each of these transcriptions of English words contains errors, in that symbols have been included that are used for English spelling but do not represent an English sound in the IPA. Spot the errors, correct them and give a VPM for the erroneous consonant symbols.

a) quick /qwVc/

b) ring /RVNG/

c) box /BVx/

2 Identify the sound represented by the following mid-sagittal section, and then label the active and passive articulators, the position of the velum and the state of the glottis.

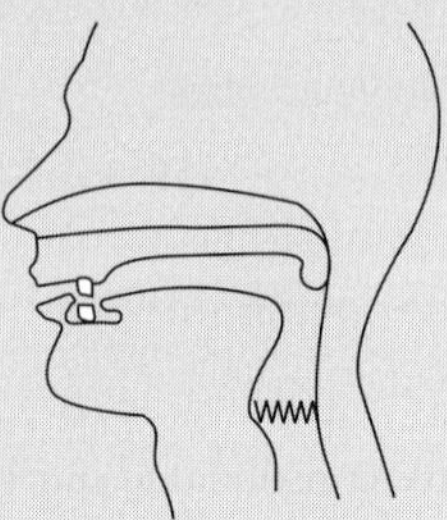

3 Spot the errors in the following diagrams and correct them.

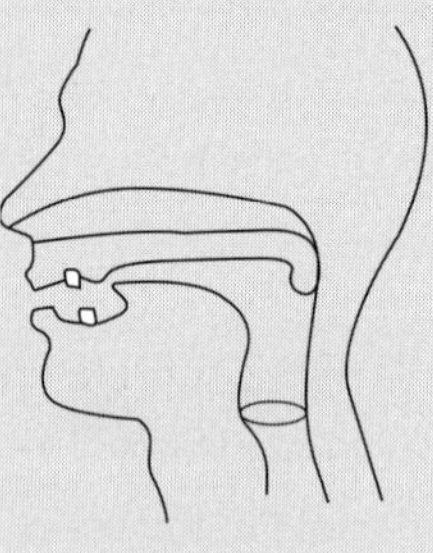

v– dental fricative

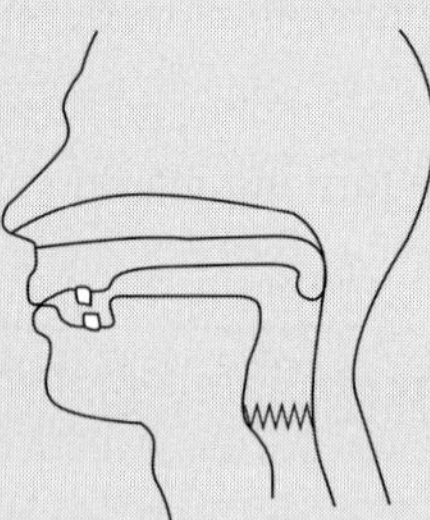

v+ bilabial nasal

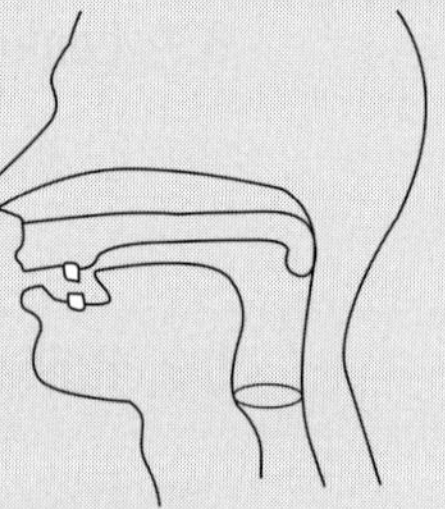

v+ alveolar fricative

UNIT 6 VOWELS

6.1 Key learning areas

In this unit we will:

- identify how vowels are similar and different to consonants
- discover how the articulation of vowels can be described
- find out how vowels can be displayed on a chart
- explore the cardinal vowels.

6.2 Introduction

So far we have concentrated on the production of consonants and we have noted that consonants have more constriction to airflow than vowels. In this unit we will see how vowels are produced, how they can be labelled and described, and we will learn about the cardinal, or reference, vowels.

We will begin by thinking about the English vowels. Just as in the case of consonants, we use English as the starting point because English is the common language for readers of this book. More specifically, we will start by considering the vowels of Standard Southern British English. This is the accent most readers will be familiar with, at least from the broadcast media. We will certainly mention other accents as we go along, however, and consider them in much greater detail in Unit 14. We will start by investigating an important division for our description of vowel sounds.

6.3 A basic distinction for English vowels

Exercise 6.1 Think about the words 'heed' and 'hide'. Isolate the vowel in each word, and then pronounce the vowel slowly out loud. Think about what your articulators (tongue, lips, vocal folds, etc.) are doing. You may also like to watch yourself in a mirror while you do this exercise. Now say the vowels immediately after one another.

What differences do you note in their production and in the way that they sound?

Comment In the majority of accents of English, the articulators stay (relatively) still during the vowel in 'heed', but move during the vowel in 'hide'. This movement of the articulators can also be heard, as the **quality** of the vowel (the way it sounds) changes as the articulators move. The final part of the vowel in 'hide' is rather like the vowel in 'heed', but the initial part of the vowel in 'hide' has the jaw more open, and the tongue lower down in the mouth. In fact, all types of vowels in English are either like the 'heed' type, which are called **monophthongs**, or like the 'hide' type, which are called **diphthongs**.

6.4 Monophthongs

First, we will look at monophthongs in more detail. The word 'monophthong' comes from Greek, with *mono* meaning 'one', and *phthong* meaning 'sound'. So, a monophthong is a single sound, with the articulators in one position throughout and therefore no change in the sound quality.

The monophthongs in SSBE are as follows. The example words are taken from those frequently used when describing differences between accents, and we will revisit them when we think about accents in more detail later on in the book.

/i/ in fleece
/ɪ/ in kit
/ɛ/ in dress
/æ/ in trap
/ʌ/ in strut
/ɜ/ in nurse
/ɑ/ in palm
/ɒ/ in lot
/ɔ/ in thought
/ʊ/ in foot
/u/ in goose
/ə/ (the final sound) in comm**a**

Exercise 6.2 Look at the words above which illustrate SSBE monophthongs.

Isolate the vowels in them and then say them out loud, looking at the symbol.

Then try to think of other words containing each vowel.

Now pick an example word to help you remember each vowel (for example, you may find it easier to remember that /ɑ/ is the vowel in 'car' rather than in 'palm').

Comment Once you have picked an appropriate word for each vowel, you will be able to use these words when you transcribe. For example, if you want to transcribe the word 'heart', you can isolate the vowel in this word and then match it to your example word 'car' or 'palm', or whichever word you have chosen for this vowel. You then know that in order to transcribe the vowel in this word you need to use the symbol /ɑ/. You can also add these words to your vowel flash cards, which you can copy from the back of the book (page 290–3). Do be careful, however, that the example word you have chosen really does contain the appropriate vowel. If you are unsure, ask a teacher to check for you.

Exercise 6.3 For each of the following words and phrases, fill in the missing vowel symbols, using your example words from the previous exercise, and your flash cards if necessary.

tent	/t _ nt/
camp	/k _ mp/
flask	/fl _ sk/
water bottle	/w _ t _ b _ t _ l/
sleeping bag	/sl _ p _ ŋ b _ g/
canteen	/k _ nt _ n/
cooker	/k_ k _ /
food	/f _ d/
thermals	/θ _ m _ lz/
mug	/m _ g/

Comment tent = /tɛnt/; camp = /kæmp/; flask = /flɑsk/, or /flæsk/ for speakers of many northern varieties; water bottle= /wɔtə bɒtəl/, or /bɒtl/ if you use a syllabic /l/; sleeping bag = /slipɪŋ bæg/; canteen = /kæntin/; cooker = /kʊkə/, or /kukə/ for certain Lancastrian varieties; food = /fud/ in SSBE, or /fʊd/ in some accents; thermals = /θɜməlz/, or/θɜrməlz/ for rhotic speakers; mug = /mʌg/, or /mʊg/ for speakers with northern accents. There are actually even more differences in the vowels for different accents, which we do not have space to cover here. Please check with a teacher if you have particular queries about your own pronunciation.

You now know the symbols for all the monophthongs in SSBE. The next step is to think about similarities and differences in how these vowels are produced, and how these distinctions affect their quality – that is, the way they sound.

6.5 Articulatory features of vowels

Exercise 6.4 All the words below start with /b/ and end with /d/, and only differ in terms of their vowels. Concentrate on the vowel in each case and think about the position of the articulators (tongue and lips) and the action of the vocal folds, and how these are similar or different between members of each pair or set.

a) bid bed bad
b) bad barred
c) bead bud booed

Tip At first, it may help you to exaggerate the vowel sounds in order to feel and hear any differences more easily.

Comment First of all, you may have noticed that all the vowels are voiced, as they all have vocal fold vibration, which can be felt in the larynx.

a) In the first set, you may have noticed that there is a difference in the position of the jaw and the height of the tongue. The major difference between the vowels for our purpose is the height of the highest part of the tongue. In 'bid', you might feel the sides of your tongue touching your upper molars, while this is less the case for 'bed' and 'bad'. In 'bad', not only is the tongue lower, but the jaw is also lowered.
b) In 'bad' and 'barred', there is a difference in how far forward in the mouth the highest part of the tongue is. In 'bad', the highest part of the tongue is towards the front, while in 'barred' it is towards the back. You may have also noticed that the vowel in 'barred' is longer.
c) In the third set, the major difference is in the position of the lips. They are spread for 'bead', in a neutral position for 'bud' and rounded for 'booed' (and there is also a difference in the position of the tongue).

Exercise 6.5 Think back to our previous units, and the voice, place and manner dimensions that we identified as important for the description of consonants. Then think about Exercise 6.4 and try to decide if VPM labels are also appropriate for describing vowels.

Comment From Exercise 6.4, you will have realised that we need a different set of features to describe vowels than those we use to describe consonants. Our VPM labels are not especially useful for vowels. Firstly, this is because all vowels are voiced. Secondly, in terms of manner, all vowels are rather like approximants, in that the narrowing in the vocal tract is not enough to cause friction. Thirdly, the place of articulation for vowels takes place in a rather restricted area of the oral cavity, roughly between the hard and soft palates. This is why it can be difficult to feel the differences between some vowels as you produce them. Finally, it is always some part of the front or back of the tongue (rather than the vocal folds, or tip or blade of the tongue) that is the active articulator, while the lips may also make an important contribution.

In fact, the features that you identified in Exercise 6.4 are the very features that we use to describe the articulation of vowels. As just explained, the tongue is always involved in producing vowels. In terms of our classification system, we are interested in the location of the highest part of the tongue. This part may be

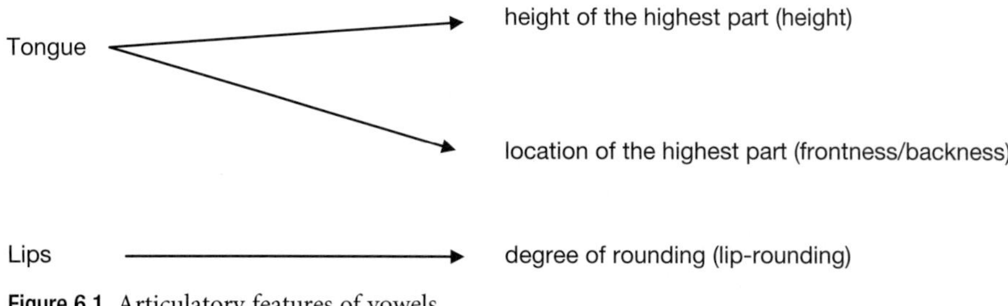

Figure 6.1 Articulatory features of vowels

towards the front of the tongue (roughly in line with the hard palate), as for /i/, the middle of the tongue, as for /ɜ/, or the back of the tongue (roughly in line with the velum), as for /ɑ/. This is the tongue **frontness** (or backness, in some contexts) dimension, and we can describe vowels as being front vowels, back vowels or central vowels.

We are also interested in the *height* of that highest part of the tongue. For /i/, the highest part of the tongue is very high, in that it is very close to the roof of the mouth. For /ɑ/, not only is the highest part of the tongue further back than for /i/, it is also lower down in the mouth. For /ɜ/, it is between these two extremes. We refer to this as the tongue **height** dimension, and we can refer to vowels as being high, mid or low (you may also see the terms 'close' and 'open' used for high and low, respectively).

Finally, we have the **lip-rounding** dimension. Lips may be rounded, as for /u/, spread, as for /i/, or neutral, as for /ɜ/.

Therefore, we can summarise the features of articulation of vowels as shown in Figure 6.1.

Of course, all of these dimensions are really continua, so vowels can be produced with tongue height between that of /i/ and /ɜ/, and where the lips are less spread than for /i/ but more so than for /ɜ/, for example. While the dimensions we use to describe vowels may suggest that there are discrete categories of tongue position and lip-rounding, we should try to remember that actually these are continuous dimensions.

These three features of articulation serve to affect the shape of the vocal tract while the vowel is produced. This means that the air inside the vocal tract vibrates at different frequencies, so that different sounds are produced. Just as blowing into differently shaped bottles will produce different sounds, setting the vocal tract into different shapes will produce different vowels.

Exercise 6.6 Experiment with producing the vowels described earlier in this section: / i ɑ ɜ u/.

Can you feel the differences in the height and frontness of your tongue and the position of your lips?

Try to produce intermediate vowels – for example, vowels between /i/ and /u/, and /u/ and /ɑ/. Move the tongue and lips between the vowels while voicing continuously, and listen to the vowels you produce.

Comment It can be very difficult to feel the small differences in tongue position that produce different vowels. Do persevere, however, as practice will help. While producing intermediate vowels you may hear vowels that sound like other English vowels, and also some that sound like non-English vowels. Try to appreciate the continuum of tongue and lip positions that can produce vowels.

6.6 Graphic representations of vowels

As you will remember from Unit 5, the IPA chart for pulmonic consonants allows us to organise the consonants of the world according to three defining features of voice, place and manner. We can also use a chart to summarise vowels according to frontness, height and lip position.

For example, a table of the English monophthongs might look like Figure 6.2.

Exercise 6.7 Look at Figure 6.2 and produce each of the vowels.

a) What do you think the bolding of certain symbols represents?
b) Can you see any problems with this particular layout?

Tip Think about the fact that some cells contain two symbols and about the issues of continua raised above.

	Front	Central	Back
High	i ɪ		ʊ u
Mid	ɛ	ɜ	ɔ
Low	æ	ʌ	ɑ | ɒ

Figure 6.2 The SSBE monophthongs represented in a table

Comment a) The bolding represents vowels with rounded lips. You will notice that all the rounded vowels in English are back vowels. This is not true for all languages, as we will see, but is the most typical situation across the languages of the world.

b) The major problem with a chart laid out like that in Figure 6.2 is that it does not show fine gradations of tongue and lip position, which is what we need for vowels. It sticks too closely to the idea of discrete categories of vowels, such as high, back or rounded, rather than allowing us to show more continuous differences. So, for example, English /i/ and /ɪ/ do not have exactly the same tongue height or frontness (try producing these sounds and feel the difference between them), but in this type of chart there is no way to show this. Likewise, /u/ and /ɒ/ do not have the same degree of lip-rounding, but in this type of chart there is only a way to show rounded as opposed to unrounded vowels. Of course, we could use different degrees of bolding to represent degrees of rounding, but this would still be rather difficult to see.

6.6.1 The vowel quadrilateral

A solution to these problems is to allow vowels to sit in different positions within and between cells. This is the approach taken by the **vowel quadrilateral**, shown in Figure 6.3, with /i/ marked.

Exercise 6.8 a) What do you think the horizontal and vertical dimensions might represent?

Tip Compare this to Figure 6.2 (page 68).

b) Why do you think the leftmost line is sloping rather than straight?

c) Using what you know already, try to place the vowels /u ɑ/ and /ɜ/ on the quadrilateral.

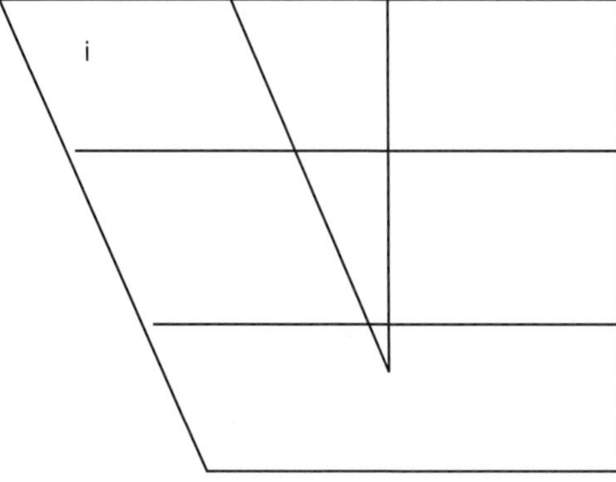

Figure 6.3 The vowel quadrilateral, with /i/ marked

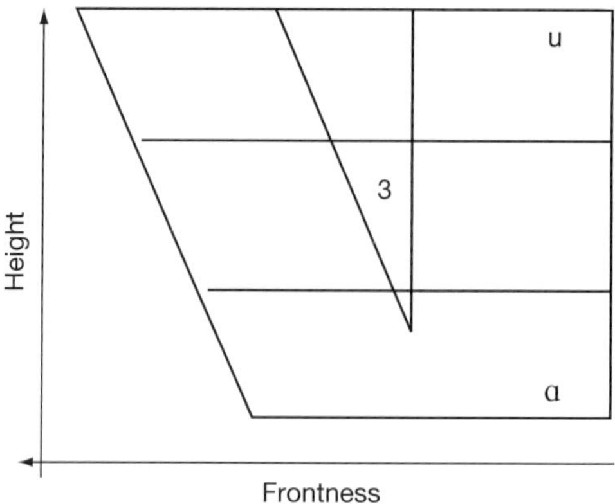

Figure 6.4 A vowel quadrilateral with /ɜ/ /ɑ/ and /u/ marked

Comment

a) The horizontal dimension is tongue frontness, with the left of the line being the front of the part of the oral cavity used to produce vowels (the **vowel space**), and the right being the back of this space. The vertical dimension represents height, with the top being a high tongue position and the bottom a low position. The rounding dimension is not shown especially well in this type of chart, when only a few vowels are present, so we will return to this point when we discuss the cardinal vowels later on in this unit.

b) The leftmost line is sloping to represent how far it is possible to move the tongue when it is raised or lowered. A tongue in a high position can move further forward than one in a lowered position. The middle triangle simply divides the top line into three, in order to show additional reference points.

c) If we fill in all the monophthongs, the quadrilateral looks like that shown in Figure 6.5.

6.6.2 Acoustic classification of vowels

We are discussing the vowel quadrilateral in relation to articulation, but it can also be thought of as an *acoustic* map of vowel quality. Although this book does not deal in detail with acoustic phonetics, it is worth saying something about this here. Each vowel has a number of important resonant frequencies called formants, which are related to the shape of the vocal tract. The lowest two of these, called F1 and F2, are especially important for distinguishing the vowels we hear. Simply put, F1 is related to tongue height, with high vowels having a lower F1 than low vowels. This seems difficult to remember, but low vowels have a high F1, and high vowels have a low F1! F2 is related to the frontness of

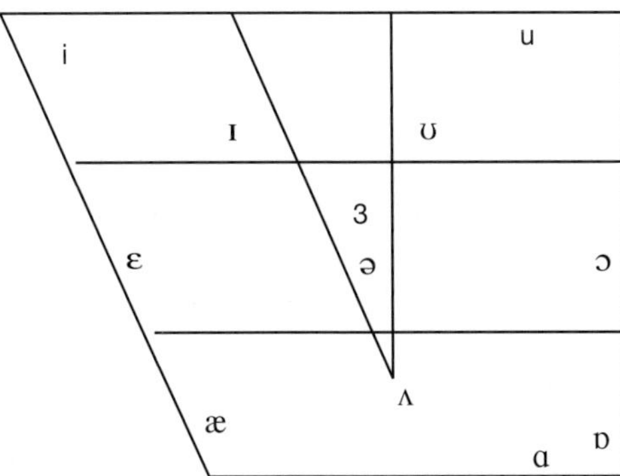

Figure 6.5 A vowel quadrilateral showing approximate positions of the SSBE monophthongs

the tongue, so back vowels have a lower F2 than front vowels. Lip-rounding also affects F2, with rounded vowels having a lower F2 than their unrounded equivalents. In this way, the vowel quadrilateral also relates to an acoustic map of vowel space.

6.7 The special case of schwa

The vowel /ə/, known as **schwa**, has a somewhat special place in English. Partly, this specialness is because it is the most common vowel in English. A related, and more important, reason for it special status is because it only ever occurs in unstressed syllables. We will visit stress and syllables in much more detail in Unit 8. All you need to know for now is that all speakers carry a store of words, like a dictionary, in their heads. This dictionary is called the **mental lexicon** and it contains information about the way a word is pronounced, such as which vowels and consonants it contains.

In addition, all words have a stressed syllable as part of their dictionary entry in your mind, and this information is just as important as knowing which segments a word contains. For example, in 'quantum', the first syllable, which contains /kwɒn/, is stressed, as it is louder and longer than the other syllable. The second syllable is unstressed and contains the vowel /ə/, which can *only* occur in unstressed syllables. Schwa can be represented in spelling by a wide variety of letters. The emboldened letters in each of the following words represent a schwa: 'gath**er**', 'gamm**o**n', 'pet**a**l', 'candl**e**' (for 'petal' and 'candle', note that no schwa, or in fact any vowel, will be produced in the second syllable if /l/ is syllabic). This variety in spelling can make it hard for beginning transcribers to feel confident in recognising schwa, especially as there is a tendency to stress every syllable in a word when 'sounding it out' for transcription. Therefore, it is important to listen out for schwa, rather than being guided by a word's orthography, and to try to say all words in a natural way when transcribing. As we will see in later units, schwa occurs even more commonly in running, connected speech than it does in single words in isolation. In fact, other vowels can even turn into schwa under the right conditions.

Exercise 6.9 For each of these words, find the stressed syllable and then transcribe the entire word in full, noting the position of any /ə/ vowels (which will only occur in unstressed syllables). Be aware that not all words will contain schwa, so say each one aloud and listen carefully.

pattern
aloof
penguin
travel
traveller
cat

Comment Stress can be indicated in transcription by adding the symbol / ˈ / immediately before the stressed syllable. /ˈpætən/, /əˈluf/, /ˈpɛŋgwɪn/, /ˈtrævəl/ and /ˈtrævələ/ ('pattern', 'travel' and 'traveller' might also be produced with syllabic consonants). 'Traveller' may also be pronounced with two syllables as /ˈtrævlə/, a point we will return to in Unit 15 when we think about compression.

Note that schwa is never within a stressed syllable. However, an unstressed syllable does not *have* to contain schwa. In 'penguin', for example, the unstressed syllable contains /ɪ/.

For words containing only a single syllable, such as 'cat', /ˈkæt/, that single syllable is always stressed when the word is spoken in isolation, and will therefore never contain schwa. This situation may change for certain words (like 'and', 'from' and 'has') in connected speech, however, as we will see later in Unit 15.

6.8 Vowel length

In some books and classes, you may see that certain vowels are transcribed with a following [ː] symbol to represent **length**. So, for example you may see /ɑː/ rather than /ɑ/ to represent the vowel in 'palm'. In this book we will not use extra marks to represent length in transcription. This is because, in English, there are no pairs of vowels that differ *only* in their length. For example, as we have seen, /i/ and /ɪ/ are rather similar, but do differ in the height and frontness of the tongue. Since they are represented by different symbols (/i/ and /ɪ/), it seems unnecessary to distinguish them further by adding a length mark to the longer vowel (that is, /iː/). There are good reasons for using either type of system, and historically both types have been used, but in this book we will consistently *not* use length marks. The only time this can really cause us problems is when we transcribe vowels in unstressed syllables, like that at the end of 'happy'. Systems that use length marks will transcribe this vowel as /i/, but the vowel in 'sheep' as /iː/. In this book we will transcribe both vowels as /i/, while remembering that there is in fact a difference in duration between the two.

6.9 Vowels and approximants

Towards the start of the unit we said that the production of vowels is rather like the production of approximant consonants, in that the tongue is not close enough to other articulators for friction to result. In particular, the approximants /j/ and /w/ are rather similar to two English vowels; in fact, so much so that /j/ and /w/ are sometimes referred to as **semi-vowels**.

Exercise 6.10

a) Which vowels do you think are similar to /j/ and /w/? Try producing the approximants and making them rather long, and seeing what vowels result. Also consider what you know about the tongue and lip position for vowels and these approximants.

b) If the articulation of /j/and /w/ is so much like that of vowels, why do you think we refer to them as consonants?

Comment

a) /i/ is similar to /j/, as the high front vowel is very similar to a palatal approximant. /w/ is similar to /u/. As you will remember, /w/ is labial-velar in its place of articulation. The labial element is basically lip-rounding, which also occurs for /u/, and the velar place of articulation is rather similar to that of a back vowel such as /u/.

b) In terms of articulation, then, the vowels and semi-vowels are really rather similar. However, the semi-vowels actually *function* as consonants. They take up positions around the edges of syllables, just like other consonants, such as /p v g/, rather than in the centre of syllables, like the vowels /ɑ/ or /æ/, for example. In addition, they are treated like consonants by some rules of spoken English. So, when we put the word 'the' in front of a noun, its pronunciation changes depending on whether that noun starts with a consonant or a vowel. When the noun begins with a consonant, the form of 'the' is /ðə/, as in 'the pear'. When the noun starts with a vowel, the form of 'the' is /ði/, as in 'the apple'. We see that the semi-vowels pattern with consonants, as in 'the watermelon', where 'the' is pronounced as /ðə/. This can be taken as evidence that the semi-vowels should in fact be treated as consonants, despite their articulatory similarity to vowels.

6.10 Diphthongs

As we discovered back at the start of the unit, some vowels are produced by moving the articulators during the vowel, and this leads to a change in the quality, or sound, during the vowel. Such vowels are called diphthongs. The word 'diphthong' comes from the Greek, with *di* meaning 'two' and *phthong* meaning 'sound'.

Because the articulators move between two positions, and the sound changes between two qualities, the symbols for diphthongs are made up of two parts, as illustrated below for the diphthongs in SSBE.

/eɪ/ as in face
/əʊ/ as in goat
/ɛə/ as in square
/ɔɪ/ as in choice
/ɪə/ as in near
/aʊ/ as in mouth
/ʊə/ as in cure (for some speakers, /ɔ/ may be used instead)
/aɪ/ as in price

Exercise 6.11 Looking at the symbols for the diphthongs above, and thinking about the sounds they represent, can you divide the diphthongs into three logical sets of sounds?

Comment You may have noticed that the final part of the diphthong symbol is only occupied by three different symbols. We can divide our diphthongs into three sets accordingly.

Ending in /ɪ/	**Ending in /ʊ/**	**Ending in /ə/**
/eɪ/ as in face	/əʊ/ as in goat	/ɪə/ as in near
/aɪ/ as in price	/aʊ/ as is mouth	/ɛə/ as in square
/ɔɪ/ as in choice		/ʊə/ as in cure

6.10.1 Diphthong classification

In fact, many phoneticians divide the diphthongs into two types, closing (which combines two of the sets we identified above) and centring. **Closing diphthongs** are those that end in /ɪ/ or /ʊ/, where the tongue moves from a low to a high (or close) position in the mouth. **Centring diphthongs** are those where the tongue moves from a higher or lower position to a central, schwa-like position.

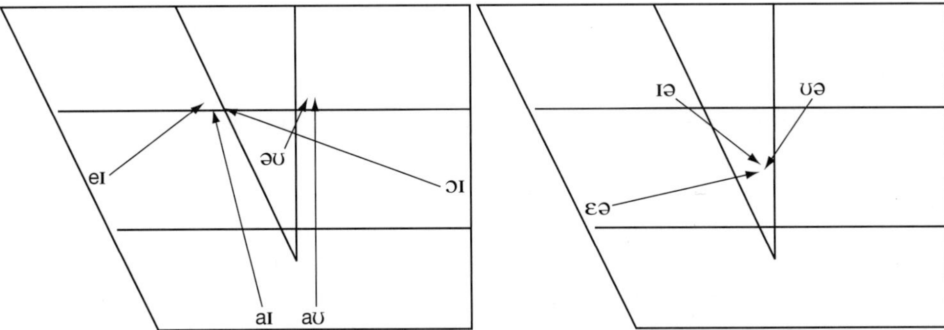

Figure 6.6 Vowel quadrilaterals showing SSBE closing diphthongs (left) and centring diphthongs (right)

The movement within a diphthong can also be shown on the vowel quadrilateral, as in Figure 6.6.

Exercise 6.12 For each of the diphthongs, say them slowly and see if you can see, feel and hear the movement of your tongue, and relate it to the diagrams in Figure 6.6.

Do any of the vowels seem not to be diphthongs in your pronunciation?

Comment There are two major potential differences between your productions and those represented in Figure 6.6. Firstly, many speakers no longer use the diphthong /ʊə/ in words like 'cure', and use the /ɔ/ vowel instead, as we suggested when we introduced this vowel above. That is to say, they produce the same vowel in 'thought' and 'cure'. In addition, some of the other diphthongs may be produced more as monophthongs in particular accents (the process of diphthongs becoming monophthongs is called **monophthongisation**). So, my (vaguely London) production of 'square', for example, has very little change in quality during the vowel. Likewise, for Cockney speakers, the vowel in 'mouth' is rather like the first part of the SSBE diphthong, but with very little upward movement of the tongue or lip-rounding. As well as being regional differences in pronunciation, the lack of the /ʊə/ vowel and monophthongisation are more common in younger than older speakers. We will address more of these differences, and the reasons for them, in Unit 14, which deals with speech sound variation.

Exercise 6.13 You now know all the symbols you will need for making your first full transcriptions of English. You can celebrate your success by making transcriptions of the following:

a) Have you got anything alcohol-free?
b) The birds are on the feeders in the garden.
c) I believe she's got eleven units left to write.

Comment At the moment, we are transcribing each word as it would be produced in isolation, and the answers below reflect SSBE. After working through a few more units, you will see that some words change their pronunciation when they are in running speech, and that sounds may be added, changed or deleted. For now, the answers given below are as if each word were produced in isolation, and therefore given its pronunciation from the mental lexicon, rather than produced in connected speech. However, if you read the transcriptions back, you will likely note that they sound quite unnatural. You may, therefore, wish to revisit these answers once you have read Units 15–17 and learnt about some of the things that can happen in connected speech.

a) /hæv ju gɒt ɛniθɪŋ ælkəhɒl fri/
b) /ðə bɜdz ɑ ɒn ðə fidəz ɪn ðə gɑdən/(or 'garden' could have a syllabic /n/)
c) /aɪ bɪliv ʃiz gɒt ɪlɛvən junɪts lɛft tu rɑɪt/

6.11 The cardinal vowels

While we have completed our survey of SSBE vowels, we also need to consider another set of vowels called the **cardinal vowels**. The cardinal vowels were devised by the English phonetician Daniel Jones in 1917. He proposed them as a set of reference vowels to which other vowels could be compared. It is very important to remember that these vowels do not actually occur in any languages, although languages can, and do, have vowels which are *similar* to some of the cardinal vowels.

Jones wanted to mark the limits of the vowel space, whereby sounds produced in more extreme positions are either physically impossible or are in fact consonants, since the air is restricted enough for friction to occur. When we think about the cardinal vowels, therefore, we can start with two reference points defined by articulation:

[i] = the highest and most front without causing friction
[ɑ] = the lowest and most back that the tongue can go.

These reference points are shown on the quadrilateral in Figure 6.7, alongside the numbers by which we often refer to them. So [i] is referred to as 'cardinal 1', for example.

The six other cardinal vowels also mark the edges of the vowel space and are auditorially equidistant from the two vowels we placed on the chart in Figure 6.7.

Because these vowels mark the limits of the vowel space, they sound more extreme than those found in the languages of the world. However, they can be used as reference vowels and compared to vowels in languages. In this way, the

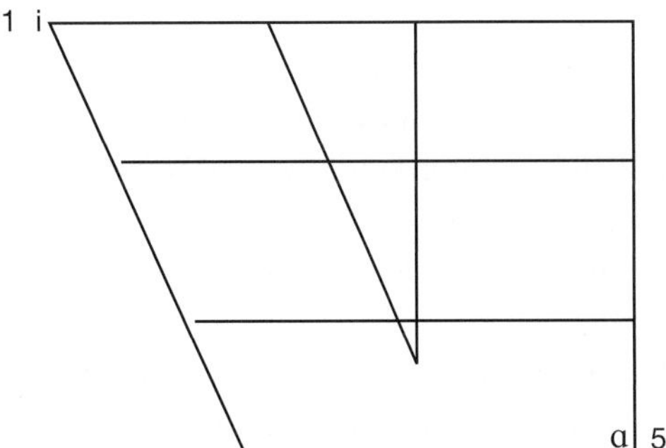

Figure 6.7 The articulatorily defined cardinal vowels

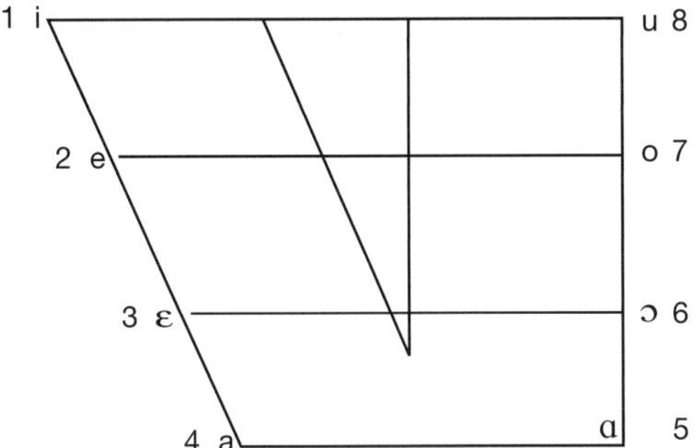

Figure 6.8 The primary cardinal vowels and the numbers used to refer to them

vowel quadrilateral acts like a map and the cardinal vowels like landmarks. So, in the same way as we might describe a café in Paris as 'halfway between Notre Dame and Sainte-Chapelle', we might describe a vowel in a language as being 'in between cardinals 2 and 3'.

6.11.1 Cardinal vowel symbols

Exercise 6.14 Why do you think many of the cardinal symbols are the same as those used for the English vowels, even though the articulation and sounds of the cardinal vowels are, by definition, not the same as English vowels?

Comment When we symbolise the vowels in any language, we (usually) use the cardinal symbols. In particular, we use the symbol for the cardinal vowel to which a 'real' vowel is closest in terms of sound and articulation. English /i/ is most like cardinal 1; therefore, we use the same symbol for both the English vowel and the cardinal vowel, even though the English /i/ is less extreme in its articulation, being less high, less front and with less spread lips. Likewise, the English vowel in 'bed' has a quality between that of cardinal vowels 2 and 3, and we choose to use one of these symbols (/ɛ/) to represent this sound (some transcription systems choose the symbol for cardinal 2 [e]). This dual use of the symbols for cardinal vowels and vowels in languages can be confusing. However, try to bear in mind that we are using the cardinal vowels as reference vowels, and therefore use their symbols to represent vowels within a language which are similar to those reference points.

There are some exceptions, however. For example, in this book we use /æ/ for the vowel in 'trap', rather than the symbol for the closest cardinal vowel, which is cardinal 4 [a]. This is purely a matter of history and convention, and in fact some phoneticians do use /a/ to symbolise the vowel in 'trap'. So, in general, when we symbolise the vowels of a language, we use the symbol for the closest cardinal vowel.

6.11.2 Secondary cardinal vowels

For the cardinal vowels above, notice that the lips are spread for /i/, become steadily more neutral between cardinals 2 and 5, and then become increasingly more rounded for cardinals 6 to 8. This situation represents the most common lip positions, as in most languages, including English (as we have seen above), front vowels have spread or neutral lip positions, and back vowels are somewhat rounded. However, it is also possible to have more uncommon tongue and lip combinations, which occur in fewer languages, such as the front rounded vowels of French or German, for example. Jones, therefore, also devised the **secondary cardinal vowels**. These have the same tongue positions as the primary cardinal vowels, but opposite lip-rounding. So, the secondary version of cardinal 1 has closely rounded lips, for example. The secondary cardinal vowels also have their own numbers and symbols, as shown in Figure 6.9 (they might also be referred to by the number of their primary equivalent – for example, [y] can be cardinal 9 or secondary cardinal 1).

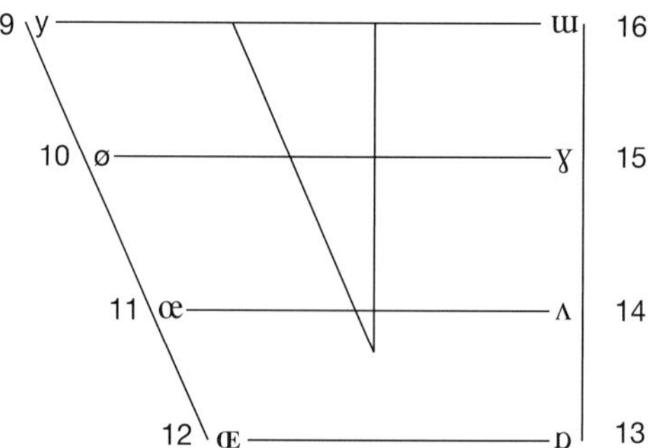

Figure 6.9 The secondary cardinal vowels and the numbers used to refer to them

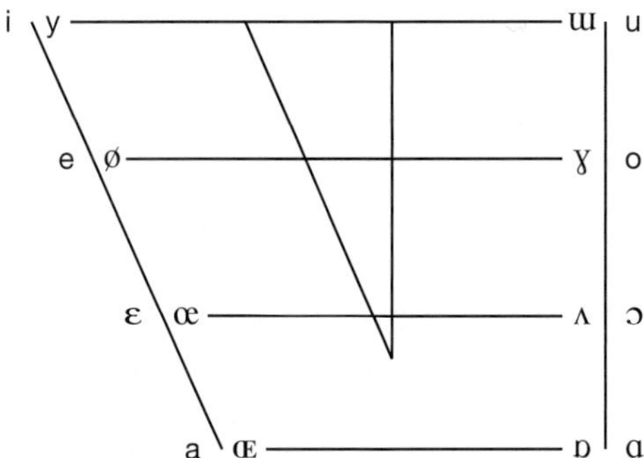

Figure 6.10 Primary and secondary cardinal vowels

When the primary and secondary vowels are shown on the same chart, they occur in pairs, with the more rounded vowel to the right. You will remember earlier that we said rounding was rather hard to show in our initial table-like representation. Rounding is also rather difficult to show in the vowel quadrilateral, unless vowels appear in pairs. Note, though, that this layout also relates to the acoustic properties we discussed earlier. As lip-rounding lowers the second formant (F2), it makes some sense for rounded vowels to occur to the right of their unrounded equivalents (return to the discussion in 6.6.2 if you need a reminder about formants and the acoustic properties of vowels, page 70).

Exercise 6.15 Try to find a recording of the cardinal vowels. These are quite easily available on the internet, and links to some sites are given in the Resources section (see page 280). Alternatively, ask a phonetics teacher to produce them for you.

Try imitating the vowels as best as you can, first of all as a sequence, and then individually.

Comment It can be very difficult to produce the vowels accurately, and it can take a long time to learn to do so. To do so accurately, you really need to learn the vowels by getting advice and correction from an experienced phonetician, and to practise producing and recognising the cardinal vowels.

6.12 Vowels on the IPA chart

A vowel quadrilateral showing all the cardinal vowels plus additional reference points is shown towards the bottom of the full IPA chart, as you can see in Appendix 1 (page 281). That part of the chart is also reproduced here for ease of reference (see Figure 6.11).

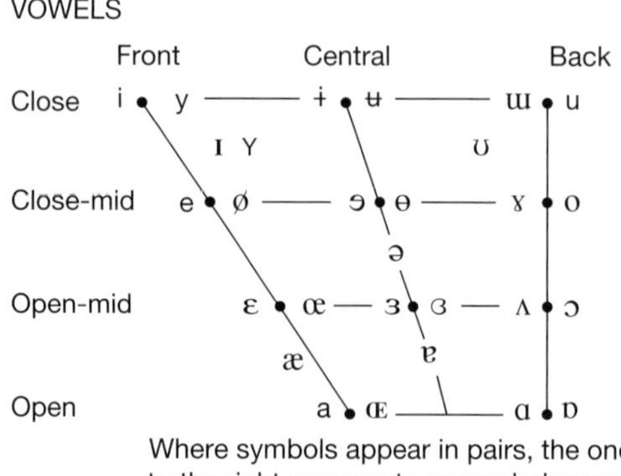

Figure 6.11 The vowels section of the IPA chart

6.13 Summary

We have now seen that vowels can be described in terms of the height and location of the highest part of the tongue, and the position of the lips. We have discussed monophthongs and closing and centring diphthongs, and learnt the symbols for vowels in SSBE. We have considered the cardinal (or reference) vowels, and have seen how vowels can be plotted on a chart. We have also given our first complete transcriptions of English words.

6.14 Looking forward

So far, all our thinking has been about sounds produced using air from the lungs. In the next unit we will look at (mainly non-English) sounds produced using other sources of air.

6.15 Review questions

Have a look at these questions to see if you have understood the main points to be learnt from this unit.

- What features are used to describe the articulation of vowels?
- What are the symbols for all the vowels in SSBE?

- In what way can the cardinal vowels be thought of as reference vowels?
- Add information about the English vowels to your flash cards if you have not done so already: example words, frontness, tongue height and lip-rounding for monophthongs, and centring or closing for diphthongs.

6.16 Review exercises

1 Match the symbols on the left to the appropriate word on the right. Assuming SSBE, there will only be one match for each one.

/ɪə/	part
/ɑ/	boy
/ɛə/	cow
/u/	mass
/æ/	hair
/ɪ/	gin
/ɔɪ/	plume
/aʊ/	hear

2 Write the symbols, and one example word, for the SSBE vowels a–h represented in the quadrilateral below.

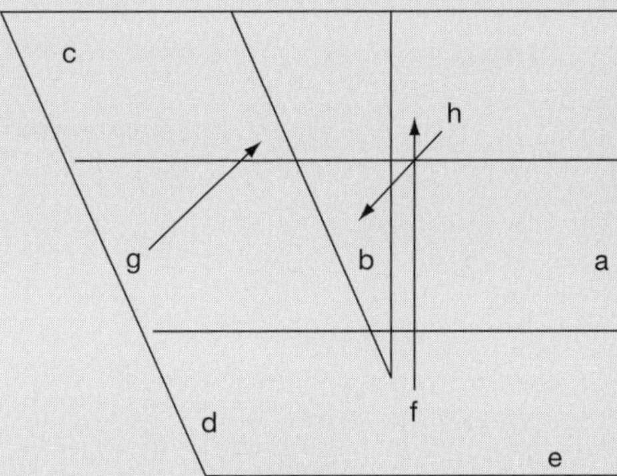

3 For each vowel below, generate some sentences which contain only that vowel. Make the sentences as long as possible; they should contain at least four words. These get progressively harder, as the later vowels are less common in English than the early ones, making it more difficult to think of appropriate words.

For example, for /i/ you could write, 'Steve Green meets Gene each week he needs tea'.

/ɛ/

/aɪ/

/ɑ/

/ɜ/

/ɔɪ/

UNIT 7 AIRSTREAM MECHANISMS

7.1 Key learning areas

In this unit we will:

- recap the importance of air for the production of sounds
- identify sources of air used to produce sounds across the world's languages
- explore how implosives, ejectives and clicks are produced.

7.2 Introduction

In this unit we will be looking at a number of sounds that do not occur in everyday English speech. They do, however, occur in other languages, and sometimes in English in ways that do not contribute to the meaning of individual words.

7.3 Pulmonic egressive and ingressive airstreams

To start with, we are going to think about how we usually use the air from the lungs and what happens when we breathe in while speaking.

Exercise 7.1 Pick a phrase that you know and can easily repeat, such as the first line of 'Twinkle, twinkle, little star', or 'the quick brown fox jumps over a lazy dog'. Produce the phrase as you normally would, several times in succession, taking only one breath at the start. Then, try to repeat the same phrase, but this time breathing in. What do you notice?

a) Is the phrase still intelligible?
b) Does it sound the same in both cases?
c) Is one version more effortful than the other?

Comment a) Your experiment above will have demonstrated that you can, in fact, talk while you breathe in, and that the speech you produce while doing so is largely intelligible.

b) However, you will also have noticed that speech in the two conditions does not sound identical – for example, the quality and pitch of the utterance will sound different.

c) In addition, you probably found the 'breathing in' condition to be quite difficult, and that you could repeat your phrase fewer times before you needed to return to normal breathing.

Exercise 7.2 Think again about the differences you observed in Exercise 7.1. Why do you think there are differences between the two conditions?

Comment First of all, the 'breathing out' condition is much more practised. We have all been doing it since we first began to speak; therefore, it feels easier and more efficient. Obviously we can speak while breathing in, but, as the air now passes in a reverse direction through our vocal tract, the quality of the sound produced is different. There is, however, no difference in meaning between the words produced in these two different ways.

Exercise 7.3 a) Do you think people ever speak while breathing in under normal circumstances (that is, not when they are doing an exercise such as that in Exercise 7.1)?

b) Might speech produced while breathing in be used for particular purposes or in particular situations?

Comment a) Speaking while breathing in is certainly much more unusual than speaking while breathing out. However, there are some occasions when we might speak while breathing in, such as if we are surprised. Imagine the word 'oh' spoken in shock, for example. Speaking on an inward flow of air has also been associated with Scandinavian languages, where the words for 'yes' are often produced in this way. Even then, however, the inward flow of air will only be very short, and we will return very quickly to speaking while breathing out.

b) Because the sound of the speech produced changes considerably when breathing in, it can be used for vocal disguise, such as by ventriloquists, for example.

7.4 Describing airstreams

As we have seen in earlier units, airflow is crucially important for speech. An **airstream mechanism** is how air is set into motion for speech to occur. By far the most common airstream mechanism in the languages of the world is the outward flow of air from the lungs. The technical term for this type of airstream is **pulmonic egressive**; 'pulmonic' refers to the lungs and 'egressive' means that air flows out of the body. This outward flow happens because muscular activity contracts the ribcage, thereby compressing the lungs and thorax, which causes the air inside the lungs to be under higher pressure than in the surrounding air. As always, air flows from an area of higher pressure to an area of lower pressure.

The other type of airstream mechanism that we considered above is termed **pulmonic ingressive**. The lungs are still responsible for the movement of air, but this time the air flows *into* the body. This happens because muscular activity lifts the ribcage, allowing the lungs to expand, and creating a lower pressure inside the lungs than in the air outside the body.

As you can see, then, there are two things that we need to name when describing an airstream mechanism. Firstly, we need to describe the part of the body that causes the movement of air. This part of the body is called the **initiator**, which is the lungs in the two airstreams we have looked at so far. Next, we need to describe the direction of airflow in relation to the body, which can be inwards (ingressive) or outwards (egressive).

7.5 Non-pulmonic airstreams

It may surprise you to learn that airstreams other than pulmonic airstreams can be used to produce speech. These can be referred to as **non-pulmonic airstreams**. Although they are not used to create meaning in English, they may be used in other contexts and are used to produce meaningful speech sounds in other languages. They exist in about 13 per cent of languages and are quite common in languages in Africa and Asia, although less so in Europe.

Exercise 7.4 The sounds we will look at below are produced using the following airstream mechanisms. Using just what you know already, what do you think are the initiators and directions of airflow in the following airstream mechanisms?

Glottalic ingressive
Glottalic egressive
Velaric ingressive

Comment Looking at the names for these airstream mechanisms, you will see that two are ingressive, so air flows into the body, while one is egressive, so air flows out of the body. Your knowledge of terminology so far will suggest that the first two have the glottis (which you may remember from Unit 3 is the space between the vocal folds) as an initiator, while the last mechanism has the velum as the initiator. We will now look at each of the airstream mechanisms in turn, to see how they work, and the type of sounds they produce.

7.5.1 The glottalic ingressive airstream mechanism and implosives

The **glottalic ingressive airstream** mechanism produces sounds called **implosives**. Implosives are not meaningful sounds in English, but can be used to imitate sounds in the environment, as we will see in Exercise 7.5.

Exercise 7.5 What noise do you make when you imitate someone drinking out of a bottle (glug-glug), or the sound a chicken makes (bok-bok)?

Comment These sounds are very hard to describe in writing, and it is possible that different readers might use a variety of different sounds to imitate drinking and chickens. Many readers, however, will make velar and bilabial implosives as part of their imitations of these noises. Implosives have a distinctive 'gulping' sound, and we will describe their production in detail below. It would be worth asking your teacher to produce them for you, or to listen to some of the recordings mentioned in the Resources section, so that you know what these sounds are like.

The diagrams and explanations below describe how an implosive is produced.

1. Firstly, a closure is made in the oral tract. In Figure 7.1 we have a bilabial closure, so the resulting sound will be a bilabial implosive. You also see that the velum is raised. This is because pressure needs to build in the vocal tract, and this cannot happen if the velum is open (see Unit 4 on manner of articulation if you need a reminder about this).
2. In the next step (Figure 7.2), the vocal folds vibrate while the whole larynx, including the glottis and vocal folds, which are inside the larynx, moves downwards, as indicated by the downwards arrow in Figure 7.2. This downwards movement is achieved by a number of muscles which allow the larynx to be raised and lowered. The downwards movement of the larynx increases the space between the bilabial closure and the vocal folds, which, in turn, reduces the pressure in the oral cavity. Importantly, pulmonic egressive flow continues throughout the production of the implosive, so that voicing can occur. This is the case for most implosives, which are usually voiced.
3. The oral closure, bilabial in this case, is released. As the air outside the vocal tract is now at a higher pressure than that inside, it flows into the area of lower pressure inside the vocal tract, as indicated by the arrow in brackets in

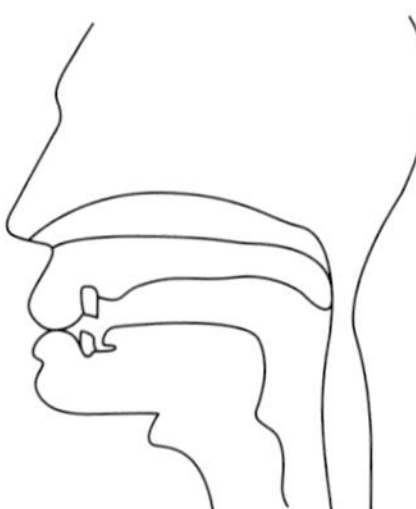

Figure 7.1 The first stage of a bilabial implosive

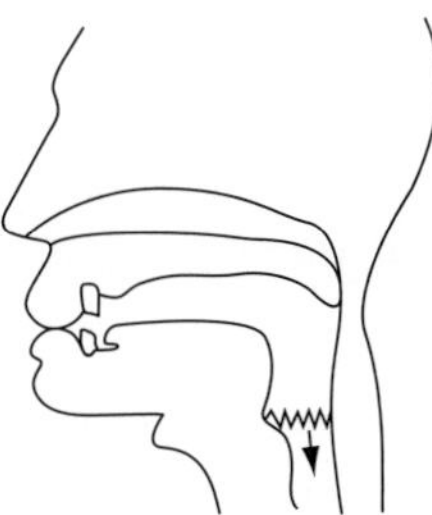

Figure 7.2 The second stage of a bilabial implosive

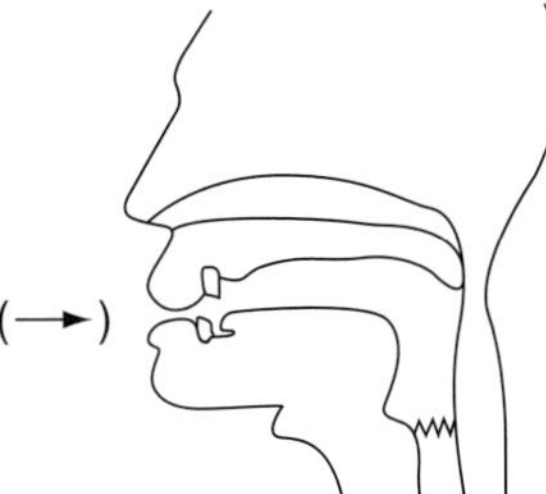

Figure 7.3 The third stage of a bilabial implosive

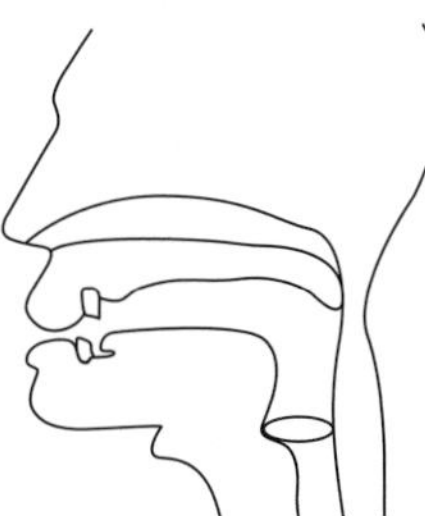

7.4 The fourth stage of a bilabial implosive

Figure 7.3. As air from the lungs continues to flow throughout, all voiced implosives are actually produced using two simultaneous airstreams, glottalic ingressive and pulmonic egressive.

4. Finally, the larynx returns to its normal position, and, if no other sound follows, the vocal folds open for normal breathing (see Figure 7.4).

Exercise 7.6 Try to produce an implosive. You may wish to imitate your teacher or a recording, or try to copy the steps above. The trick is to move the larynx down while there is a closure in the oral cavity (not before or after this closure). You can practise moving your larynx up and down by pretending to sing high and low notes, respectively. You can watch yourself in the mirror, and when you can move your larynx down at will, try to do it with the lips closed while voicing.

Comment Many people find it quite difficult to produce implosives, especially from anatomical instructions such as those given above. It is worth persevering, ideally getting help from a teacher.

Exercise 7.7 Which of the diagrams above (Figures 7.1 to 7.4) would look different if we were showing a voiced *alveolar* implosive? Draw those diagrams as they would appear.

Comment The final stages of the process will look the same, as the closure has been released. However, the first two stages will look different, as the place of articulation has changed, as shown in Figures 7.5 and 7.6.

The symbols for implosives look very similar to the symbols for voiced plosives, but have a rightwards hook at the top. So, a bilabial implosive is [ɓ] and an alveolar implosive is [ɗ]. These symbols, and all those explored in this unit can be seen in the consonants (non-pulmonic) section of the main IPA chart, as

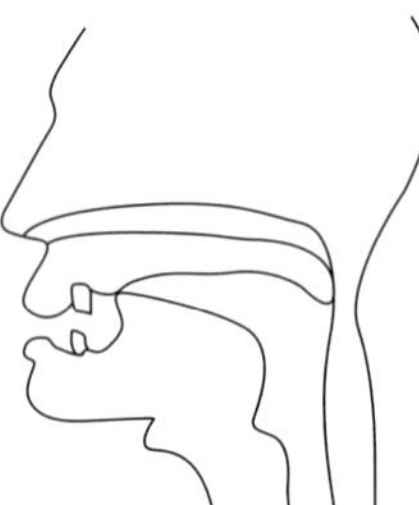

Figure 7.5 The first stage of an alveolar implosive

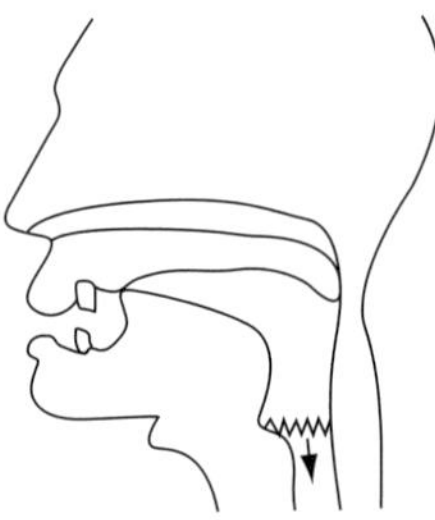

Figure 7.6 The second stage of an alveolar implosive

shown in Figure 7.16 (page 97) and on the main IPA chart in Appendix 1 (page 281).

7.5.2 The glottalic egressive airstream mechanism and ejectives

In 7.5.1, we saw that the glottis can be the initiator of an airstream, as its movement causes pressure changes in the vocal tract. We saw that, for implosives, the larynx moves down, and, of course, the glottis moves down too, as it is inside the larynx. This movement leads to pressure differences, which, in turn, move air and create an airstream flowing into the mouth.

Now we will continue to look at glottalic airstreams, but this time we will look at sounds produced on a **glottalic egressive airstream**. Sounds produced on a glottalic egressive airstream are called **ejectives**. They exist in about 15 per cent of the world's languages and are quite common in North American and African languages. They are not found linguistically in English, so they never make a meaning difference. However, they can be found as one way of producing voiceless plosives (/p t k/) at the end of a phrase, especially if the speaker is being particularly forceful.

Exercise 7.8 a) Try saying the word 'quick' loudly and forcefully. Listen carefully to the final /k/.

b) Now compare the forceful production to that when the word is said quietly and gently. What do you notice?

Comment (a) and (b) If you succeeded in producing an ejective, then the /k/ at the end of 'quick' will have sounded quite different when it is produced loudly and forcefully. Of course, it is difficult to describe sounds in writing, but it will have sounded sharper and more explosive. As you did for the implosives, it is worth listening to some examples from your teacher or the internet (see the Resources section, page 279). You will then be able to listen out for ejectives in speech you hear around you, and in your own speech (we will think about where ejectives can occur in English in Unit 11).

Exercise 7.9 Bearing in mind what you know about the glottalic ingressive airstream, what do you think might happen to the glottis to initiate a glottalic *egressive* airstream?

Comment Above, we saw that the glottis moves down to bring air into the vocal tract. To move air out of the vocal tract – that is, to produce an egressive airstream – the glottis moves up, as we shall see shortly.

We now turn our attention to the stages of production for ejectives. We will illustrate this with the velar ejective, which is the most common ejective in the languages of the world.

1. The first stage when an ejective is produced is for two closures to form more or less simultaneously, in addition to velic closure. One of these closures must be a glottal closure, whereby the vocal folds become tightly shut. This closure of the glottis is shown by the straight line in the larynx in Figure 7.7, just as for a glottal plosive. The other closure is elsewhere in the vocal tract, such as the velar closure in Figure 7.7. Air is therefore trapped between these two closures.
2. The next stage is for the larynx (and the glottis, which is inside the larynx) to move up, while both closures remain in place. This is shown by the upward arrow near the larynx in Figure 7.8. As the glottis is closed, it acts like a piston and pushes up the air trapped between the two closures. The air cannot escape, so is squashed into a smaller space, and therefore under higher pressure than before the larynx rose.
3. Then the closure in the oral tract is released (see Figure 7.9), and the pressurised air flows quickly out of the vocal tract towards the ambient air, which is of lower pressure. This quick movement of air gives the ejective its distinctive sharp sound.
4. Finally, the larynx lowers, and, if no sound follows, the glottis opens to return to normal breathing (see Figure 7.10).

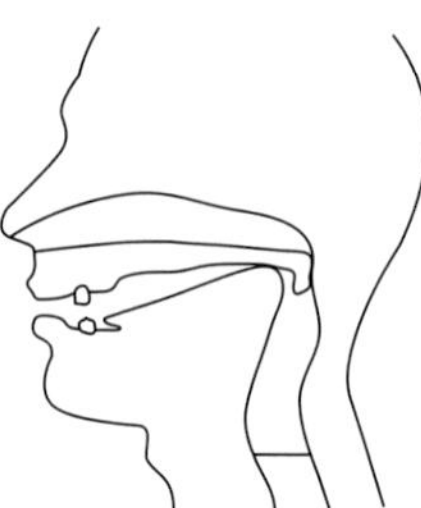

Figure 7.7 The first stage of a velar ejective

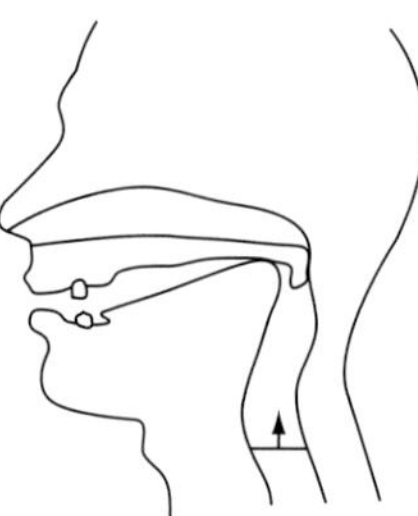

Figure 7.8 The second stage of a velar ejective

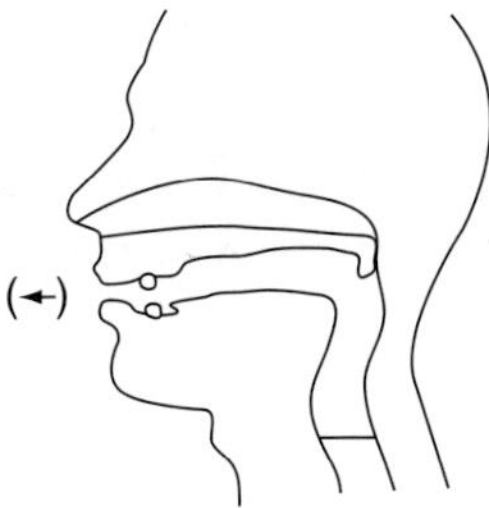

Figure 7.9 The third stage of a velar ejective

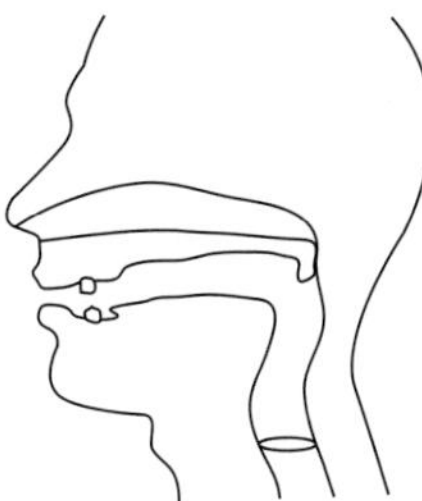

Figure 7.10 The fourth stage of a velar ejective

Exercise 7.10

a) Attempt to replicate the stages above and see if you can produce ejective sounds. Try to make velar, alveolar and bilabial ejectives.

b) Do you think it is possible to produce voiced ejectives? Why, or why not? Try it!

Comment

a) As we suggested above, it is worth practising the ejectives and trying to find a teacher to help you. Some of the clickable IPA charts recommended in the Resources section (page 279) will allow you to listen to ejectives and try to imitate them.

b) Voiced ejectives do not exist in the languages of the world. You can give them a try and hear that you do not get the distinctive ejective sound if the vocal folds are vibrating. While most voiceless sounds have an open glottis, ejectives have a firmly shut glottis, like [ʔ]. If the glottis is to act as an efficient piston, it needs to be tightly closed, and if it is tightly closed, it cannot also be vibrating to produce voice. Conversely, if the glottis is not tightly closed, it does not move the air very efficiently.

Importantly, any voiceless obstruent can be produced as an ejective. So the languages of the world contain ejective plosives, ejective fricatives and ejective affricates. There are no new symbols to learn for ejectives, as all ejectives can be symbolised by adding the symbol [’] to the equivalent pulmonic egressive symbol. So, the velar ejective plosive from above is symbolised as [k’], a bilabial ejective plosive is [p’] and an alveolar ejective plosive is [t’]. The symbols for ejectives are shown with the other non-pulmonic sounds on the IPA chart (see page 281).

7.5.3 The velaric ingressive airstream mechanism and clicks

The final airstream mechanism we will consider is the **velaric ingressive airstream**, which is responsible for the production of click sounds. **Clicks** only exist in southern and eastern African languages. Click sounds are not part of the sound inventory of English, but they occur frequently when English speakers try to imitate sounds in the environment, or to express certain emotions, so will probably be familiar to all readers.

Exercise 7.11 What sounds would you make to do the following?

Blow a kiss
Tut your disapproval
Imitate the sound of horses’ hooves (at a Nativity play, for example)
Tell a horse to giddy-up (this one may be familiar only to those who have learnt to ride horses).

Comment All of the sounds above are click sounds and therefore have a number of similarities in their production. We will consider the production of a voiceless alveolar click below, and then think about the labels for the other clicks in Exercise 7.15.

1. Firstly, two closures form almost at the same time. One of these closures is always a velar closure, just as for a /k/, and gives its name to the velaric airstream mechanism. The other closure is further forwards in the vocal tract, and the closure shown in Figure 7.11 is alveolar. This traps a pocket of air between the two closures.

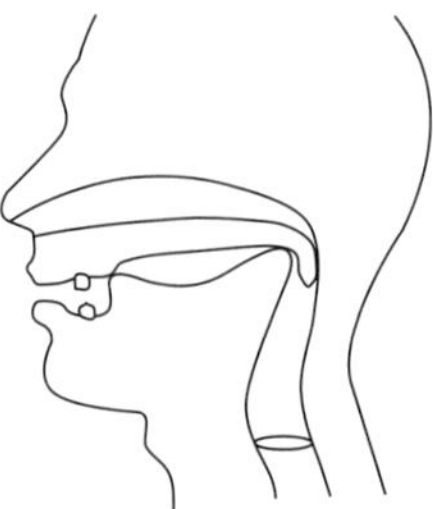

Figure 7.11 The first stage of an alveolar click

2. Next, the tongue moves back and down, but both closures are maintained, so that no air can enter or leave the pocket. As the cavity has changed shape, the trapped air is now in a larger space, and therefore under lower pressure, than before. (See Figure 7.12.)
3. Now, the front-most closure is released so that the pocket of air is no longer trapped. As the pressure inside the vocal tract is lower than that outside, ambient air is sucked into the vocal tract. (See Figure 7.13.)
4. Finally, the velar closure is released, so that, if no other sounds follow, the articulators return to their resting positions. (See Figure 7.14.)

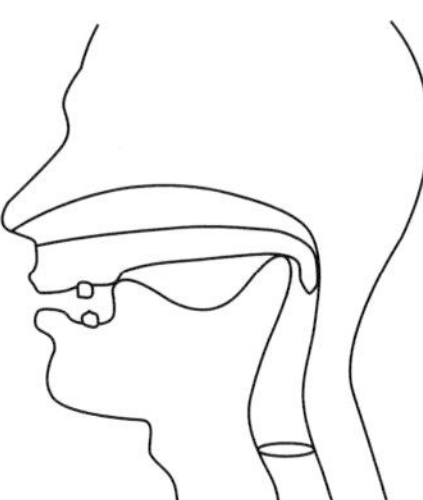

Figure 7.12 The second stage of an alveolar click

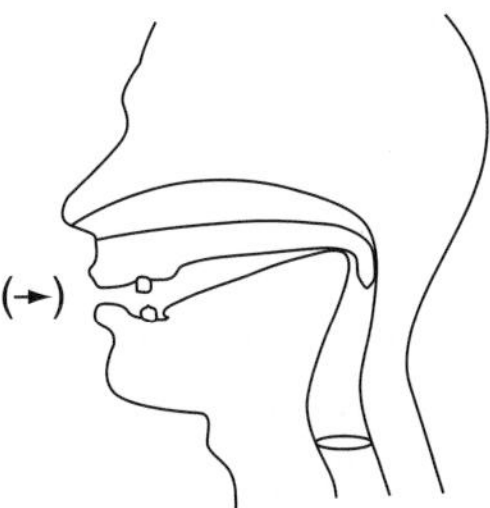

Figure 7.13 The third stage of an alveolar click

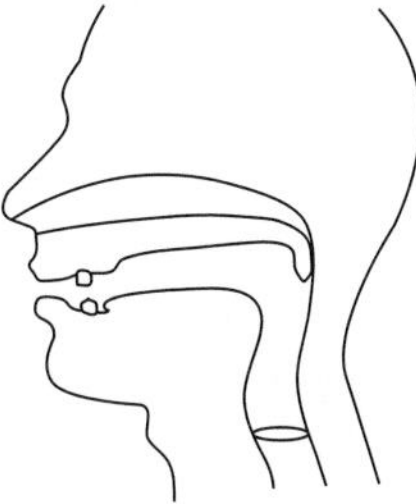

Figure 7.14 The fourth stage of an alveolar click

Exercise 7.12 The place of articulation for the 'tut' sound is either alveolar, as illustrated in Figures 7.11 to 7.14, or dental. What do you think are the places of articulation for the other clicks?

a) Blowing a kiss
b) Imitating the sound of horses' hooves
c) Telling a horse to giddy-up

Comment a) Kisses are bilabial clicks. It is important to remember for bilabial clicks that the tongue is still involved in the articulation. If you make a slow and deliberate kissing motion, you should feel that you make a velar closure with the back of your tongue, even though the *tip* of the tongue is not involved, as it is for many other clicks. This velar closure is the crucial feature of clicks, and gives its name to the velaric airstream mechanism, as we have said above.

b) The sound used to imitate horses' hooves is usually a postalveolar click, with lips spread and then rounded to imitate 'clip' and 'clop', respectively (think back to Unit 6, vowels, on to work out why that should make a difference to the sound produced).

c) The giddy-up noise is an alveolar lateral click. So, the head diagram would look very similar to those in Figures 7.11 to 7.14. However, rather than the tongue tip lowering to produce the click, the sides of the tongue lower, so that air escapes laterally (see Unit 4 on manner of articulation if you need a reminder about lateral airflow).

The symbols for these clicks are as follows:

[kʘ] voiceless bilabial click
[kǀ] voiceless dental click
[kǁ] voiceless alveolar lateral click
[k!] voiceless alveolar or postalveolar click.

Exercise 7.13 Why do you think these symbols have two parts? Specifically, why do you think the symbols contain a [k]?

Comment The part on the right of the symbol indicates the place of articulation of the click – bilabial, alveolar, and so on – and these can be seen on the full IPA chart under 'Consonants (non-pulmonic)' (see page 281). The part on the left, [k], reminds us about the velar closure that all clicks must have, and also tells us about the voicing and nasality of the click, as we will investigate further below. Note that some transcription systems do not show the leftmost [k] part of the symbol for voiceless clicks. We will use the two-part symbol throughout this book, however, for consistency with the symbols used for voiced and nasal clicks, which we will turn to now.

7.5.3.1 Click accompaniments

All the clicks described above are voiceless, as the vocal folds are not vibrating, and oral, as the velum is raised, sealing off the nasal cavity. However, it is also possible to produce voiced and nasal clicks.

Exercise 7.14

a) Why can clicks be voiced and nasal when ejectives and implosives are much more restricted?

b) How would our diagrams change to show voiced and nasal clicks? Specifically, what would the diagram look like for the second stage of a voiced, nasal, alveolar click?

Comment

a) As the larynx does not have any involvement in initiating a click, the vocal folds can either vibrate for voiced clicks or remain open for voiceless clicks. Importantly, voiced clicks make use of two airstream mechanisms simultaneously. The velaric airstream mechanism takes care of the click part, as we have seen above. Voicing, however, occurs when air flows up from the lungs and through the vibrating glottis, so voiced clicks are actually produced on two airstreams simultaneously: velaric ingressive and pulmonic egressive.

As you can see from Figures 7.11 to 7.14, the nasal cavity is also independent from the actions of the oral cavity during click production, because all the air is trapped in front of the velum. Therefore, the velum can be lowered while the click is produced, without affecting the pressure in the space between the two closures, and a nasal click will result.

b) Figure 7.15 shows the second stage of a voiced, nasal, alveolar click.

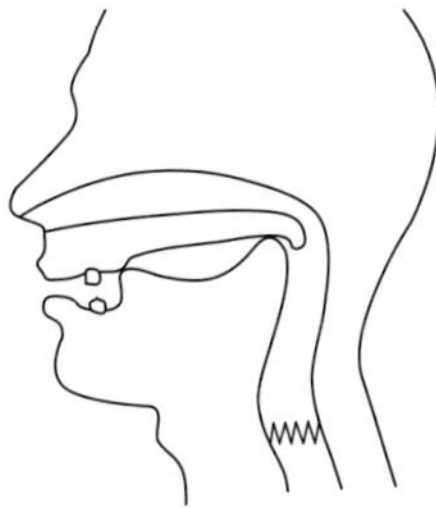

Figure 7.15 The second stage of a voiced nasal alveolar click

Exercise 7.15 a) How might our symbols change to symbolise clicks that are voiced or nasal?

b) How would we symbolise:

a voiceless dental click?
a voiced bilabial click?
a voiced nasal postalveolar click?

Tip Remember the role of [k] in the click symbols we have already seen above.

Comment a) As you will remember from Exercise 7.13, the initial part of the symbol indicates voicing and nasality, while also reminding us about velar closure. This is why a velar symbol (such as [k]) is used, rather than, say, an alveolar or bilabial symbol. We can, therefore, use other velar symbols to indicate voiced and nasal clicks.

b) So, while [k] indicates the click is voiceless and oral, [g] indicates it is voiced and oral, and [ŋ] indicates it is voiced and nasal. The rightmost part of the symbol simply indicates the place of articulation (and the manner for laterals) of the click, as we noted earlier.

A voiceless dental click	[k|]
A voiced bilabial click	[gʘ]
A voiced nasal postalveolar click	[ŋ!]

7.5.4 The velaric egressive airstream

In order to fully cover all the logical combinations of initiators and directions, we should mention the **velaric egressive airstream**. While it is possible to produce sounds (sometimes known as reverse clicks) using this airstream, no such sounds are found in human languages, so we will not discuss these further here.

7.6 Non-pulmonic consonants on the IPA chart

Figure 7.16 shows the symbols for non-pulmonic consonants, as they appear on the IPA chart. They can be seen on the full IPA chart in Appendix 1 (page 281).

7.7 Summary

In this unit we have looked at the production of implosives, ejectives and clicks, which are all produced on non-pulmonic airstreams. We have also learnt the symbols for these sounds and seen where they can be found on the IPA chart.

Consonants (Non-Pulmonic)

Clicks	Voiced implosives	Ejectives
ʘ Bilabial ǀ Dental ! (Post)alveolar ǂ Palatoalveolar ǁ Alveolar Lateral	ɓ Bilabial ɗ Dental/alveolar ʄ Palatal ɠ Velar ʛ Uvular	’ Examples p’ Bilabial t’ Dental/alveolar k’ Velar s’ Alveolar fricative

Figure 7.16 The non-pulmonic consonant section of the IPA chart

This means we have reached the end of the first section of the book, focussing on individual speech sounds.

7.8 Looking forward

In the next section, we will go on to think about what happens when we combine sounds into words, and we will begin by thinking about syllables and stress.

7.9 Review questions

- What is the most common airstream mechanism in English and in the languages of the world?
- Which two features need to be described when we name an airstream mechanism?
- Which of the physically possible airstream mechanisms is not used to produce sounds in any human language?

7.10 Review exercises

1 Fill in the following chart, naming the sounds produced using each type of airstream mechanism.

Initiator direction	Pulmonic	Glottalic	Velaric
Ingressive			
Egressive			

2 Write VPM labels for the following:

[kʘ]
[ɗ]
[ɡǁ]
[p’]
[ŋ̥ǀ]

3 Draw a head diagram for a voiced velar implosive, then turn your diagram into a voiceless dental click, and finally into a voiceless dental ejective plosive. In each case, draw the phase of maximum constriction. You can either draw three separate diagrams, or draw one in pencil and make alterations for each separate sound.

2 Putting sounds together

UNIT 8 SYLLABLES AND STRESS

8.1 Key learning areas

In this unit we will:

- investigate how words can be divided into syllables
- explore the constituent parts of a syllable
- learn some of the rules governing sound patterns in English
- discover the nature of stress.

8.2 Introduction

In this section of the book we start to think about what happens when we put sounds together to make words. Later we will see that sounds that we think of as being the same can be produced quite differently if we listen closely enough.

Firstly, however, in this unit, we will be looking at syllables and stress. We will try to define these terms and concepts, and will find that people generally have quite a good idea about these notions, even if they do not know much about phonetics.

8.3 Syllables

Exercise 8.1 Without looking anything up in a book, or thinking too hard about it, put these words in order of how many syllables they contain:

indigo orange aquamarine red

Tip Start by counting the syllables in each word.

Comment Most people agree that 'red' has one syllable, 'orange' has two syllables, 'indigo' has three, and 'aquamarine' has four. This is likely to be the case for all native English speakers, including those who have never studied phonetics. Ask your friends and family, to see if they agree with you.

So, hopefully you agreed with the comment above about how many syllables each word contains. But how did you complete the exercise?

Exercise 8.2 a) What did you do in order to come up with the correct answer in Exercise 8.1?

b) Based on your answer to (a), how would you define a syllable?

Comment (a) and (b) Most people struggle to answer these questions. They might mention feeling the rhythm of a word, or dividing it into beats, or tapping their finger for each syllable. All of these are useful in describing how a listener can count the syllables in a word, but do not really help us to describe a syllable to someone or to define the concept. It is interesting that people can essentially agree on how many syllables there are in words, even though they are unable to explain what a syllable is. However, our knowledge of phonetics can help us to work out what we are really doing when we count syllables.

Exercise 8.3 a) Transcribe the words below and then divide them into their component syllables, thinking about which sounds 'belong' to which syllable. You can show syllable division by adding a full stop character in between syllables within your transcription.

indigo orange aquamarine red

b) Can you see a pattern? What does a syllable have to contain, and what is optional?

Comment a) Your transcriptions may have looked rather like those shown below, but do not worry just now if you put the consonants in different syllables; we will think about that soon.

/rɛd/
/ɒ.rɪndʒ/
/ɪn.dɪ.gəʊ/
/æ.kwə.mə.rin/

b) All the syllables contain a single vowel, but the syllables may or may not contain consonants on either side of that vowel.

8.3.1 A phonetic definition of the syllable

We can define the **syllable** as a unit containing an obligatory centre part which is a sonorant (look back at Unit 4 if you need a reminder about obstruents and sonorants). This centre is usually a vowel (although in some circumstances it can be another sonorant, as we will see later).

As the vowel-like centre of the syllable is the only obligatory part, there are syllables made up entirely of vowels which contain no consonants at all, such as the words 'eye' /aɪ/ and 'are' /ɑ/ (for non-rhotic speakers). In our words above, the first syllables of 'orange' /ɒ/ and 'aquamarine' /æ/, both consist only of a vowel. This obligatory vowel-like part is called the **nucleus**. The term 'nucleus' comes from biology and physics, where the nucleus is the centre of the cell or atom, just as the nucleus here is the centre of the syllable. A nucleus contains one and only one vowel (or other sonorant), and diphthongs count as a single vowel, as the change in articulator position happens within a syllable. Therefore, a word containing two vowels also contains two syllables, and vice versa.

As we can see from Exercise 8.3, however, syllables can also start with a consonant, like the final syllable in 'indigo' /ɡəʊ/. Syllables can also end in a consonant, like the first syllable in 'indigo' /ɪn/, or have consonants both before and after the vowel, as in the final syllable of 'aquamarine' /rin/. The portion of a syllable that contains consonants before the nucleus in a syllable is called the **onset**, and the portion that contains consonants after the nucleus is called the **coda**.

Exercise 8.4 Here are some CVC words for you to divide into their constituent parts. What sound forms the onset, nucleus and coda in each word?

duck bath calm phone

Tip You may wish to transcribe these first, so that you are not misled by the spelling.

Comment In 'duck', /d/ is the onset, /ʌ/ is the nucleus, and /k/ is the coda. In 'bath', /b/ is the onset, /ɑ/ is the nucleus, and /θ/ is the coda. In 'calm', /k/ is the onset, /ɑ/ is the nucleus, and /m/ is the coda. In 'phone', /f/ is the onset, /əʊ/ is the nucleus, and /n/ is the coda. These transcriptions assume SSBE, but while the vowel symbols may differ for other accents, the division into the components of the syllable will be the same. Note, for now, that consonants are in the onset and coda, and vowels are in the nucleus. We will look at some more complicated examples in Exercise 8.6, and will now turn our attention to nuclei that contain a sonorant other than a vowel.

8.3.2 Syllabic consonants

As we have implied earlier in the book, /n/ and /l/ can form a nucleus instead of a vowel. When /n/ and /l/ occur in this way, they are known as **syllabic consonants**, because they, rather than a vowel, form the nucleus of a syllable. However, in all cases where a syllabic consonant can occur, an alternative pronunciation is also possible, where that consonant occurs as a coda and a schwa occurs as the nucleus. For example, in the word 'television' (which we looked at back in Unit 1), both /tɛlɪvɪʒən/ (where /ə/ is the nucleus of the final syllable, and /n/ is the coda) and /tɛlɪvɪʒn̩/ (with a syllabic /n/) are heard in SSBE.

There is also a special symbol that we can apply in transcription if we want to note explicitly that a consonant is syllabic. This is a single bar underneath the consonant in question – for example, /tɛlɪvɪʒn̩/. However, this symbol is not strictly necessary for our purposes, as we know /l/ and /n/ will be syllabic if there is no vowel to form the nucleus of the syllable; therefore, we will not use it further in this book.

Exercise 8.5 Try to work out if you have a tendency to use syllabic consonants or not.

Produce the following words as naturally as you can, while concentrating on the emboldened syllable. For each emboldened syllable, try to work out if you produce a syllabic consonant or a schwa followed by the consonant.

televis**ion** pudd**le** midd**le** heav**en**ly

Comment There is often variation between and within speakers as to whether or not they use syllabic consonants. Neither version is more correct than the other, but speakers may vary according to their accent, individual preferences, who they are talking to, and the situation, all aspects of variation that we will consider in Unit 14. We will also return briefly to syllabic consonants a bit later, when we think about elision in Unit 15.

8.3.3 Syllables in English and other languages

English allows many different types of syllable. As we have seen in the examples above, English has syllables consisting of just a nucleus, syllables with an onset and a nucleus, syllables with a nucleus and a coda, and syllables with all three constituents.

English also allows onsets and codas that contain more than one consonant. For example, the coda of the second syllable of 'orange' contains a cluster (or group) of two consonants, (/ndʒ/), as does the onset of the second syllable of 'aquamarine' (/kw/).

Exercise 8.6 Take the following words (which all consist of just one syllable) and divide them into onset, nucleus and coda. As usual, remember to transcribe them first.

phone street grand eve lamps

Tip You may find it easiest to start by finding the nucleus in each syllable.

Comment 'Phone' has one consonant in the onset /f/, a nucleus /əʊ/, and one consonant in the coda /n/, as we saw above. 'Street' has three onset consonants /str/, a nucleus /i/, and one consonant in the coda /t/. 'Grand' has two consonants in the onset /gr/, a nucleus /æ/, and two consonants in the coda /nd/. 'Eve' has no onset (also known as an **empty onset**), a nucleus /i/, and one consonant in the coda /v/.

'Lamps' has one onset consonant /l/, a nucleus /æ/, and three consonants in the coda /mps/.

In fact, English can allow up to three consonants in the onset, and four consonants in the coda of a syllable.

Exercise 8.7 What is the longest syllable you can think of in English?

Tip Make sure you are thinking of a single syllable, and not a long word with multiple syllables.

Comment The longest syllable will have three consonants in the onset and four in the coda. A syllable like 'strengths' represents the longest syllable in English, if you pronounce a /k/ in the coda, which many speakers do – that is, /strɛŋkθs/.

Other languages allow different sorts of syllables, and we can distinguish three broad categories of complexity. English is considered to exhibit complex syllable structure, as it allows more than two consonants in onset and coda position, but not all languages do so. For example, in languages like Darai (spoken in Nepal), considered to have moderately complex syllable structure, the most complex syllable allowed is CCVC (where C is a consonant and V is a vowel). Other languages are considered to have simple syllable structure. For example, Hawaiian has only CV syllables, and Igbo (spoken in Nigeria) has only CV or V syllables. (See www.wals.info if you would like to read more about this.)

8.3.4 Syllable affiliation in English

Exercise 8.8 Earlier we suggested that you might have had difficulty working out which syllable some consonants belong to, and we will explore this difficulty further now.

a) Think about the /p/ in happy. Do you think it is the coda of the first syllable /hæp.i/, or the onset of the second syllable /hæ.pi/, or can you not tell?
b) Ask some other people and see what they think.

Comment (a) and (b) This type of exercise is interesting and tends to draw different responses from people. In terms of theory, researchers also sometimes disagree about the syllable affiliation of these **intervocalic** consonants (consonants in between vowels). Some people think that stress attracts intervocalic consonants, so that the /p/ in 'happy' would belong to the first syllable, as it is stressed (louder and longer than the second syllable). Some people even think that the /p/ in 'happy' belongs to both syllables at the same time (that is, as the coda of the first syllable and the onset of the second) and say it is **ambisyllabic**.

In this book, we will take a different approach, based on the maximal onset principle; but to do that we need to know a few things about phonotactics and distribution, areas that we will now explore.

8.4 Phonotactics and distribution

Phonotactics refers to which sequences of sounds are allowed within a syllable in any particular language; and **distribution** refers to which sounds can occur in which positions within a syllable or word. We have already seen some examples of these in the book. For example, we have said that only three consonants are allowed in onsets in English (phonotactics) and that schwa cannot occur in stressed syllables (distribution).

Exercise 8.9 a) Look at the following transcriptions. None of them is a real word of English. However, for this exercise, you should work out which ones *could* be words of English. For example, if a new product came on to the market tomorrow, which of these could be new words for the name of that product, and which do not seem like words of English at all?

b) When you have worked out which ones can not be words of English, try to work out what is wrong with them.

/dɛm/
/ŋʊdəl/
/splim/
/spfid/
/ʒɔdʒ/
/bɑh/
/sɪŋt/

Comment (a) and (b) /dɛm/ and /splim/ are both perfectly good English words, which just happen not to exist in the language at the moment.

All the others, however, violate some important rules of English. These are rules that English speakers store internally in their minds about what is permissible in the language, and not conscious rules of what is right and wrong. /ŋʊdəl/ is problematic because words in English can never begin with /ŋ/. Words can end with this sound and it can occur intervocalically (between two vowels), but it never occurs at the start of a word. The status of /ʒɔdʒ/ is a bit less clear. In general, English words can not begin with /ʒ/. However, there are a few exceptions, such as 'genre', which have usually been borrowed into the language from French. It is still unlikely that newly invented words would begin with this sound, as many speakers would turn the initial /ʒ/ into the affricate /dʒ/. /spfid/

is also problematic as an English word because of its onset consonants. Onsets like /sp/ are fine in English, as in 'spin', and /sp/ can also be followed by /l/ or /r/ in English, as found in 'splint' and 'sprint'. However, /sp/ cannot be followed by another obstruent, such as /f/, in the onset. /bɑh/ is an impossible English word because the syllable ends in /h/. Likewise, /sɪŋt/ is impossible because of its coda. In English, nasals can be followed by voiceless plosives in the coda, as long as they agree in place of articulation. Hence, we have words like 'rank', 'ramp' and 'rant', where both coda consonants are velar, bilabial and alveolar, respectively. It is not possible to mix places of articulation for the nasal and voiceless plosive, however, so /sɪŋt/, with a velar nasal and alveolar plosive, is not a possible word of English.

Exercise 8.10 Try to produce /sɪŋt/.

Can you produce it? If so, how does it feel? If not, what do you do instead?

Comment Some speakers will be able to produce the non-word /sɪŋt/, but will find it feels very awkward. Others will find it so difficult that they change it to /sɪnt/ or /sɪŋk/, to fit the rules of English.

Of course, other languages make different choices about the sounds they allow to combine, and where sounds can occur within a syllable. We have already seen that many languages allow fewer consonants to occur in the onset and coda than English does, and Thai, for example, allows [ŋ] in the onset position.

8.4.1 The maximal onset principle

We now return to our question about syllable division from Exercise 8.8. Just how do we decide whether the /p/ in 'happy' forms the coda of the first syllable or the onset of the second? Throughout this book, we will use a rule called the **maximal onset principle**. This means that if an intervocalic consonant or consonant cluster *can* form the onset of a syllable in English, it is assigned to the onset of the second syllable. To make this kind of decision, we need to use our knowledge of English phonotactics and distribution. So, in 'happy', we know that /p/ is a perfectly fine onset (because it is the onset to real words like 'pen' and pin'). Therefore, in this instance, we say that it is the onset to the second syllable in 'happy'. In a word like 'lengthy', /ŋ/ and /θ/ both occur intervocalically. Using the maximal onset principle and our knowledge of phonotactics and distribution, we would say that /θ/ is the onset to the second syllable, but that /ŋ/ must be the coda to the first syllable, as the cluster /ŋθ/ cannot be an onset in English (by the same reasoning, the syllable division would be /lɛŋk.θi/ if you pronounce a /k/ in this word).

By comparison, in a word like 'restore', both the /s/ and the /t/ belong in the onset of the second syllable, because /st/ is an acceptable onset in English. So, using this principle, consonants and consonant clusters always go into the onset of a syllable, unless doing so disobeys the phonotactic or distributional rules of English.

Exercise 8.11 Divide the following words into syllables, paying particular attention to the intervocalic consonants and the maximal onset principle. Do not forget to transcribe the words first.

Baltimore Portland Austin Branson Washington Memphis
Kansas Aspen Detroit

Comment /bɒl.tɪ.mɔ/ or /bɒl.tɪ.mɔr/, /pɔt.lənd/ or /pɔrt.lənd/, /ɒ.stɪn/, /bræn.sən/, /wɒ.ʃɪŋ.tən/, /mɛm.fis/, /kæn.zəs/, /æ.spən/, /dɪ.trɔɪt/.

8.5 Stress

Now that we know what constitutes a syllable, we can move on to think about stress, which is an important property of syllables. We have already thought about stress when we introduced schwa in Unit 6, but we will now look at the phenomenon in much more detail.

Exercise 8.12 Think about the following words. Say them out loud and see if one of their syllables sounds more prominent than the others. Check with friends too, and see what they think.

cassette gramophone record disc video television

Tip It may help to work out how many syllables each word has first.

Comment The syllables that you have picked out, which seem to stand out in relation to the others, are known as the **stressed** syllables. As we mentioned when we introduced /ə/ in Unit 6, the stressed syllable can be indicated in transcription by using a raised straight line before the onset of that syllable; for example, /kəˈsɛt/ /ˈgræməfəʊn/ /ˈdɪsk/ /ˈvɪdiəʊ/ are probably fairly uncontroversial. 'television' may be stressed on the first or third syllable, depending on the speaker. For 'record', it may be harder to decide which is the stressed syllable, as the word's pronunciation depends on whether it is a noun or a verb. The other items in the group may have led you to believe that the intended word was a noun (i.e. 'a record'), in which case, the stress is on the first syllable /ˈrɛkɔd/. If the word is a verb, however (i.e. 'to record'), then the stress is on the second syllable /riˈkɔd/. Recall that stress is as much a part of our mental representation of a word as the vowels and consonants it contains.

Exercise 8.13 Listen again to the words in Exercise 8.12 and compare the stressed and unstressed syllables. What are the properties of stressed syllables that make them stand out and sound more prominent?

Comment Stressed syllables are different in several ways from unstressed syllables. Typically, they are both louder and longer, and cannot contain /ə/. They may also be associated with pitch prominence (as we will see in Unit 20).

Exercise 8.14 Look at the following two-syllable words. All of these can be stressed on the first or second syllable, depending on whether they are a noun or a verb. Try pronouncing them first with stress on the first syllable, and then with stress on the second, and work out which version is the noun and which is the verb.

present
refuse
import
invite (this may be rather colloquial as a noun for some speakers)
permit

Tip If you find it difficult to produce the two versions, try putting the word after 'a' or 'the' to make it a noun, and after 'to' to make it a verb.

Comment There are lots of pairs like this in English. For the majority of them, including those above, the pattern is like 'record', where the noun is stressed on the first syllable and the verb is stressed on the second syllable. However, the pattern is changing for some speakers, so that both members of the pair are stressed on the same syllable. For example, 'finance' is often stressed on the first syllable for both noun and verb.

8.5.1 Finding stressed syllables

Some students of phonetics have quite a lot of difficulty hearing stress, whereas others find it rather easy. If you find it difficult to pick out stressed syllables, there are a couple of things you can try. One trick is to cover your ears and say the word loudly. The stressed syllable should sound much more prominent than the others. Another trick is to shout the word across the room. You will automatically lengthen the stressed syllable and make it even louder than the rest of the word. Alternatively, try producing the word several times, each time stressing a different syllable, and working out which one sounds most like the word when it is spoken naturally. Just remember not to do any of these in an exam situation! To practise, you can take some words at random and check their stress pattern using a pronunciation dictionary.

8.5.2 Rules for stressed syllables

Stressed syllables are generally louder and longer than other syllables, as we have seen. Every word has a stress pattern (a specification of which syllables are stressed and which are unstressed) as part of its entry in our mental lexicon, the part of the brain where the pronunciation of all words is stored. In English, stress is largely unpredictable and can occur on any syllable of the word, as we saw in Exercise 8.12. This means that we need to listen really carefully to every word to work out its stress pattern. This is not the case for all languages, however, as some have the same stress pattern in all words. For example, Hungarian always has stress on a word's first syllable, and Polish words always have stress on the penultimate syllable.

So, English words can have any of their syllables stressed. Stress location may also be affected by the **affixes** that we add to words. Some of these affixes attract stress to themselves. For example, in the word 'themselves' that we have just used, the suffix 'selves' is stressed. Other affixes attract stress to the syllable before them. For example, the word 'athlete' is stressed on the first syllable, but in 'athletic' the stress moves to the second syllable, directly before the suffix '-ic'. Other affixes have no effect on the stress of the word to which they attach. These include most **prefixes**, which attach at the start of a word (such as 'pre-' and 'ex-') and lots of suffixes, too (such as '-ing' and '-ed').

8.5.3 Lexical and rhythmic stress

So far we have only discussed **lexical stress**, which refers to the stress pattern of words when they are produced in isolation (the term 'lexical' simply refers to individual words). However, we can also think about the stress pattern of syllables in sentences, and this is called **rhythmic stress**. While we will not explore this issue much further here, what you need to know for now is that rhythmic stress can sometimes override lexical stress.

Exercise 8.15

a) Think about the following phrases. Mark two stressed syllables in each phrase, one in each word.
   Chinese takeaway
   Waterloo station
b) Now find the *lexical* stress when the first word of each phrase is said in isolation.
   Chinese
   Waterloo
c) Compare the stress in the words in (a) with the stress in the words in (b). What do you notice?

Comment

a) Stress likely falls on the first syllable of each element: ˈChinese ˈtakeaway and ˈWaterloo ˈstation.

b) When we say the initial words in isolation, however, the stress is on the final syllable: Chiˈnese and Waterˈloo.

c) This phenomenon is known as **stress shift**, because stress shifts from the lexical stress position to somewhere else. This happens because another stressed syllable occurs immediately afterwards – that is, at the start of ‘takeaway’ and ‘station’. English likes stressed syllables to be separated by some unstressed syllables, and stress shift is one of the techniques the language employs to do just that. This may also be known as the ‘thirteen men’ rule, as this is often the example used to illustrate the phenomenon (compare the stress pattern on ‘thirteen’ in isolation and in the phrase).

Just as for lexical stress, it is not entirely possible to predict where rhythmic stress will occur in a sentence. However, there are a few generalisations to bear in mind. Firstly, it is more usual for **content words** (e.g. nouns, adjectives, verbs) to be stressed than **function words** – words that make an utterance grammatical, but do not add to its meaning (e.g. pronouns, conjunctions, determiners).

Secondly, notwithstanding our illustration of stress shift above, content words will normally be stressed on their lexically stressed syllable (as stated in our mental dictionary entry for these words). Finally, any syllable that contains a schwa cannot be stressed in English. You will still need to listen to sentences carefully, though, to work out which syllables are stressed. We will return to think briefly about rhythmic stress and the effect this can have on vowels and consonants in Unit 15, when we consider weak forms.

8.6 Summary

We have seen in this unit how we can define syllables and their component parts (onset, nucleus and coda). We have thought about phonotactics and distribution, as a way to decide how to divide words into syllables. We have also seen that all words have a stressed syllable as part of their entry in our mental lexicons, and that stressed syllables are louder and longer than unstressed syllables.

8.7 Looking forward

In the next units, we will move on to look at allophonic variation, starting with variations of voicing. We will discover that such variation is often affected by stress and syllable position.

8.8 Review questions

Have a look at these questions to see if you have understood the points to be learnt from this unit.

- What is the only obligatory part of a syllable in English?
- How do stressed syllables differ from unstressed syllables?
- How do we decide which syllable an intervocalic consonant belongs to?

8.9 Review exercises

1 Group the following words according to which syllable is stressed (i.e. put all those with a stressed first syllable together, and so on).

guitar recorder trumpet piccolo clarinet bassoon
cello triangle trombone harpsichord viola
violin tuba

2 Match the words on the left to the syllable structures on the right, where C is a consonant, V is a vowel and a full stop (.) represents a syllable boundary. There will be only one match for each, and the maximal onset principle is obeyed in each case. SSBE pronunciation is assumed, and syllabic consonants are not used.

kiwi	CV
guava	CCCV.CCV
grapes	V.CVC
melon	CV.CV
apple	CCV.CV
coconut	CV.CVC
pineapple	CVC
orange	CCVCC
lime	CV.CV.CVC
raspberry	V.CVCC
pear	CVC.CCV
plum	CV.CV.CVC
apricot	CVC.CV
mango	V.CCV.CVC
strawberry	CCVC

3 Transcribe each of the following words, noticing if and how the addition of affixes has any effect on the stress pattern of the word 'photograph'.

photograph photography photographic photographed rephotographed photographing

UNIT 9 ALLOPHONIC VARIATIONS OF VOICE

9.1 Key learning areas

In this unit we will:

- discover that the same phoneme can occur in a number of different forms
- explore how allophonic variation is conditioned by the environment and relates to coarticulation
- investigate why there is a need for two levels of transcription.

9.2 Introduction

So far we have looked at how individual sounds can be described and how we can transcribe English words. In this unit, we will see that there are a number of differences between sounds, which speakers of a language hardly ever notice. These variations are usually related to the surrounding sounds, and it is crucially important to know about them when studying phonetics.

9.3 Allophonic variation

Exercise 9.1 a) Make a transcription of the words 'pin' and 'spin'.
b) Are the two /p/s the same?

Comment a) Your transcriptions should be /pɪn/ and /spɪn/.
b) It is very likely that you have commented that the two /p/s are the same, but your opinion might change once you have completed Exercise 9.2.

Exercise 9.2 Take a single sheet of paper and hold it in front of your mouth. Now say the word 'pin' loudly and watch what happens to your piece of paper around the time you are producing the /p/. Now, keeping the paper where it is, say the word 'spin' loudly and watch the paper again.

Comment You probably found that your piece of paper moved after the /p/ in 'pin', but not after the /p/ in spin, demonstrating that, in fact, the two /p/s are *not* identical. This will be easy to observe for speakers of many accents of English, such as SSBE. However, for some other accents of English, such as some

Northern accents, there may have been little difference between the two. In this case, you might like to ask some friends with different accents to try the same experiment, to see what happens.

9.4 Aspiration

The effect you observed when the paper moved in 'pin' is the result of something called **aspiration**. Aspiration is an audible puff of air that occurs after another sound; it sounds rather like a short /h/. The /p/ in 'spin', on the other hand, is unaspirated. This means that there is no /h/-like friction after the release of the /p/. We will consider the detailed phonetics of aspiration and unaspiration shortly.

Aspiration is present in English not only for /p/, but also for the other voiceless plosives /t/ and / k/. There is a 'rule' for when aspiration occurs, which is related to the position of /p t k/ in the syllable, and the stress of that syllable. The rule is that aspiration occurs any time a voiceless plosive (i.e. /p t k/) occurs at the very beginning of a stressed syllable. However, /p t k/ are always unaspirated when they follow an /s/ in the onset of a stressed syllable – that is, when they are in an /s/-cluster. Note that these rules are not conscious rules that speakers deliberately follow, but unconscious rules, stored in their minds, which they learnt as they acquired English as a child.

Exercise 9.3 Look at the following words and work out from the rules above which voiceless plosives are aspirated and which are unaspirated when these words are produced in isolation, and therefore stressed.

tan king spend ski stand pen

Comment 'king' has an aspirated /k/, 'pen' has an aspirated /p/, and 'tan' has an aspirated /t/. 'stand', 'ski' and 'spend' all contain the unaspirated version of those consonants, as they come after /s/ in a cluster.

9.5 Diacritics

Now that we know there is a difference between the /p/ sounds in words like 'pin' and 'spin', we need a way to transcribe this difference. For most differences of this kind, we will add a small symbol to the symbol that we have already learnt for the sound. These small additional symbols are known as **diacritics**, and there is a special section for them on the full IPA chart. We will use a large number of diacritics in this book, but they are summarised in Appendix 3 for ease of reference (page 283). Aspiration is transcribed with a superscript – (that is, a small, raised) 'ʰ', and unaspiration is transcribed with a superscript 'equals' sign '⁼'. This is a different level of transcription to that which we have concentrated on so far, in that it shows more detail. For example, it shows aspiration and unaspiration, rather than transcribing all /p/s as the same. For this new type of transcription, we will need to use a different type of brackets, for reasons that will be explained more fully below. So, 'pin' is transcribed as [pʰɪn] and 'spin' is transcribed as [sp⁼ɪn]. You may remember that we also learnt how to show more detail for /r/ sounds, using [ɹ] and [ʋ], back in Unit 3.

9.6 Meaning differences

At this point, you may be feeling a bit confused. You have spent a long time (and several units of this book so far) learning about the sounds in SSBE, and now it turns out that there are more differences that you were not even aware of. Actually this is perfectly normal, particularly if English is your first language. As native speakers of a particular language, we learn to ignore small difference between sounds – for example, the difference between aspirated and unaspirated plosives. The reason is that these small differences never make a difference in meaning, as we shall see now.

Exercise 9.4 Remember that an aspirated /p/ has an audible puff of air before the following vowel, which sounds a bit like an /h/. An unaspirated /p/ has no puff of air. Try to swap these sounds around in words that you produce. For example, say 'spin' with an aspirated /p/, and 'pin' with an unaspirated /p/. This can be done quite easily with a bit of practice, or you could ask your teacher to say it for you, or to demonstrate it on a computer by splicing sounds together.

What do you notice about the meaning of the word? Does 'spin' still mean 'spin' even with an aspirated /p/? And what about 'pin'? Does its meaning change when the /p/is unaspirated?

Comment You should have found that, although the words might sound a bit odd, there is no meaning difference between 'spin' or 'pin' when they are produced with an aspirated /p/ or an unaspirated /p/. We will carry this idea further by thinking about phonemes and allophones.

9.7 Phonemes, allophones and minimal pairs

Phonemes are the smallest units that can make a meaning difference in a language, but they occur in slightly different forms depending on their **environment** (the other sounds around them, and factors such as stress and their position in the syllable). We can tell if two sounds are variants of the same phoneme by replacing one for another in a word and seeing if they make a meaning difference. If they do not, then we know they are different versions of the same phoneme. These different versions are called **allophones**. The aspirated and unaspirated sounds we have looked at in 'pin' and 'spin' are both allophones of the phoneme /p/, but we could easily have used different examples for the allophones of phonemes /t/ and /k/. In fact, every time we speak, we are actually producing allophones. The native listener simply categorises these according to which phoneme they belong to, and is very unlikely to even notice that different allophones of a single phoneme exist. This seems quite a surprising idea for many students, but hopefully it will become clearer and less odd as we work through the next few units.

In terms of transcription, then, we can transcribe the same speech at different levels of detail (and we will return to this idea in Unit 13). At one level, we can give a **broad transcription**, by including only enough detail to show which phonemes are present, and encase our transcription in slash brackets / /. We can also make more detailed transcriptions, known as **narrow transcriptions**, which we enclose in square brackets [ ]. One type of narrow transcription, for example, shows which allophones of phonemes are present, and would indicate, therefore, whether plosives are aspirated or unaspirated. This type of transcription is known as **allophonic transcription**. So, a broad transcription of 'spin' is /spɪn/, and an allophonic transcription is [sp$^{=}$ɪn]. Both transcriptions represent the same speech, but at different levels of detail.

Swapping one sound for another to look for meaning differences is a really useful tool and is referred to as a minimal pairs test. **Minimal pairs** are pairs of words that only differ by one sound and mean different things. So, 'pin' and 'tin' are a minimal pair, as are 'spin' and 'skin'. If a minimal pair can be found, it demonstrates that the two different sounds ([p^{h}] and [t^{h}], or [p$^{=}$] and [k$^{=}$]) are variants of different phonemes, because they make a meaning difference.

As we have already seen, there is no meaning difference when we swap allophones of the *same* phoneme, like aspirated and unaspirated /p/, even if the resulting words sound a bit odd. Thus, it is impossible to find a minimal pair involving aspirated and unaspirated /p/, because they are allophones of the same phoneme and never make a meaning difference in English.

Exercise 9.5 What phonemes are illustrated by the following English minimal pairs? For example, 'pin' and 'tin' illustrate phonemes /p/ and /t/.

a) ban and man
b) cat and rat
c) tin and tan
d) ram and ran
e) belated and berated

Comment a) /b/ and /m/
b) /k/ and /r/
c) /ɪ/ and /æ/
d) /m/ and/n/
e) /l/ and /r/

These pairs show that the two sounds which distinguish words in a minimal pair can differ by one feature (such as manner in (a)), or many (such as voice, place and manner in (b)). The test works for vowels (see (c)) as well as consonants, in onsets (a), (b), (e) and codas (d), and in multisyllabic words (e). As long as only one sound is changed, and that sound is in the same position in each word, then the words form a minimal pair.

We can also find minimal sets, such as 'ran', 'ram' and 'rang', which illustrate three (or more) separate phonemes, /m n ŋ/ in this case.

Exercise 9.6 Find minimal pairs to illustrate that the following pairs of sounds belong to separate phonemes in English. For example, for [t]–[d], you could say 'tangle' and 'dangle'.

[p]–[b]
[s]–[z]
[θ]–[ð]
[z]–[ʒ]
[g]–[ʒ]
[ŋ]–[h]

Comment You probably found this task harder as the list progressed. That is because there are more minimal pairs in the language for the pairs of sounds at the start of the list than those at the end. So, while the first two pairs are pretty easy, things get harder as you go along. For [θ]–[ð] you might have said 'thigh' and 'thy', for [z]–[ʒ], 'baize' and 'beige', and for [g]–[ʒ] 'mega' and 'measure', which is possibly the only minimal pair for these two sounds. You can see lists of minimal pairs at http://myweb.tiscali.co.uk/wordscape/wordlist/. Importantly, you will not have been able to find any minimal pairs for /ŋ/ and /h/, a point that we will explore further now.

Exercise 9.7 There are no minimal pairs in the English language for [ŋ] and [h].

a) Can you think why not?

Tip Remember what we learnt about the distribution of these sounds in Unit 8.

b) Do you think this means [ŋ] and [h] are allophones of the same phoneme?

Comment There are no minimal pairs for these sounds because they never occur in the same environment. This is a situation known as **complementary**

distribution. In this example, [ŋ] only occurs in codas and [h] only occurs in onsets. When two sounds are in complementary distribution, we often use this as evidence that they are allophones of the same phoneme, because it means that a minimal pair cannot be found (remember that minimal pairs differ by one sound in the same position in the word). Using our earlier example of aspiration, notice that aspirated and unaspirated sounds occur in different environments (in stressed simple onsets and stressed /s/-clusters, respectively). For [ŋ] and [h], however, most native speakers intuitively think they are allophones of *separate* phonemes, even though they are in complementary distribution and can never make a meaning difference between English words.

Exercise 9.8 Why do you think most speakers think of [ŋ] and [h] as different phonemes, rather than as allophones of the same phoneme?

Tip Think about the VPM labels for each one.

Comment The reason that these sounds are classed as separate phonemes, even though they are in complementary distribution, is that they are not phonetically similar. If we think about aspirated and unaspirated /p/, they are not only in complementary distribution, but are also phonetically similar, sharing the same voice, place and manner of articulation. So, to be classed as allophones of the same phoneme, sounds must be in complementary distribution *and* be phonetically similar.

Exercise 9.9 Imagine that a new language is discovered. This language might be on a newly explored island in the middle of the ocean or on a planet outside our solar system (in which case, it would likely be very different phonetically to most human languages, but we can imagine that the principles discussed in this unit still hold).

How will you work out which sounds are separate phonemes in this new language and which are allophones of the same phoneme? Think about practical considerations, such as the task you will ask your participants to perform, any equipment you might need and any analysis you will carry out.

Comment The crucial test will be to find minimal pairs in the language. In order to elicit words to analyse for minimal pairs, you might ask informants to name concrete objects (those that can be seen in the surroundings), as these are easier to consistently identify than abstract concepts, like 'truth' and 'justice'. Producing words individually has the advantage of breaking up the speech stream somewhat, so that you can tell where word boundaries are, and what each word refers to. You may also wish to record your participants, so you can listen several times to their speech, and possibly analyse it acoustically.

Exercise 9.10 Imagine that, after eliciting some speech from your informants, you get the following results.

[p^{h}an] means ‘belligerent’
[p$^=$an] means ‘birthmark’
[ban] means ‘to bloom’

The informants clearly use [p^h] [p=] and [b], but are they used in the same way as in English?

Comment [p^h] and [p$^=$] make a meaning difference in the language, so must be classed as allophones of different phonemes. We know this because there is a minimal pair involving these sounds in our data set. This is a good example of how different languages can use the same sounds in different ways. English also uses the allophones [p^h] and [p$^=$] as part of its sound system, but they are allophones of the same phoneme /p/. The language illustrated above is, in fact, Thai, where [p^h] and [p$^=$] are allophones of separate phonemes, both of which **contrast** (make a meaning difference) with [b]. This is the most typical example of this contrast in Thai, which you will find in many textbooks, but the same situation also exists at the alveolar POA, with a three-way contrast between [t^h] [t$^=$] and [d].

The details of the articulation and auditory effect of different allophones are a matter of phonetics. However, once we start to think about how sounds function in a language we are in the realm of **phonology**. In this book, we will concentrate on the phonetic aspects of different allophones and where they occur in English. While this will involve some aspects of phonology, we will leave detailed description of phonological theory to other textbooks, some of which are suggested in the Resources section (page 278).

9.8 Allophones of voicing

The remainder of this unit will be devoted to thinking about some of the allophones of English. We will concentrate on the articulatory aspects of these allophones, and the environment in which they typically occur in Standard Southern British English.

The allophones we will investigate in this unit all have something to do with voicing. As we will see, the voice label we have learnt for the phoneme may be modified somewhat, depending on the environment, when we examine the sound in more detail.

9.8.1 Recap of facts about voicing

Exercise 9.11 Fill in the gaps in the following paragraph for a reminder of the essential facts about voicing.

Whether a sound is classified as voiced or voiceless depends on the action of the ______ ______, situated in the larynx. For voiced sounds, the vocal folds are

_____ and are positioned close together so that they _____ in the airstream from the _____. For voiceless sounds, the vocal folds are usually _____ and held far apart, so that they do not vibrate. All vowels are _____, but _____ may be described as either voiced or voiceless.

Comment Whether a sound is classified as voiced or voiceless depends on the action of the vocal folds, situated in the larynx. For voiced sounds, the vocal folds are adducted and are positioned close together so that they vibrate in the airstream from the lungs. For voiceless sounds, the vocal folds are usually abducted and held far apart, so that they do not vibrate. All vowels are voiced, but consonants may be described as either voiced or voiceless.

So, in earlier units, we learnt that sounds can be categorised as either voiced or voiceless. What we will see now, however, is that the situation is rather more complicated. In particular, the label that we learnt for certain sounds may differ or be modified due to the environment in which those sounds occur.

9.8.2 Obstruent devoicing

In some environments, sounds that we have classified as voiced can in fact be produced without vocal fold vibration for some or all of their duration. We refer to this process as **devoicing**. One class of sounds whose voicing can be affected by the environment in this way is obstruents (see Unit 4.6 if you need a reminder of this term). In transcription, a small circle directly above or below a symbol indicates that a sound is devoiced. In this book, we will mainly use the diacritic above the symbol, for ease of reading.

Exercise 9.12 Look at the following sets of data, which are allophonic transcriptions. In these sets, we assume each word is spoken in isolation and thus surrounded by silence.

What is the rule for obstruent devoicing demonstrated in each set?

Set 1	Set 2
[g̊əʊld̊]	[wɛb̊saɪt]
[sɪlvə]	[b̊æg̊paɪp]
[b̊ɹɒnz̊]	[hɒtd̊ɒg̊]

Tip Firstly, find all the obstruents you have previously classified as voiced, and divide them into two sets, depending on whether or not they have been transcribed with the diacritic indicating devoicing.

Comment In set 1, the devoiced obstruents are at the beginning and end of words; hence the /v/ in 'silver' is not devoiced. In set 2, there are again some devoiced obstruents at the start and ends of words, but others appear next to voiceless

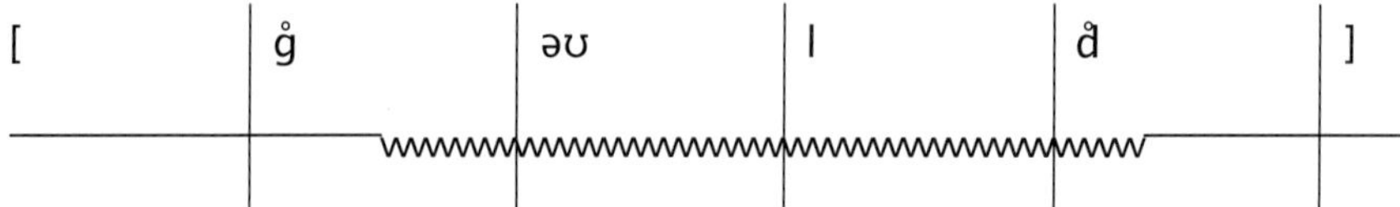

Figure 9.1 Parametric diagram of vocal fold vibration in 'gold'

obstruents. So, in set 2, obstruents are devoiced preceding or following silence or voiceless consonants. It is important to remember here that the words in set 1 are transcribed as if they were in isolation. If these words were pronounced in a phrase or sentence, things would be a bit different. For example, in the phrase, 'gold and silver and bronze', only the /g/ and /z/ would be devoiced, as they are next to silence. The /d/ and/b/ would no longer be next to silence, as we do not leave silent gaps between our words when we talk.

Exercise 9.13 Why do you think sounds classified as voiced might get devoiced next to silence and voiceless sounds? Why are they not devoiced next to *voiced* sounds?

Comment Many of the allophones that we will investigate come about due to the influence of surrounding sounds. We tend to think of sounds as individual discrete units, but, of course, they run together with sounds next to them, and because these sounds are produced with the same articulators, the sounds affect each other's production. Back in Unit 1, we said that speech is really like a movie, but that we can think of it as a number of still snapshots. Each of our snapshots, however, will be influenced by what happens before or after in the movie.

After silence or a voiceless sound, it can take some time for the vocal folds to start vibrating, so a sound we think of as voiced may not have vocal fold vibration the whole way through. Likewise, before a voiceless sound or silence, the vocal folds prepare to stop vibrating, and may stop early, while the rest of the articulators are still in position for the voiced sound. This process is called **coarticulation**, in which the articulations for successive sounds overlap, and therefore sounds change to accommodate features of the sounds that are around them.

We can draw a diagram to illustrate where vocal fold vibration takes place within a word. As you can see in Figure 9.1, a 'slot' is assigned to each segment, so the vertical lines indicate notional beginnings and ends of segments. The horizontal line represents the action of the vocal folds across the utterance. Vibrating vocal folds are indicated by the wiggly line, and lack of vibration by a straight line.

What we see here is that the vocal fold vibration does not begin immediately when the other articulators are in position for /g/. In addition, the vibrations of the vocal folds stop before the other articulators have moved out of position for /d/.

This type of diagram is called a **parametric diagram**, as it shows parameters such as vocal fold vibration, and can also be used to show the changing position of the velum across the course of an utterance, which we will do in Unit 11.

9.8.3 Direction of coarticulation

In the example in Figure 9.1, we see that sounds can be influenced by what comes before or after them. So, the /g/ in 'gold', when the word is produced in isolation, is devoiced because of the silence that comes *before* it. The /d/ of 'gold', when the word is in isolation, is devoiced because of the silence that comes *after* it. These two directions of influence have different names. If a sound is affected by what comes before, this is called **perseverative** (or progressive) coarticulation. If a sound is affected by what comes after it, this is called **anticipatory** (or regressive) coarticulation. You will see that these terms can also be used to describe the direction of assimilation in Unit 17.

9.8.4 Approximant devoicing

Obstruents are not the only sounds that are devoiced in English. Approximants are also devoiced, but in different environments to obstruents.

Exercise 9.14 See if you can spot when approximants are devoiced by looking at the following allophonic transcriptions.

[tɹ̊i] [lif] [ˈflaʊə] [pl̊ɑnt] [ˈkl̊əʊvə] [g̊ɹɑs] [wid̊] [ˈpɹ̊ɪvət] [ˈkʌntɹi]

Tip Divide the list into two, separating those words with and without approximant devoicing.

Comment Approximants are devoiced when they occur in a cluster after a voiceless plosive in the onset of a stressed syllable. Thus there is a devoiced /r/ in 'tree' and 'privet', and a devoiced /l/ in 'plant' and 'clover'. The /l/ in flower is not devoiced because it follows a fricative. The /r/ in grass is not devoiced because it follows a voiced plosive (even though this plosive is itself devoiced, the fact that the phoneme is *classified* as voiced means it does not trigger devoicing in the /r/). The /w/ in 'weed' is not devoiced because it does not follow a voiceless plosive in a cluster. Finally, the /r/ in 'country' is not devoiced because /tr/ is not the onset of a stressed syllable.

Again, coarticulation explains why there are different allophones of approximants. After voiceless plosives, the voicelessness carries over into the next sound, as can be seen in Figure 9.2; so a voiceless version of an

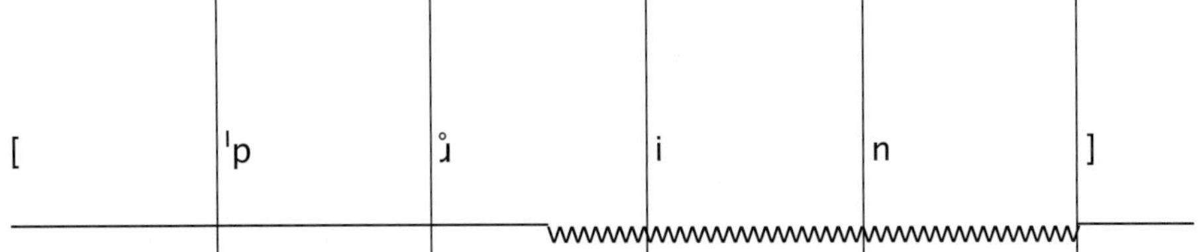

Figure 9.2 Parametric diagram of vocal fold action in 'preen'

approximant is heard, even though approximants are voiced in most other environments. Figure 9.2 shows how devoicing affects the /r/ in the word 'preen'.

9.8.5 Aspiration and unaspiration

We have already seen earlier in the unit that some sounds are aspirated and some are unaspirated. Now we will recap these phenomena. For Exercise 9.15, you need to remember that the symbol for aspiration is [^{h}], while that for unaspiration is [$^{=}$].

Exercise 9.15 Look at the following words. Try to work out in which environments sounds are aspirated and in which they are unaspirated. We have covered most of this briefly already, but the rule is slightly more complicated than that explained above.

[kəm'p^{h}æʃən] [pə't^{h}eɪtəʊ] [ə'st$^{=}$ɒnɪʃ] [spɛkju'leɪʃən] ['stɹɒŋgɪst]

['sk$^{=}$ul] ['skɹudʒ]

Tip Are there some sounds that are not marked with either diacritic?

Comment First of all, you should notice that aspiration and unaspiration only apply to the voiceless plosives /p t k/. This is true for English, but is not the case in all languages, as fricatives and affricates can be aspirated too. Secondly, you will have seen that stress and syllable position are crucial, as the aspirated and unaspirated allophones only occur in stressed onsets, as we have already said. You will also have seen that aspirated consonants occur when they are alone in the onset of a stressed syllable, while the same sounds are unaspirated in /s/ clusters. If an approximant follows in an /s/ cluster, such as in 'strongest', neither diacritic is used. Finally, you will note that when /p t k/ are in the onset of an *unstressed* syllable, neither diacritic is used. Thus, we can think of there being three levels of aspiration in English (aspirated, unaspirated, and a third level, called weak aspiration, which we will revisit below).

9.8.5.1 The phonetics of aspiration

Exercise 9.16 Look at Figure 9.3, which shows the vocal fold activity in the word 'Pam'. What do you notice about the vocal fold activity in the vowel?

Comment The vocal folds do not vibrate all the way through the vowel, even though we think of vowels as 'voiced' sounds. Rather than starting as soon as the articulators have released the bilabial closure, there is a delay in vocal fold vibration,

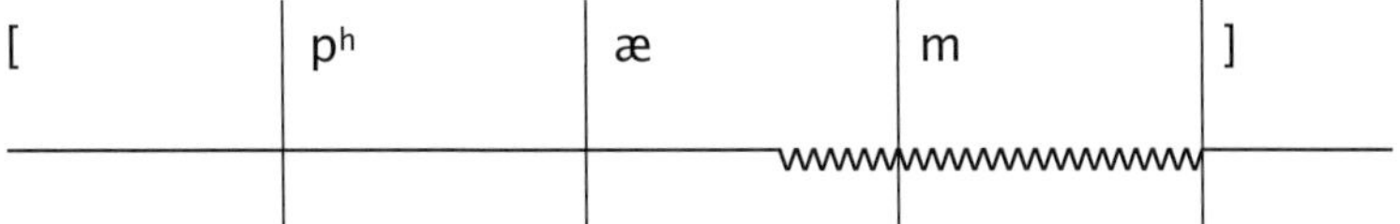

Figure 9.3 Parametric diagram of vocal fold vibration in 'Pam'

meaning that part of the vowel is voiceless. The time between the release of the plosive and the start of the vibration of the vocal folds is called **voice onset time** (VOT), which is measured in milliseconds. A delay in voicing is referred to as a positive voice onset time. We hear the delay in voicing as [h]-like friction, because air is still flowing through the vocal tract, even though there is no voicing; we call this friction aspiration.

It can be quite confusing to realise that the variation in voicing is actually associated with the following vowel, even though we talk about the *consonant* being aspirated and apply the diacritic to the consonant in transcription. This situation is really due to tradition, and is a consequence of us thinking about speech as a string of individual sounds, rather than as a more continuous stream. While we will follow the convention of talking about aspiration in relation to consonants, it is worth remembering that, phonetically, the effects of aspiration are present in the following vowel, as we can see in the parametric diagram (for example, Figure 9.3).

Exercise 9.17 If you compare the diagrams for aspiration in Figure 9.3 and devoicing of an approximant in Figure 9.2, you will note that they look very similar, in that both have a delay to the start of voicing. Why do you think we use different terms, and different diacritics, for these two phenomena?

Comment While the action of the vocal folds is delayed in both, the action and position of the other articulators (i.e. those above the larynx) is different. So, for a devoiced approximant, the articulators are in position for that approximant and a voiceless version can be heard. For example, for a devoiced /l/, the tongue is in the position for [l], but the vocal folds do not vibrate throughout. For aspirated plosives, in comparison, the following sound is a vowel, so the articulators are in position for that vowel during the voiceless period after the release of the plosive. Voiceless vowels sound like [h]. (You can test this yourself by whispering a few vowels and listening to them.) So, although the action of the vocal folds is similar in each case, the positions of the articulators *above* the larynx are different, as is the auditory effect. For this reason, we use two different descriptive terms (aspiration and devoicing) and two different diacritics.

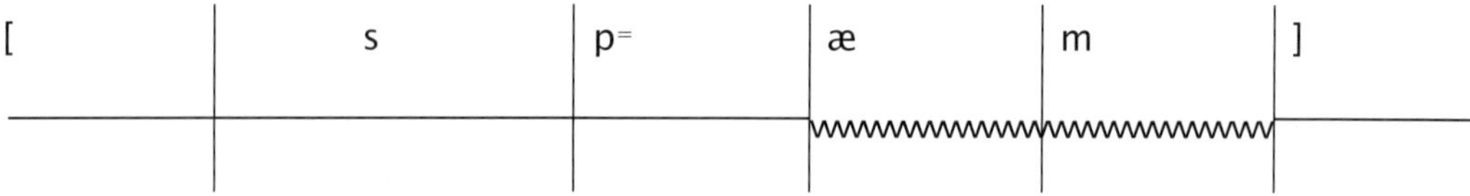

Figure 9.4 Parametric diagram of vocal fold action in 'spam'

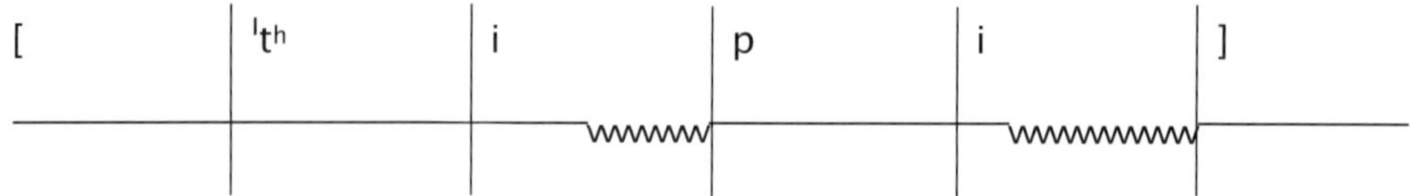

Figure 9.5 Parametric diagram of vocal fold vibration in 'teepee'

9.8.5.2 Phonetics of unaspiration

For the **unaspirated** /p/ in Figure 9.4, you will notice that vocal fold vibration begins immediately at the onset of the vowel, as soon as the bilabial closure for /p/ is released. There is no interval between the release of the plosive and the start of voicing, and we say there is zero VOT. Therefore, there is no interval where we can hear voiceless friction.

9.8.5.3 Phonetics of weak aspiration

As we noted above, however, we can also distinguish a third level of aspiration in English.

As you can see from the voicing diagram for 'teepee' (Figure 9.5), there is some delay in voicing for the vowel after the /p/, but that /p/ is not transcribed as aspirated. Again, this is largely a matter of convention. Voiceless plosives in unstressed onsets are followed by a shorter voice onset time than those in stressed onsets. While there is in fact a continuum of VOTs, we tend to divide this into three distinct categories for allophonic transcription, and only transcribe the plosives in stressed syllables as aspirated. So, in SSBE, we refer to three levels of aspiration for voiceless plosives: aspirated, unaspirated and weakly aspirated, as for /p/ in the example of 'teepee' in Figure 9.5. These weakly aspirated plosives occur as singleton onsets in unstressed syllables, and weak aspiration is not symbolised with any additional diacritic. Weak aspiration is also frequently not shown in parametric diagrams, and we will not show it in the remainder of the diagrams in this book.

9.8.6 Voicing of /h/

A final allophonic variation concerning voicing relates to sounds that are voiceless in most environments, but occur as voiced variants in certain situations. This is actually rather rare in English, and primarily affects /h/.

Exercise 9.18 a) Try producing the following words and listening to the /h/ sound. Do you hear any voicing for the /h/ in any of these words? In particular, compare the words on the left with those on the right,

hind	behind
head	ahead

b) Why do you think voicing of /h/ occurs where it does?

Comment a) /h/ can be voiced when it occurs between two vowels, in words like 'behind' and 'ahead'.

b) Here the voicing spreads from the surrounding vowels, which is another instance of coarticulation.

The symbol for a voiced glottal fricative is [ɦ], as can be seen on the IPA chart, and this symbol can be used to represent a voiced /h/ in an allophonic transcription. If you listen closely to the sound of the [ɦ], you might hear that it sounds breathy, with lots of air escaping each time the vocal folds part, rather than the smoother, less breathy voicing we hear for other 'voiced' sounds.

Exercise 9.19 Why do you think [ɦ] has a breathy quality?

Tip Think about its place of articulation.

Comment [ɦ] is breathy because not only do the vocal folds have to vibrate to produce voicing, they must also be in the correct position to produce friction, as the place of articulation is glottal.

Figure 9.6 illustrates the action of the vocal folds for /h/ in 'head' and 'ahead'.

9.9 Allophones and phonemes again

Finally, you may have wondered why we learnt labels and symbols for English sounds in the early units of the book, which have now changed. For example, why did we learn that /z/ is voiced, when in fact it can be devoiced, as we have seen here? The labels and symbols that we have learnt already only reflect quite general characteristics of the sounds in question. So, /z/ is frequently voiced, frequently alveolar, and frequently fricative. If it has all three of these characteristics, then it is represented as [z] in a narrow transcription. Under some circumstances, aspects of its articulation can change. The labels and symbols in the early units allowed us to think about sounds in general terms, but now we

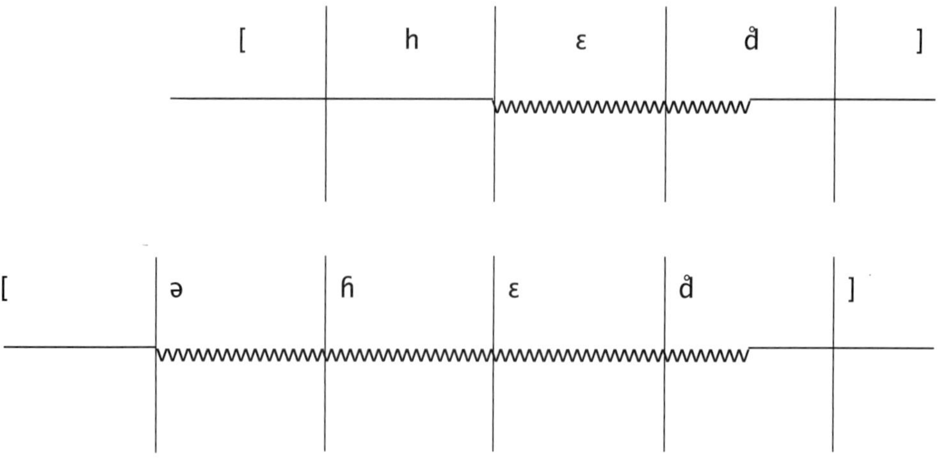

Figure 9.6 Parametric diagrams of vocal fold vibration in 'head' (upper) and 'ahead' (lower)

can add much greater detail, which can be shown in our allophonic transcription.

9.10 Summary

In this unit, we have looked at how the VPM labels we learnt for consonants may be modified according to a sound's environment, and we have considered variations in voicing, such as aspiration and unaspiration, devoicing of obstruents and approximants, and voicing of /h/. We have seen how such variations can be noted in an allophonic transcription and shown on a parametric diagram. We have also considered the difference between phonemes and allophones, and introduced the idea of coarticulation and allophonic transcription.

9.11 Looking forward

In the next unit, we will investigate allophonic variations of place of articulation.

9.12 Review questions

Have a look at these questions to see if you have understood the main points to learn from this unit.

- In any given language, how can we tell whether two sounds are allophones of the same phoneme or allophones of different phonemes?
- What are the three levels of aspiration we distinguished for SSBE, and how do they differ phonetically?

- In what environments are obstruents and approximants devoiced in English?

9.13 Review exercises

1 Look at the following words and think about the consonants that are emboldened. Remembering the rules for aspiration above, divide the words into three groups, depending on whether the emboldened consonant is aspirated, weakly aspirated or unaspirated, when each word is said in isolation.

a**pp**endix **k**idney s**t**omach intes**t**ines u**t**erus **p**ancreas

2 Now divide the following words into three sets, depending on whether they contain a devoiced approximant, a devoiced obstruent, or neither. Assume all words are spoken in isolation.

bladder brain prostate vein heart lung

3 Now give full allophonic transcriptions for all of the words in questions (1) and (2), including the diacritics we have started to use for aspiration, unaspiration and devoicing.

UNIT 10 ALLOPHONIC VARIATIONS OF PLACE

10.1 Key learning areas

In this unit we will:

- find out how allophones of a phoneme can vary in terms of place of articulation
- see how these allophones can be divided into primary and secondary types
- explore further how most allophonic variation is the result of coarticulation.

10.2 Introduction

In the last unit we saw that when we speak, we produce allophones. Phonemes are made up of a number of different allophones, and the allophones are produced in predictable ways according to the environment in which they occur. In the last unit, we also saw that there are voicing variations, such as aspiration and devoicing, which often occur due to coarticulation. In this unit, we will see that within a phoneme there may also be variations in place of articulation.

10.3 Variations in POA

10.3.1 Dental realisations

Exercise 10.1 Let us think about the phoneme /t/.

a) What place label have you learnt for this sound?
b) Now think about /t/ in the following words and try to decide if its POA is the same in each one.

eighth   track   leant

Comment You will probably have remembered that we normally label /t/ as alveolar. And in the word 'leant', its POA is indeed alveolar (unless you have replaced it with a glottal stop [ʔ]). However, in 'eighth', you will probably have found that the tongue touches the upper teeth, so the POA is dental; whereas in 'track', the tongue is further back in the mouth, closer to the postalveolar region (unless you use a labiodental [ʋ] in 'track', in which case /t/ is likely to be alveolar).

The /t/ in 'eighth' is dental due to the following dental fricative /θ/. This is due to coarticulation, as the features of one sound influence an adjacent sound. We use a diacritic to symbolise this allophone, in the same way that we use diacritics to transcribe aspiration and devoicing. The diacritic indicating that a sound's POA is dental is [̪] underneath the symbol for that sound. You will notice that the direction of coarticulation is anticipatory because the allophone comes before the trigger sound.

Exercise 10.2 We have seen that /t/ is realised as [t̪] in 'eighth'. However, we know from looking at other allophones in the previous unit that the same processes of coarticulation often apply to *classes* of sounds – that is, sounds with the same voicing, manner or place. For example, devoicing occurs in the same environment for all voiced obstruents in English.

a) What other sounds do you think might be realised as dental before dental fricatives?
b) Produce the following words, paying particular attention to the sound before the dental fricative. Which of them are produced with a dental POA?

wealth menthol everything rose-thorn breakthrough

Comment (a) and (b) The /k/ of 'breakthrough' and the vowel /i/ in 'everything' are unaffected by the following dental. The /l/ of 'wealth' and the /n/ of 'menthol' are both produced as dentals, so at first it may appear that the process is open to all alveolar sounds. However, the /s/ of 'rose-thorn' is unaffected. We can therefore summarise the rule by saying that alveolar stops (both plosives and nasals) and /l/ are realised as dental before a dental fricative. You will have noticed that we are learning about lots of different allophones and you may be finding them difficult to remember. Recall that you have a list of these allophones in Appendix 3, for ease of reference (page 283).

10.3.2 Retraction

We have just seen that sounds we have initially classified as alveolar can in fact be realised as dentals in a particular environment. In Exercise 10.1, we also saw that the POA for /t/ in 'track' was further back in the mouth than we might expect for a sound we classify as 'alveolar'. When a sound is produced with a POA that is further back in the mouth than most other allophones of that phoneme, we call this process **retraction**. We symbolise retraction using the diacritic [̠] underneath another symbol in an allophonic transcription.

Exercise 10.3 We have seen that /t/ is retracted before /r/, but, again, we need to see if our rule should be any broader. In particular, we need to see if it is only /r/ which triggers retraction of alveolars.

Produce the following words, concentrating particularly on the alveolar stops and /l/. Before which sounds are they retracted?

pi**n**ch **d**raw hea**d**s we**l**sh wi**d**th

Comment You should find that /n/ is retracted before /ʃ/ (or /tʃ/, depending on your pronunciation) in 'pinch'. /d/ is retracted before /r/ in 'draw' (unless you use [ʋ] in this word), and /l/ is retracted before /ʃ/ in 'welsh'. The alveolar /z/ of 'heads' does not affect the /d/, and we know that the /θ/ in 'width' will actually cause the /t/ to be realised as a dental. Therefore, we can summarise by saying that alveolar stops and /l/ are retracted before postalveolar sounds (such as /ʃ ʒ tʃ dʒ/ and [ɹ]). Again, this process is anticipatory. The alveolar fricatives sometimes behave in a similar way, but, for various reasons, we will leave these until Unit 17, where we deal with place assimilation.

Exercise 10.4 Alveolars are not the only consonants that can be retracted. Sounds that we classify as velar phonemes can also be retracted, but in different environments to the retraction of alveolars. We use the same symbol as for retraction of alveolars, but this time the symbol means that the POA is approaching the uvular region.

Think about and produce the following words, concentrating on the emboldened velar phonemes.

queen **g**eese **g**houl **G**went **c**aught **c**rab **g**et

a) In which words are the velars retracted? Think about whether your tongue touches the velum or further back in the mouth.
b) How might we summarise the environment for retraction of velars?

Comment a) Hopefully, you have found that /k/ and /g/ are retracted in 'queen', 'ghoul', 'Gwent' and 'caught'.

b) If we look closely at these words, we see that the environment for retraction is before back vowels (/u/ and /ɔ/ in these examples) and /w/. Of course, this makes sense when we think about coarticulation. An upcoming back tongue position affects the POA of a previous 'velar'. We know that /w/ is produced in almost the same way as /u/, which explains why /w/ has the same effect as the back vowels. Again, this is an anticipatory process, as the velar is affected by the following sound.

10.3.3 Advancement

Conversely, velar sounds can also be produced at a POA further forward in the mouth than the phoneme's place label would suggest, which is known as **advancement**. We use the diacritic [̟] underneath another symbol to signify that that sound is advanced.

Exercise 10.5 a) In what environments do you think velars might be advanced?

Tip Keep in mind the rule for *retraction* of velars.

b) Produce the following words, concentrating on the velars to see if you are correct.

cute   cake   **g**irl   cube   **g**eese

Comment a) You may have worked out, by comparison with the environment for retraction, that velars will be advanced before front vowels, and thus advancement is an anticipatory process.

b) Advancement of velars happens in 'cake' (where the first element of the diphthong /eɪ/ is a front vowel) and 'geese' (where the vowel /i/ is a front vowel). As /j/ is so similar in articulation to the front vowel /i/, we find that velars are also advanced in front of /j/, as in 'cute' and 'cube'. When velar sounds are advanced, the place of articulation is actually near to the palatal region.

We saw previously that velars are retracted before back vowels, and advanced before front vowels. But what about central vowels? As you will notice if you think carefully about /g/ in 'girl', velars have a truly velar POA before central vowels.

10.3.4 A note about advancement and dental realisations

As just explained, for articulations further back in the mouth than VPM labels suggest, we use the same term, retraction, and diacritic [̠] for both velars and alveolars. We do this, even though the resulting POA is different: close to uvular for velars, and postalveolar for alveolars. However, for articulations further *forward* in the mouth, we use two different terms and diacritics: advancement [̟] for velars and dental [̪] for alveolars. In the latter case, it would not be strictly incorrect to use the term 'advancement' instead of 'dental', but the term 'dental' is more specific and we will continue to use it in this book.

Exercise 10.6 You now know the rules for advancement, retraction and dental realisations.

Have a look at the following words, and produce them while concentrating on the velar and alveolar consonants emboldened. Work out for each word whether you need to add a diacritic for dental realisations, retraction or advancement in allophonic transcription, or if the consonant in question is in fact produced at the place of articulation that we learnt in Unit 3.

course **c**raze hea**l**th **k**een **g**arbage **c**ue **c**age **t**rams be**ll**s

Tip Remember to bear in mind the environments for each allophone that we have investigated above.

Comment 'course' has a retracted /k/ as it occurs before the back vowel /ɔ/. In 'craze', there are no place variations, as the /k/ is not affected by postalveolar sounds such as /r/. 'health' has a dental /l/ due to the following dental fricative. 'keen' has an advanced /k/, as the following sound is the front vowel /i/. 'garbage' has a retracted /g/ due to the following back vowel /ɑ/. 'cue' has an advanced /k/, as does 'cage', due to the following /j/ and /eɪ/, respectively. 'trams' has a retracted /t/ due to the following postalveolar /r/. The /l/ in 'bells' is alveolar, as stated in its VPM label.

Note that for speakers who use a labiodental realisation of /r/ in *all* positions, this sound will not trigger retraction of preceding alveolars in words like 'trams'. However, many speakers with labiodental /r/ everywhere else (myself included), actually use a postalveolar realisation of /r/ when following /t/ or /d/, and retract the alveolars accordingly.

10.3.5 Labiodental realisations

There is another type of place variation that we need to look at. When sounds classified as bilabial /p b m/ come immediately before the labiodental fricatives /fv/, their place of articulation may in fact be labiodental.

Exercise 10.7 Think about the /m/ in 'triumph' and work out if you can see and feel that the POA of the /m/ is indeed labiodental. Try the same exercise with the bilabials in 'o**b**vious' and 'ty**p**eface'.

Comment For some speakers, the /m/ in 'triumph', /b/ in 'obvious' and /p/ in 'typeface' are all labiodental, due to the presence of the upcoming labiodental sound. Again, this realisation is due to anticipatory coarticulation, where the articulators anticipate the following sound.

The diacritic for these labiodental realisations is the same as that for dental realisations, [̪], which can be somewhat confusing. It is important to remember, however, that the diacritic means labiodental when it occurs under an otherwise bilabial symbol, and dental when it occurs under an otherwise alveolar symbol. In addition, the IPA provides a unique symbol for a voiced labiodental nasal, which is [ɱ], as can be seen on the IPA chart in Appendix 1 (page 281). Thus, [ɱ] and [m̪] symbolise the same sound.

10.4 Secondary articulations and variations of place

In all the examples we have looked at above, the place of articulation of a sound is different to that stated in the VPM label that we give by default to the phoneme. So, those phonemes that we would classify as alveolar can in fact be realised as postalveolar or dental, according to their environment. Similarly, velars can be realised with places of articulation near to the uvular or palatal regions, and bilabials can be labiodental. The labels that we learnt in Unit 3 relate only broadly to the phonetic detail that we now know about.

As you know, the term 'place of articulation' refers to the greatest constriction in the vocal tract, and this can also be referred to as the **primary articulation**. For the allophonic variations we have just considered, the primary articulation is different to most other allophones of the phoneme in question, and we can refer to these as **primary variations of place**.

There is another type of variation of place that does not relate to the location of the primary articulation, but in which an extra, or secondary, constriction is added in the vocal tract. This **secondary articulation** is always of a lesser degree of stricture than the primary articulation. So, for example, the primary articulation may be a plosive, and the secondary articulation an approximant. We will refer to these types of variation as **secondary variations of place**, and will look at several types.

10.4.1 Labialisation

Labialisation is the technical term for lip-rounding. Any consonant can be labialised before rounded vowels or before /w/. We use the diacritic [ʷ] to the right of a symbol to symbolise labialisation, as shown in the 'Diacritics' section of the full IPA chart in Appendix 1 (page 281).

Exercise 10.8 Let us compare 'teak' and 'tweak', by producing them and thinking about the initial alveolar in each case.

a) Firstly, see if you can reassure yourself that the primary place of articulation for /t/ is alveolar in both words.
b) Now try to work out if you can see or feel lip-rounding during the /t/ in either of the words. It may help to look in a mirror, or to ask someone else to say the words for you.
c) Now do the same exercise for 'spoon' and 'span', concentrating on the /p/.

Comment
a) You should find that the primary articulation for /t/ is alveolar in both words.
b) However, if you look in a mirror you should see that there is lip-rounding during the /t/ in 'tweak', due to the influence of the following /w/, but not during 'teak'.

c) In both 'spoon' and 'span', /p/ is bilabial, but you will likely see lip-rounding during the /p/ of 'spoon', due to the influence of the following rounded vowel /u/.

In fact, labialisation applies to any consonant when it occurs before a rounded vowel or /w/, and, as we have said, we use the diacritic [ʷ] to indicate labialisation in allophonic transcription. Because consonants are affected by the following sound, this is an anticipatory process. Labialisation does not affect the primary articulation of the sound, but adds another constriction. This constriction is a secondary articulation, because it is less extreme than the other, primary, articulation. For example, the primary articulation for /t/ in 'tweak' is at the alveolar ridge, and, as it is a plosive, this is a stronger constriction (that is, the articulators are closer together) than the lip-rounding, in which there is wide approximation between the articulators.

We now know that sounds are labialised before rounded vowels or /w/. In fact, as we know, all the rounded vowels in English are also back vowels. Therefore, labialisation occurs in the same environment in which velars are retracted – that is, before back vowels and /w/.

Exercise 10.9 Think about the word 'course' from Exercise 10.6 (page 133) and try to answer the following.

a) Do we expect the velar to be retracted?
b) Do we expect there to be lip-rounding during the velar?
c) Do we know of any other variations of /k/ that will apply in this word when it is spoken in isolation?
d) Can more than one allophonic variation apply to the same phoneme at the same time?

Comment (a) and (b) We know that /k/ will be retracted before the back vowel /ɔ/. We also know that /k/ will be labialised, because /ɔ/ is rounded. In fact, the /k/ is both retracted and labialised in this word.

c) You may also have noticed that the /k/ will be aspirated, as it is a voiceless plosive at the start of a stressed syllable.

d) Thus, allophones of a phoneme can actually differ from each other in several different ways, and an allophonic transcription notes all these variations. So, in 'course', /k/ is realised as an aspirated voiceless retracted velar plosive with lip-rounding, and it could be transcribed allophonically as [k̠ʷʰ]. Remember that an allophone is the actual sound that we produce, and we include as much detail about it as possible in our allophonic transcriptions.

Of course, not *all* allophonic variations can combine, because some articulations are mutually exclusive. An allophone of /t/ cannot be both retracted and dental, for example, or both aspirated and unaspirated, as these have mutually incompatible articulations (and they occur in mutually exclusive environments). As a rule of thumb, a single realisation might have one difference of voice, one of primary articulation, one of secondary articulation, and one of manner from most other allophones of that phoneme.

10.4.2 Palatalisation

We have seen that labialisation does not affect the primary POA of a sound, but instead adds a secondary articulation at the lips. **Palatalisation** is similar to labialisation in this regard, but a secondary articulation is added in the palatal region of the vocal tract. We use the diacritic [ʲ] to the right of another symbol to symbolise palatalisation.

Exercise 10.10 Think about the words 'noon' and 'news' and transcribe them broadly. Be very careful to think about whether you produce a /j/ after the /n/ in 'news'. Most speakers of SSBE will, but some American speakers, those with some British accents, and younger British English speakers may never produce /j/ in this and similar words. This exercise will only work for speakers who *do* produce a /j/ in 'news', so you may wish to get a friend to say them if this exercise does not work for you.

a) Concentrate on the /n/ in each of these words. In particular, think about how your tongue feels, and which parts of the tongue are high in the mouth.
b) Do you notice a difference between /n/ in the two words?

Comment (a) and (b) If you do produce a /j/ in 'news', you will have felt that the front of the tongue comes close to the palatal region of the mouth during /n/, whereas this did not happen in 'noon'. Again, this is an effect of anticipatory coarticulation as the tongue prepares to produce /j/ during the /n/. In fact, any non-velar sound is palatalised before /j/.

Exercise 10.11 Think about the statement above, 'any non-velar sound is palatalised before /j/', and about the primary POA allophones we have already discussed in this unit.

a) Why are only *non-velar* sounds palatalised before /j/?
b) What happens to *velar* sounds in this environment (before /j/)?

Comment (a) and (b) As we have seen in 'news', /n/ is alveolar, as in most other environments, but gains a secondary articulation in the palatal region. However, *velar* sounds are *advanced* before the palatal approximant /j/, as we saw above. In a word like 'queue', therefore, the presence of the palatal actually affects the *primary* POA of the velar, which we say has been advanced to nearer the palatal place of articulation.

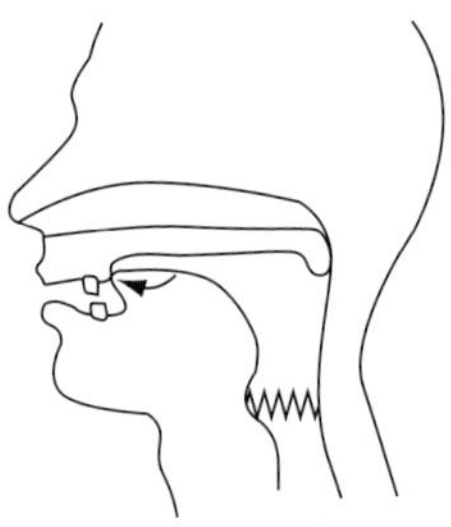 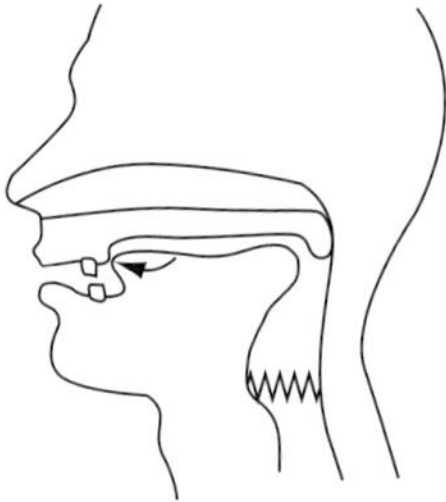

Figure 10.1 Mid-sagittal sections showing the production of non-velarised (left) and velarised (right) /l/

10.4.3 Velarisation

Exercise 10.12 Given your knowledge of palatalisation and labialisation, what do you think velarisation might mean?

Comment **Velarisation** means a secondary articulation in the velar region of the vocal tract. Like palatalisation and labialisation, velarisation is a secondary POA variant, so will not influence the primary POA of any sound it affects. Velarisation applies primarily to /l/ in English, but only occurs in certain environments.

Exercise 10.13 Think about and produce the words 'little' and 'lulled'. In each word, compare the /l/ in the onset with the /l/ in the coda, and concentrate on the shape of your tongue, particularly towards the back.

What do you notice?

Comment This can be quite difficult to feel, but hopefully you noticed that the back of your tongue comes close to the velar region of the mouth for the /l/s that are in the coda, but that there is no such approximation for the onset /l/s. The two tongue shapes are shown in Figure 10.1. In SSBE, /l/s are velarised when syllabic or when in the coda of a syllable (see Unit 8 for a reminder of these terms), provided they are not immediately followed by a vowel. Another name for velarised /l/ is **dark /l/**, and we can use the diacritic [ˠ] to the right of a symbol to show velarisation in general, or the special symbol [ɫ] to indicate a velarised /l/. In this book, we will not use the use the [ɫ] symbol, to avoid confusion with the symbol for a voiceless alveolar lateral fricative [ɬ]. Instead, we will use the [ˠ] diacritic, for consistency with other allophonic variations, such as palatalisation [ʲ] and labialisation [ʷ]. Note that non-velarised /l/s are called **clear /l/s**, and no diacritic is added to the symbol we use for the phoneme: [l] signifies a clear /l/. Take care to remember that [l] *is* an allophone of /l/, just as [lˠ] is, even though it does not have any diacritics added in an allophonic transcription.

Consonants before the [lˠ] can also be velarised – for example, in 'hustle', both the /s/ and the /l/ are velarised: [hʌsˠlˠ]. When /l/ occurs between two vowels, it tends to be clear.

Exercise 10.14 We have seen that labialisation and palatalisation are the result of coarticulation. Labialisation occurs due to an upcoming sound with lip-rounding, and palatalisation occurs due to an upcoming palatal sound.

Let us think again about 'little' and 'lulled', and about the rule mentioned above for velarisation.

Do you think velarisation comes about because of a velar sound in the environment?

Comment Velarisation is rather different to the other secondary place allophones we have looked at. Velarisation is not the result of coarticulation due to a velar segment in the environment. Instead, syllable position determines whether /l/ is velarised or not, as we have seen above. We refer to this as a rule-based or **extrinsic allophone**, because it cannot be predicted from the surrounding sounds. Extrinsic allophones tend to be language-specific rather than universal. So, whereas labialisation will happen in many languages before rounded vowels, for example, not all languages will velarise /l/ syllable finally.

10.4.3.1 Accent-specific allophones of /l/

Different regional accents of English also have different allophones of /l/. Scottish English speakers tend to use velarised /l/ in all positions, including onsets, while Welsh and Irish English speakers tend to have clear /l/ in all positions, including codas. Many accents, such as Cockney, use a **vocalised /l/** wherever SSBE uses a dark /l/. When a consonant is vocalised, it becomes more like a vowel. For vocalised /l/, the velar approximation of dark /l/ remains, but the tongue tip contact is removed, resulting in a sound like a high back vowel, which can be symbolised as [o] or [ʊ]. These variants would be recorded in an allophonic transcription but in a broad transcription, all variants will simply be transcribed as /l/.

10.4.4 Glottal reinforcement

In Unit 3, we saw that speakers often use a glottal plosive [ʔ] as a version (we now know the term 'allophone') of /t/ in English, a situation we referred to as 'glottalling' or 'glottal replacement'. However, it is also possible to produce a glottal plosive *at the same time as*, or slightly before, the oral closure for the voiceless plosives /p t k/, when they occur at the end of an utterance. This is known as **glottal reinforcement**, or glottalisation, and can be shown by adding the [ʔ] symbol to our allophonic transcriptions before the sound that is glottally reinforced.

Exercise 10.15 Produce the following words and try to work out if you are producing a glottal plosive at the same time as (or slightly before) the final voiceless consonant.

rat rack rap

Comment It can be quite difficult to work out whether or not you are glottally reinforcing voiceless plosives, so it might be worth practising several times and asking a teacher to check for you. In addition, you may have used glottal *replacement* in 'rat' in this exercise. People also vary in whether or not they use glottal reinforcement, and this can depend on their accent, or just the situation in which they are speaking. As glottalisation varies substantially between and within speakers, we will not include it in allophonic transcriptions in the following units.

10.5 Summary

In this unit, we have explored allophones of place of articulation. We have looked at variations in the primary articulation, such as advancement and retraction, and variations when a secondary articulation is added, such as labialisation and velarisation.

10.6 Looking forward

In the next unit we will explore allophonic variations of manner.

10.7 Review questions

See if you can answer the following questions, based on the key learning areas for this unit.

- What is the difference between primary and secondary allophonic variations of place?
- Name, and give examples of, all the types of primary and secondary place variations discussed in this unit.
- What is an extrinsic allophone?

10.8 Review exercises

If you would like further practice, try the following.

1 Match each diacritic to the relevant allophonic process.

retraction	[ʷ]
advancement	[ˠ]
dental/labiodental realisations	[̠]

labialisation	[ʲ]
palatalisation	[˖]
velarisation	[˗]

2 Give full allophonic transcriptions of the following, including diacritics from this unit and Unit 9.

corners
huge
twitch
eleventh
bold
trance

3 Find the errors in the following three allophonic transcriptions, and explain why each transcription is wrong.

million	[mɪlˠɪən]
cupid	[kʲjupɪd̊]
green	[g̠ɹin]

UNIT 11 ALLOPHONIC VARIATIONS OF MANNER

11.1 Key learning areas

In this unit we will:

- explore how allophones of a phoneme can vary in manner of articulation
- discover how these allophones can relate to the approach and release phases of plosives
- investigate nasalisation.

11.2 Introduction

So far, we have looked at how a phoneme's allophones can vary in terms of voicing and place of articulation. Here, we will think about how they can vary in manner. We will start by thinking about nasalisation, a topic that we will continue in the next unit, about vowel allophones.

11.3 Nasalisation

Exercise 11.1 Just using your knowledge of the English language, and the phonetics terminology you have learnt so far, what do you think the following terms might mean?

nasal
nasalise
nasalisation

Comment You know from previous units that nasals are consonants with a complete blockage to airflow in the oral cavity, but with a lowered velum so that air escapes through the nose. The nasals in English are /m n ŋ/. The suffix '-ise' (or '-ize') means something like 'cause to be', and is used to turn a noun into a verb. In this book, for example, we use words like 'symbolise', and words like 'visualise' are common in everyday language. Therefore, 'nasalise' means something like 'to cause something to be nasal'. The suffix '-tion' is also common in English and is used to turn a verb into a noun. More specifically, it is added to a verb to mean an instance of that verb. So, for example, we have the verb 'to demonstrate', and a 'demonstration' is an instance of people demonstrating. 'Nasalisation', then, is an instance of something being nasalised.

As we have seen in the previous units, speech is not a string of separate segments, even though this is a convenient way to think about it. Speech sounds overlap, and coarticulation means that sounds affect one another. One way in which manner of articulation is affected is that sounds can be nasalised in certain environments. For these **nasalised** sounds, the velum is lowered so that air can flow through the nasal cavity. Unlike *nasal* consonants, however, there is no blockage to airflow in the oral cavity. Therefore, nasalisation means that there is simultaneous oral and nasal airflow.

Exercise 11.2 Thinking back to what you know about manner of articulation, and rereading the comment on Exercise 11.1, what manners of sounds do you think can be nasalised, and which cannot?

Tip Think back to what we discovered about obstruent and sonorant sounds in Unit 4.

Comment As you will remember from Unit 4, obstruent sounds (such as plosives, fricatives and affricates) must have velic closure, as they need pressure to build in the oral cavity. If the velum is lowered, air can escape through the nasal cavity and pressure cannot build. Therefore, obstruents cannot be nasalised. Sonorants (vowels, nasals and approximants, including lateral approximants) do not need pressure to build, which means that they do not need velic closure, and, in fact, nasals must have velic opening. For approximants, however, velic closure is optional, and when they are produced without velic closure, they are nasalised. What we will see shortly is that whether the velum is open or closed during approximant sounds is largely due to coarticulation.

Mid-sagittal sections for a non-nasalised (left) and nasalised (right) approximant /j/ are shown in Figure 11.1. Note that the position of the velum is different in the two pictures.

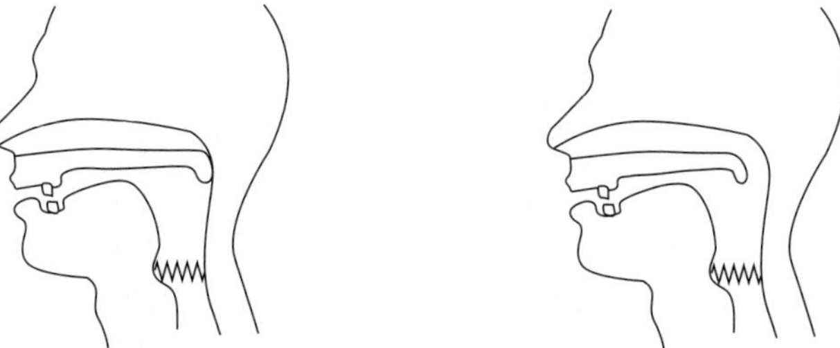

Figure 11.1 Mid-sagittal sections for a non-nasalised (left) and nasalised (right) palatal approximant /j/

Exercise 11.3 The diacritic for nasalisation is [˜] above the symbol for the sound that is nasalised. Look at the following data. Which sounds are nasalised, and in which environments?

[j̃æ̃m] [pɑsnĩp] [gɹ̃ĩn bĩn] [l̃ɛ̃ntɪl] [w̃ĩntə mɛ̃l̃ə̃n] [mũli]

Comment First of all, you should observe that only vowels and approximants are nasalised. As we said before, this is because velic closure is optional for these sounds. Importantly, these sounds are only nasalised in the vicinity of a nasal consonant in English. Nasalisation works in both directions – that is, it is both anticipatory and perseverative. However, the anticipatory effect is stronger, and we will reflect this by assuming that it affects up to two segments, whereas only one segment can be nasalised *following* a nasal (compare the two segments after the /m/ in 'mooli' with the two segments before the /n/ in 'green').

Exercise 11.4 Why do you think sounds are nasalised in the environment of a nasal consonant?

Comment The answer, of course, involves coarticulation. For a nasal consonant, the velum has to be lowered. Therefore, the vocal tract can begin to prepare for a nasal consonant by lowering the velum before the other articulators are in position for that nasal. For example, in 'yam', which we worked on in Exercise 11.3, the velum begins to lower before the bilabial closure for /m/. This results in oral and nasal airflow for the approximant and vowel, so they are nasalised. Likewise, in 'parsnip', the velum does not immediately return to a closed position after the /n/, so there is oral and nasal airflow in the following vowel. If an obstruent is next to the nasal, however, the velum must be raised throughout that obstruent, so there is no coarticulatory effect.

Note that in other languages, such as French, sounds can be nasalised (have simultaneous oral and nasal airflow) *without* being in the vicinity of a nasal consonant. Nasalisation can also make a contrast in meaning in other languages. In French, for example, /sɛ/ means 'knows', while /sɛ̃/ means 'saint'. So, nasalisation need not be a result of coarticulation, even though it is in English.

Nasalisation can be shown in a parametric diagram, in a similar way to how we showed allophonic variations of voicing in Unit 9. Figure 11.2 shows a parametric diagram of velum height in the word 'parsnip'. Again, the vertical lines represent beginnings and ends of the individual segments within the word. The height of the horizontal line in the diagram represents the position of the velum at each point in the word, with a low line representing a lowered velum and a high line representing a closed velum (velic closure). Notice that the velum moves during the nasalised /ɪ/, as shown by the sloping line. We will look at parametric diagrams, and how to draw them, in much more detail in Unit 13.

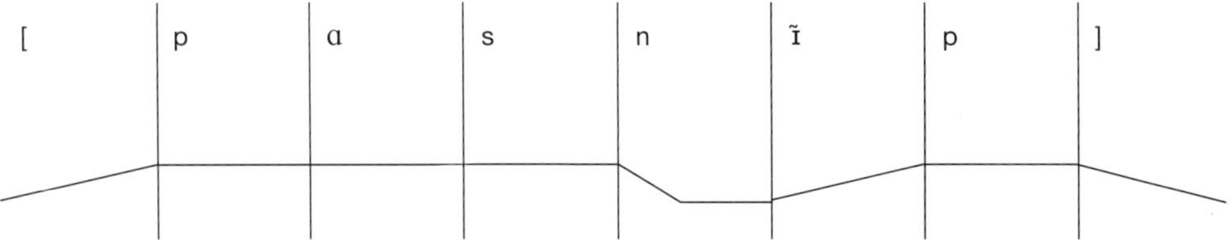

Figure 11.2 Parametric diagram of velum action in 'parsnip'

11.4 Allophonic variations of manner relating to plosives

We now turn to some allophonic variations relating to plosives, so we need to remind ourselves briefly of the articulation of plosives.

Exercise 11.5 Remind yourself about the three stages of plosive production and draw a diagram to represent these phases. Try to do this without looking back in the book, but have a look back at Unit 4 if you get stuck.

Comment In Unit 4, we talked about how plosives are produced and we distinguished three phases. Firstly, the active articulator approaches the passive articulator, in a phase called the approach phase. The middle phase is the hold phase, where two articulators are in contact, and air builds up behind this closure. After the hold phase is the release phase, where the active articulator moves away from the passive articulator and air escapes from the vocal tract. Figure 11.3 represents the three phases, with the top line showing the passive articulator, and the bottom line showing the active articulator.

We can be more detailed, however, about the approach and release phases of plosives, and refer to them as *wide* oral approach and release, when they occur as shown in Figure 11.3. We use the term 'wide' because the active articulator moves far away from the passive articulator, and 'oral' because the air is released through the oral cavity. We will see shortly that other types of approach and release are possible.

Figure 11.3 Manner diagram for a plosive

11.4.1 Nasal approach and release

Exercise 11.6

a) Produce the word 'wed'. Concentrate on the /d/ sound and the movements your articulators make to produce it. Can you feel the approach, hold and release phases?
b) Now produce the word 'when'. Concentrate on the /n/. Again, what movements of the articulators can you feel?
c) Now think about the word 'wend'. Logically, what might you expect to feel for the /n/ and the /d/ in this word, based on what you discovered for /n/ and /d/ above?
d) Try producing the word 'wend'. What do you feel? Specifically, do you feel two approach, hold and release phases?

Comment

a) For /d/ in 'wed', you probably felt your tongue approaching your alveolar ridge, making a firm closure in the hold phase, and then moving away quickly to a position of wide approximation, before the articulators return to their resting positions.
b) For /n/ in 'when', the articulators move in a very similar way, with the tongue approaching the alveolar ridge and making contact with it for a short time before moving away again. The major difference between /n/ and /d/ is that the velum is lowered for /n/, so air does build up behind the closure.
c) Given that /n/ and /d/ both have approach, hold and release phases, you might have expected 'wend' to contain two approach, hold and release phases.
d) Instead, however, you would only have felt your tongue approach and leave the alveolar ridge once.

The reason that you only feel one approach and release is that the /d/ is nasally rather than orally approached. To produce the /n/, the tongue approaches the alveolar ridge and makes firm contact with it. Meanwhile, the velum is lowered, so that air escapes through the nose. To move from an /n/ to a /d/, however, the tongue does not need to approach the alveolar ridge, as it is already in place. In fact, all that needs to happen is for the velum to raise, closing off the nasal cavity, so that air can build up behind the alveolar closure. Therefore, the /d/ is not approached orally by raising the tongue tip, but nasally by closing off the nasal cavity: this is called **nasal approach**. Try Exercise 11.6 again, to see if you can feel the stages just described in 'wend'.

Exercise 11.7

In Exercise 11.6, we looked at nasal approach. What do you think nasal release might be? Can you think of an example word where it might occur?

Comment

Nasal release means that a plosive consonant is not released orally by moving the active articulator away from the passive articulator. Instead, the velum is lowered, so that air escapes through the nose, and the sound becomes a nasal. An example might be a word like ‘hidden’, if /n/ is syllabic and there is no schwa between the /d/ and /n/ (as, obviously, the plosive and nasal must be adjacent for nasal approach or release to occur).

Exercise 11.8 The diacritic for nasal approach and release is [^{n}]. This occurs as a superscript to the left of the plosive for nasal approach, and to the right for nasal release.

Look at the data below. You will notice that not all nasal-plosive combinations result in nasal approach or release of the plosive. Can you spot the condition for the occurrence of nasal approach or release? (Other diacritics are omitted for clarity.)

[hæn^{n}d] [hæŋdɒg] [lɪm^{n}bəʊ] [kɪd^{n}nĩ] [kæmdən]

Comment You will see that nasal approach and nasal release only occur when the nasal and plosive have the same place of articulation. This makes sense, since, if the place of articulation of the two is different, the speaker must do more than simply change the position of the velum, and therefore the plosive will be approached or released orally. Another word for the same place of articulation is **homorganic**.

The examples in Exercise 11.8 all use voiced plosives, but nasal approach and release also apply to voiceless plosives, as long as they are adjacent to a homorganic nasal – for example, in ‘lint’, or ‘kitten’, produced with a syllabic /n/. Of course, to change from /t/ to /n/, or vice versa, the state of the glottis also needs to alter, but the approach and release is the same as that described for the voiced plosives.

Note that in a parametric diagram, nasal approach and release are *not* shown as nasalisation of the plosive. The velum must be lowered for the nasal and closed for the plosive, so must move rapidly between them. It cannot move during the production of the plosive in normal speech, as the plosive requires a closed velum throughout so that pressure can build, and therefore moves towards the end of the nasal, as shown in Figure 11.4 for nasal approach.

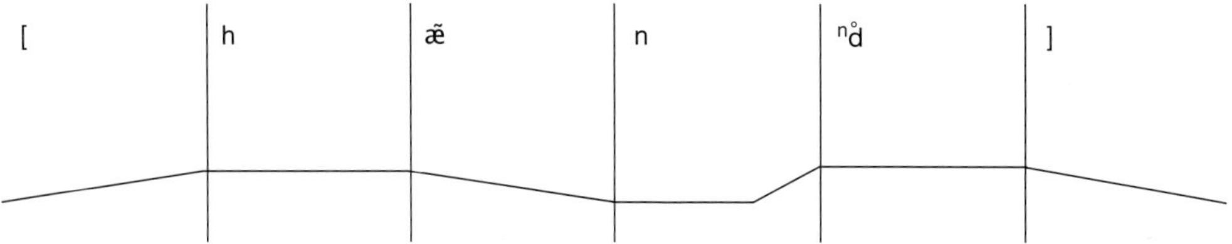

Figure 11.4 Parametric diagram for the position of the velum in ‘hand’

11.4.2 Lateral approach and release

Exercise 11.9 Given what you know about nasal approach and release, what do you think is meant by lateral approach and release, and in which environments might these occur?

Comment The label 'lateral approach and release' gives you much of the information you need to work out what types of allophonic variation are described. The 'approach and release' part of the label tells you that we are again thinking about allophonic variation of plosives. The 'lateral' part of the label suggests that the plosive is approached or released in a lateral manner – that is, by moving the sides of the tongue. You might have surmised, therefore, that plosives will be laterally approached or released when they are adjacent to a lateral consonant, which in English can only be /l/. Furthermore, you may have thought back to our discussion earlier in this chapter, and imagined that the plosive and /l/ will have to be homorganic. Consequently, as /l/ is alveolar, only the alveolar plosives /t/ and /d/ can be laterally approached or released.

Exercise 11.10
a) As in Exercise 11.6, produce the word 'wed'. Concentrate on the /d/ sound and the movements your articulators make to produce it. Can you feel the approach, hold and release phases?
b) Now produce the word 'well'. Concentrate on the /l/. Again, what articulatory movements can you feel?
c) Now think about the word 'weld'. What do you feel? Specifically, when do you feel the tongue tip approach the alveolar ridge?

Comment
a) When the /d/ is at the end of 'wed', you can feel the tongue tip approaching the alveolar ridge, making firm contact and then moving away again.
b) In 'well', we find a similar sort of articulation for /l/, in that the tongue tip rises and forms a firm contact with the alveolar ridge. Here, however, the sides of the tongue remain lowered and in wide approximation with the alveolar ridge, so that air flows over the sides of the tongue.
c) In 'weld', the tongue tip contacts the alveolar ridge for /l/ and remains there for /d/. The sides of the tongue change position, however. After being lowered for /l/, they rise for /d/ and make firm contact with the roof of the mouth. Therefore, the only change in the articulators between /l/ and /d/ is in the position of the sides of the tongue. As the tongue tip has not risen in the approach to /d/, we say that /d/ is **laterally approached**.

Lateral release is much as you would expect, given what you know already. Here, a /t/ or /d/ is followed immediately by an /l/, and is released by lowering the sides of the tongue to a position of wide approximation, so that air can flow over the sides of the tongue. For example, in 'little' or 'huddle', the alveolar plosives are laterally released (so long as the /l/ is syllabic and no schwa occurs before it), as is the /d/ in 'medley'.

Lateral approach and release are symbolised in transcription by the superscript diacritic [^{l}], which occurs to the left of the plosive for lateral approach and to the right of it for lateral release.

Exercise 11.11 Give allophonic transcriptions of the following. Concentrate on manner allophones, but also try to include allophonic details of voice and place.

mitten Santa felt metal candle molten

Comment The allophonic transcriptions are [mĩt^{n}n], [sæ̃n^{n}tə], [fɛl^{ɣ}^{l}t], [mɛ̃t^{l}l^{ɣ}], [k̟^{h}æ̃n^{n}d^{l}l^{ɣ}] and [mɒ̃l^{ɣ}^{l}t^{n}n]. You will notice that plosives can be both nasally approached and laterally released, as in 'candle', or laterally approached and nasally released, as in 'molten'. This is an exception to our rule of thumb from Unit 10, where we said that, in general, only one variation of manner would occur at any one time. This exception is because one variation affects the approach phase, and one the release phase of a plosive, and therefore the articulations are not incompatible. Of course, plosives cannot be laterally approached and nasally approached at the same time (or laterally released and nasally released), because they cannot be preceded (or followed) by a lateral and a nasal simultaneously.

Note, also, that the plosives will only be nasally or laterally released if they are *directly* followed by a nasal or a lateral, which is often the case when the nasal or lateral is syllabic, but not if a schwa intervenes. This depends very much on an individual's pronunciation, as we have seen. If a person produces 'mitten', 'metal' and 'candle' with a schwa following the plosive, then the transcriptions will be [mĩtə̃n], [mɛ̃təl^{ɣ}] and [k̟^{h}æ̃n^{n}dəl^{ɣ}].

We will now turn our attention to several more ways in which plosives may be released.

11.4.3 Narrow release

Exercise 11.12 Say the following pairs of sentences. Focus on the release of the /t/ in pair (a) and the release of the /d/ in pair (b). Do you notice a difference between the members of each pair?

a) Say cat again Say cats again
b) Say card again Say cards again

Comment In 'cat' and 'card', the plosives have a wide oral release, as we discussed in our description of 'standard' plosives in Unit 4, and at the start of this unit. In 'cats' and 'cards', however, the release phases of the plosives are much narrower. Rather than moving far away from the alveolar ridge, as in the first example, the tongue moves into narrow approximation in preparation for the following alveolar fricatives. Thus, we say the plosives are **narrowly released**.

Exercise 11.13 The diacritics for narrow release are shown in the allophonic transcriptions below.

[kætˢs] [kɑdᶻz]

a) Why do you think the diacritic is different in the different words?
b) What do you think is the environment for narrow release of plosives?

Comment a) The diacritic always takes the form of the following fricative.
b) Plosives are narrowly released when they are followed by a fricative at the same place of articulation – that is, one that is homorganic with the plosive.

Exercise 11.14 Will the /t/ in 'width' be narrowly released? Give an allophonic transcription of this word. (Depending on your pronunciation, the plosive in 'width' might be /d/, but the exercise will still work.)

Comment At first glance, it might appear that /t/ (or /d/) will have wide oral release, because it is alveolar and /θ/ is dental. However, as you may remember from Unit 10, /t/ is actually produced with a dental place of articulation when it is before a dental fricative due to coarticulation, and, consequently, both plosive and fricative are dental. As we have a homorganic plosive and fricative, therefore, the plosive will be narrowly released and the allophonic transcription will be [wɪt̪ᶿθ].

11.4.4 Ejective release

As we have already seen in Unit 7, in English, voiceless plosives can sometimes be produced as voiceless ejective plosives before a pause.

Exercise 11.15 Remind yourself of how an ejective sounds and the diacritic we use to symbolise ejectives. Try to produce ejective versions of /p t k/.

Comment We looked at ejectives in Unit 7, and demonstrated their use in English with the word 'quick' spoken with some urgency. They have a distinctive sharp sound at the release, while the approach and hold phases are much the same as for pulmonic plosives. You will remember that this distinct sound comes from the larynx being raised so that pressure increases behind the oral closure. In English, any voiceless plosive before a pause can be produced as an ejective, and the diacritic we use to symbolise **ejective release** is ['], to the right of the appropriate plosive symbol.

You may have noted by now that diacritics relating to the release phase occur to the right of a plosive symbol, and those relating to approach appear to the left. As we transcribe from left to right, you can remember this by recalling the logical order of the approach and release phases (approach comes first, so we symbolise it first – that is, on the left of the symbol).

11.4.5 No audible release

It is also possible that the release of a plosive cannot be heard, and this is known as **inaudible release** or **no audible release**. Note that this does not mean that the plosive is not released (although we will see some examples of that later), just that the release cannot be heard.

Exercise 11.16 The diacritic for an inaudibly released plosive is [̚] to the right of the plosive symbol. Plosives are inaudibly released in three environments, shown in (a) to (c) below. Can you spot what the three environments are? (Each word is assumed to be in isolation rather than part of a phrase.)

a) [ʌp̚ɡɹeɪd̚] [tʃɪk̚pi] [wæɡ̚teɪlz]

b) [bɹɛk̚fəst̚] [kʊk̚sən] [əb̚zɒlv]

c) [ɔk̚] [blit̚] [sid̚]

Comment a) The inaudibly released plosives are those that occur before a plosive at a different place of articulation.

b) The inaudibly released plosives occur immediately before fricatives with a different place of articulation.

c) They occur at the end of words, with examples of this type also seen in (a) and (b). Note that inaudible release at the end of words happens only when the plosives occur before a pause, and *not* if another word follows.

In Exercise 11.16, in (a) and (b), the plosive release is inaudible because it is covered or masked by something else. When a plosive or fricative follows at a different place of articulation (which we call **heterorganic**), the hold phase of the second plosive or the friction of the fricative overlaps with the release of the first plosive, so that the release cannot be heard, as shown in Figures 11.5 and 11.6.

Immediately before a pause, both voiced and voiceless plosives can be released inaudibly. Here, the closure is released rather slowly and gently, so the air escapes silently, rather than with the wide oral release and audible plosion found in other positions.

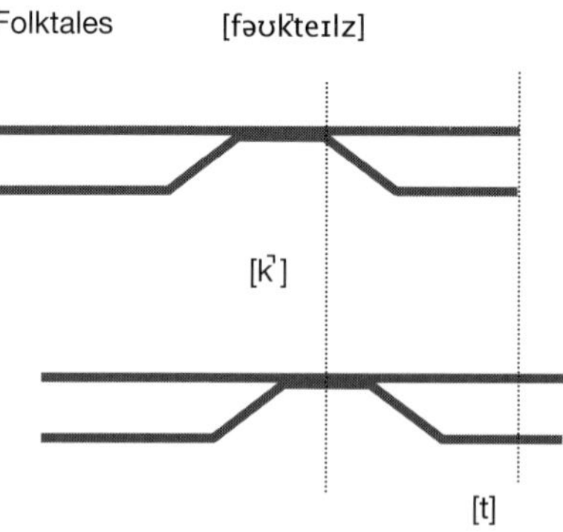

Figure 11.5 Inaudible release of /k/ due to overlap with hold phase of /t/

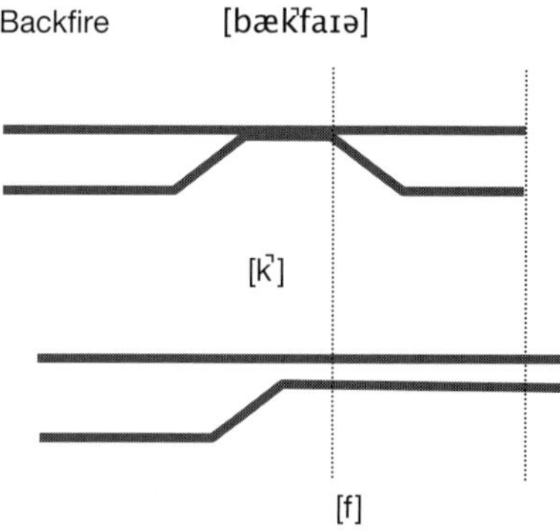

Figure 11.6 Inaudible release of /k/ due to overlap of friction in /f/

Exercise 11.17 We have just said that plosives may be inaudibly released before a pause. Does this contradict anything else we have said in this unit, and, if so, is this contradiction a problem?

Comment In the sections above, we have given two possible allophonic variations for voiceless plosives before a pause. In the first instance, we have said that voiceless plosives can be ejective before a pause (section 11.4.4), and, in the second instance, that all plosives, including voiceless ones, can be inaudibly released before a pause (section 11.4.5). This would seem to be a problem for complementary distribution, which, as we learnt earlier, means that only one allophone of a phoneme can occur in any particular environment. However, as we shall now see, there are some cases in which it *is* possible for alternative allophones of a phoneme to occur in the same environment.

11.5 Free allophonic variation and complementary distribution

In Unit 9, we first introduced the idea that there are two levels at which we can describe sounds. The broad level is that at which only meaningful units of sounds (i.e. phonemes) are recognised. However, phonemes actually occur in a number of different forms, depending on their environment. These different forms are called allophones, which are largely governed by coarticulation, and form the allophonic level. Because they are so dependent on their environment, usually only one allophone of a particular phoneme can occur in any particular environment, and this allophone can differ in many ways from other allophones of the same phoneme (remember the allophone of /k/ that we looked at in the word 'course' in Exercise 10.9). We say that allophones of a phoneme are in complementary distribution – that is, where one occurs, another cannot (the allophone of /k/ in 'course' [k̠ʷʰ], for example, is the only one that can occur in this environment).

What we have seen just now, however, is that, in some rare environments, different allophones of the same phoneme *are* possible. So, before a pause, a /p/, for example, might be pronounced as either [p̚] or [p']. This situation, where alternative allophones of a phoneme are possible, is called **free allophonic variation** (FAV).

Exercise 11.18 From what you know so far, and from what we have said above, can you think what might determine whether [p̚] or [p'] is used before a pause?

Comment In these very restricted circumstances, the speaker has some degree of choice over which allophone to use. In Exercise 7.8, where we talked about ejectives, we tried to produce them by saying the word 'quick' loudly and forcefully (page 89). This tends to be one type of situation in which ejective allophones occur, whereas the inaudibly released ones might be said when the speaker does not feel a particular desire to be overly clear or directive. In fact, before a pause, voiceless plosives with wide oral release can also occur, so the speaker actually has a choice of *three* allophones in this situation. Of course, the choice will not be a conscious one, and speakers do not wake up in the morning and think, 'Today, I am going to use only ejective plosives before pauses'. However, some speakers may have an unconscious preference for one allophone or another, and the unconscious choice at any one time might be determined by speaking style, background noise, or the proximity or identity of the listener. For example, I tend to use many more plosives with wide oral release and ejective release when I am talking to my grandmother, who is hard of hearing.

It may seem, initially, that these situations of free allophonic variation invalidate the notion of complementary distribution, which we said earlier

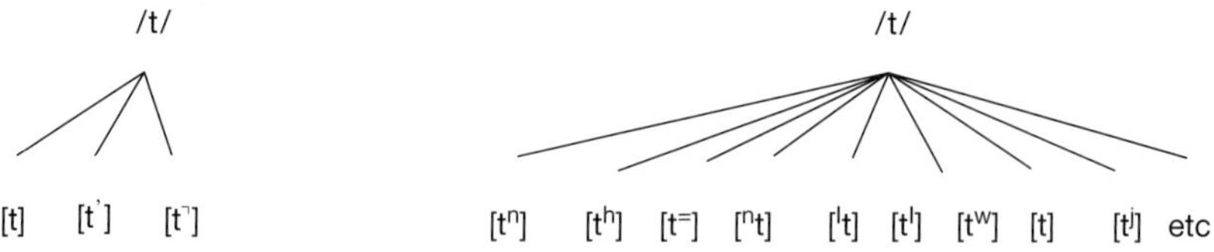

Figure 11.7 Free allophonic variation and complementary distribution for /t/

demonstrates that particular allophones 'belong' to the same phoneme. However, it is important to remember that there are only a small number of allophones that can be in free variation with each other. So, as we have just seen, there are three allophones of voiceless plosives that can occur before a pause, but also a vast number of others that cannot occur in this environment. For example, a nasally released plosive or a narrowly released plosive cannot occur, as they are not in the right environment (before a homorganic nasal or fricative, respectively). Consequently, the three allophones that *can* occur are still in complementary distribution with all the other allophones of that phoneme, which *cannot* occur in this environment. Figure 11.7 illustrates this point.

The three allophones of /t/, on the left, are in free allophonic variation before a pause, as the speaker has a choice of which to use. However, these three are in complementary distribution with all the other allophones of /t/ which cannot occur here, as shown on the right.

11.5.1 Unreleased plosives

Exercise 11.19 Produce the words 'bad' and 'day' separately, saying them quite carefully. Concentrate on the /d/s and see if you can feel the approach, hold and release phases for each. Now put the words together so that you produce the phrase 'bad day', and try to produce it fairly quickly and naturally. Again, concentrate on the /d/s. What do you notice? Can you still feel the approach, hold and release phases of each one?

Comment When you say the words separately, both /d/s have an approach, hold and release phase, although the release phase for the /d/ in 'bad' may be inaudible when the word is produced in isolation, as we have seen above, because it occurs before a pause. When the two /d/s are adjacent in the phrase 'bad day', however, it is possible that they merge together, with a single approach and release, and one long hold phase. We say that the first /d/ is **unreleased**, and transcribe it as [d˚]. Note that the diacritic is a circle and looks rather similar to the devoicing diacritic. However, it is to the right of the plosive, rather than above or below it, as for other diacritics specifying different types of release. Figures 11.8 and 11.9 illustrate the differences in /d/ between separate production of the words 'bad' and 'day', and a rapid production of the phrase 'bad day'.

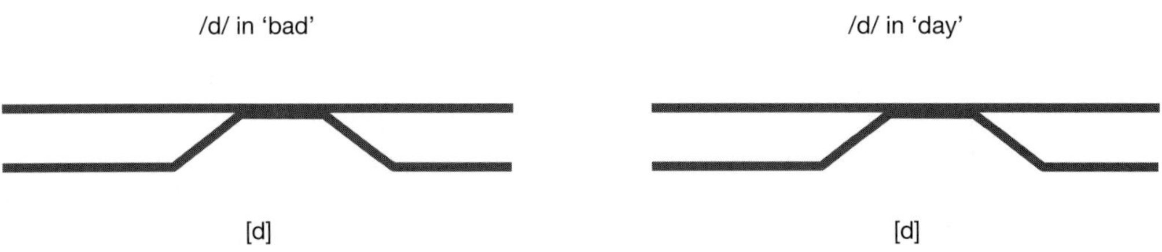

Figure 11.8 Manner diagrams for /d/s in 'bad' and 'day' when the words are spoken in isolation

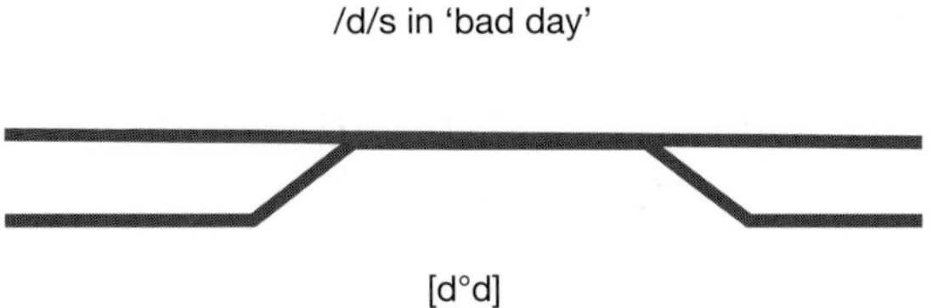

Figure 11.9 Manner diagrams for /d/s in the phrase 'bad day'

When this happens, **gemination** is said to have occurred. Notice that it is not the case that one of the /d/s has been deleted (try saying the phrase with just one /d/ and see how odd it sounds). Instead, they have merged, to have a longer hold phase than a single /d/, and only a single approach and release phase. Note that the first /d/ is entirely unreleased, and that this is rather different to a plosive with inaudible release, where the release does occur, but cannot be heard.

In any sequence of homorganic plosives, the first plosive can be unreleased. This includes voiceless plosives (for example, a sequence of /k k/) and where the two homorganic plosives differ in voicing (for example, a sequence of /k g/). However, once again, we have a case of free allophonic variation. When two homorganic plosives occur, the first *might* be unreleased, as in the example above, or it can have wide oral release, in which case, gemination does not occur, and each plosive has an approach, hold and release phase. Again, this depends on the speaker's, largely unconscious, choice.

Exercise 11.20 Try to produce 'bad day' in two ways: firstly, with an unreleased first plosive; and, secondly, with the plosive in 'bad' produced with wide oral release. Do they both sound normal and natural?

Comment As the unreleased and wide orally released plosives are in free allophonic variation in this position, they should both sound fine. The released version may sound a little more careful, but both are acceptable. However, when we visit assimilation in Unit 17, we will come across a situation where the unreleased version is the only option.

11.6 Summary

Here we have looked at variations in manner of articulation. We have looked at nasalisation of approximants, and several different variations in the approach and release phases of plosives. We have seen how to symbolise these variations in an allophonic transcription, and how to show the position of the velum using parametric diagrams. We have now covered all the major allophonic variations of consonants in English.

11.7 Looking forward

In our next unit we will look at allophonic variations of vowels.

11.8 Review questions

Have a look at these questions to see if you have understood the main points to learn from this unit.

- What is the difference between a nasal and a nasalised sound?
- What is meant by free allophonic variation?
- What are all the different ways in which plosives can be approached and released?

11.9 Review exercises

1 Focus on the (emboldened) /d/s in the words and phrases below. For each /d/, work out how it is released, and match this to the list of release types in the middle column, and to the allophonic transcription of /d/ on the right.

'broa**d**en' (produced with syllabic /n/)	narrow release	$[d^{\circ}]$
'yo**d**el' (produced with syllabic /l/)	inaudible release	$[d^{n}]$
'o**dd**s'	unreleased	$[d^{z}]$
'drea**d**ful'	lateral release	$[d^{\urcorner}]$
'brea**d** dough'	nasal release	$[d^{l}]$

2 Look at the following parametric diagram of velum height. Spot the errors and redraw the diagram.

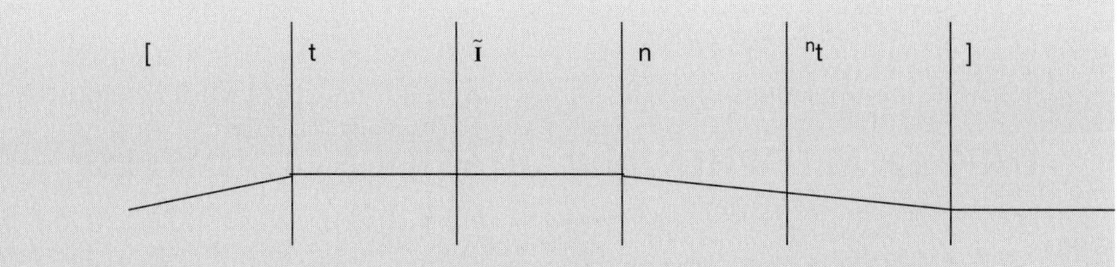

3 Try to invent a sentence that has a lowered velum throughout. You will need to include words that only contain nasals, vowels and approximants. Some words to get you started are 'men', 'milliner' and 'lemon'. This is especially hard, as few function words (such as pronouns, articles and conjunctions) fit our criteria, and pluralising most nouns will not be possible.

UNIT 12 ALLOPHONIC VARIATIONS OF VOWELS

12.1 Key learning areas

In this unit we will:

- explore how vowels can vary according to their environment
- see how these variations are related to those found for approximants.

12.2 Introduction

We have spent the last few units describing the way consonants vary according to their environment. We now turn our attention to two major allophonic variations of vowels. In fact, we have already considered one of these in Unit 11.

12.3 Brief revision from the previous unit

Exercise 12.1 Think back to the previous unit about allophonic variations in the manner of consonants. Can you remember what type of variation we said also applies to vowels?

Comment In the last unit, we saw that approximants can be nasalised when they are in the vicinity of a nasal consonant. We also said that vowels can be nasalised in a similar environment.

Exercise 12.2 Remind yourself about the facts of nasalisation from the previous unit.

a) What does it mean for a sound to be nasalised?
b) What is the role of the velum in nasalisation?
c) In what environment are sounds nasalised in English?
d) How is nasalisation shown on a parametric diagram?

Comment a) You will remember from the last unit that nasalised sounds have both oral and nasal airflow.

b) This is because the velum is lowered for nasalised sounds, so that air can flow into the nasal cavity; and, as there is not a total blockage in the oral cavity, there is oral airflow too.

c) In English, nasalisation happens in the vicinity of a nasal consonant and is due to coarticulation: the velum lowers in preparation for a nasal consonant, or stays lowered following a nasal consonant.
d) Nasalisation, therefore, appears as a sloping (or lowered) line representing the velum in a parametric diagram.

Note that all of the above facts also apply to nasalised vowels.

Exercise 12.3 Given what you know about nasalisation of approximants, which *vowels* do you think will be nasalised when the following words are pronounced in isolation? Give allophonic transcriptions of each one.

among helm help man written modern

Comment The transcriptions are as follows: [ə̃ˈmɒ̃ŋ], [hɛ̃l̃m], [hɛlp] [mæ̃n], [ˈɹɪtə̃n] or [ˈɹɪtⁿn] and [ˈmɒ̃də̃n] or [ˈmɒ̃dⁿn] (where speakers may vary in whether or not they use a syllable nasal).

The vowels that are adjacent to nasal consonants will be nasalised. So, both the vowels in 'among', the vowel in 'man', the /ɒ/ in 'modern' and the schwas in 'written' and 'modern' (if the words are produced with schwas) will be nasalised. In Unit 11, we also learnt that nasalisation can extend for two segments ahead of a nasal, since the anticipatory effect is stronger than the perseverative effect. Thus the /ɛ/ in 'helm' will also be nasalised, as the process affects both the /l/ and the vowel. The /ɛ/ in 'help', of course, will not be nasalised, as there is no nasal in the vicinity.

Exercise 12.4 Draw parametric diagrams of 'help' and 'helm', showing velum height. What do you think happens to the velum before and after these words when they are spoken in isolation?

Comment As you would expect, the velum lowers during /ɛ/ and /l/ in 'helm', in preparation for the nasal consonant. This does not happen in 'help', however, as it does not contain any nasals. Before and after the words, however, the velum is in a lowered position for normal breathing. This is because we normally breathe through our noses; therefore, the velum is low so that the nasal cavity is open and air can travel between the nose and the lungs.

Exercise 12.5 What will a parametric diagram of 'man' look like when this word is spoken in isolation? What will happen to the position of the velum before and after this word?

Comment As the first consonant is a nasal, the velum does not raise from its resting position for normal breathing. Likewise, at the end of the word, the velum is already lowered, so does not need to move in order to be in a position for normal breathing. As the /æ/ is surrounded by nasal consonants, the velum is in a lowered position, rather that moving during the vowel as it does when a nasal

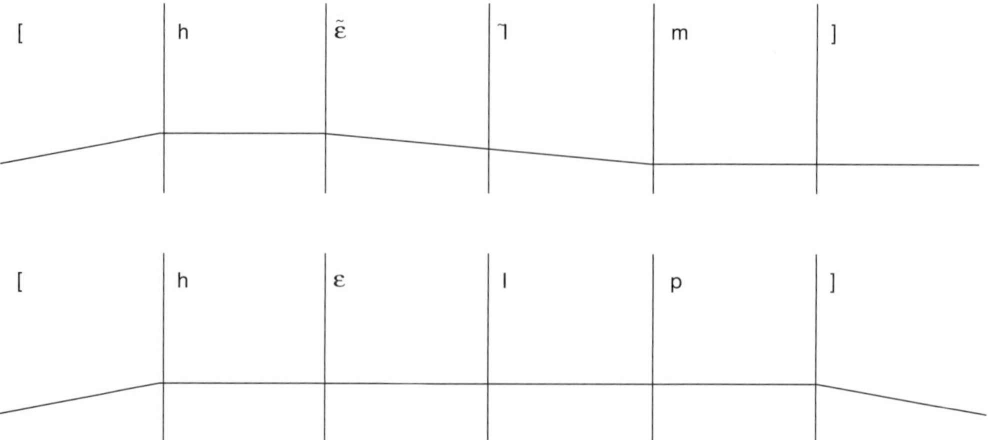

Figure 12.1 Parametric diagrams for velum action in 'helm' (upper) and 'help' (lower)

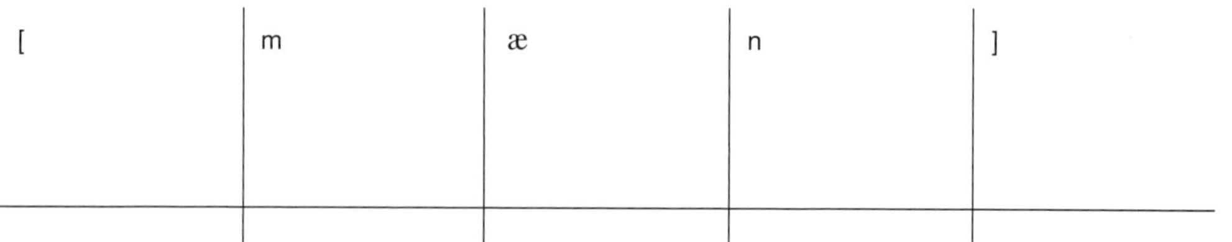

Figure 12.2 Parametric diagram for velum action in 'man'

only appears on one side. Consequently, when this word is produced in isolation, the velum is low throughout.

As with all our diagrams, we should remember that these are only approximations of the actions of the articulators. The exact movements can be affected by a speaker's accent, how carefully or quickly he or she is speaking, the degree of stress put on a word, and a variety of other factors. What is most important, however, is that we remember that speech is a continuous process, with sounds affecting one another, rather than each phoneme being produced independently and identically, regardless of context.

12.4 Pre-fortis clipping

Exercise 12.6

a) Give broad transcriptions of the words 'meat' and 'mead'. Would you agree that the vowel is the same in each case?

b) Now say these words slowly, out loud, and listen to the vowel in each case. Does the length of the vowel appear to be the same?

Comment a) A broad transcription of these words would be /mit/ and /mid/. Therefore, you probably said that the vowels in these words are the same, at least from a phonemic perspective.

b) You will probably have noticed that there seems to be some difference in vowel duration between these words. In particular, the vowel appears to be shorter in 'meat', and somewhat longer in 'mead'. This is a phenomenon that we call **pre-fortis clipping**.

Exercise 12.7 Using your knowledge of the English language, and thinking about Exercise 12.6, what do you think the term 'pre-fortis clipping' means? 'Pre-' and 'clipping' are probably quite easy to work out, but what about 'fortis'?

Comment Pre-fortis clipping means that sounds are shorter (clipped) when they come before (pre-) a voiceless (fortis) consonant in the same syllable.

There are a couple of points we need to clarify, however, about pre-fortis clipping. First of all, the term 'fortis' is new to us in this book. This term could be loosely equated with 'voiceless', as we have suggested, but then why do we need another term? Why not just say pre-voiceless clipping? *Fortis*, in fact, means 'strong' in Latin, and can be contrasted with the term *lenis*, meaning 'weak'. One aspect of this strong–weak distinction is to do with voicing, but there are also other differences between fortis and lenis sounds. For example, the fortis consonants are often aspirated in languages, as is the case for English. Fortis consonants are also longer than lenis ones, and have a shortening effect on preceding sounds, as we have just seen when we compared 'meat' and 'mead'.

One way in which these terms are particularly useful is as alternative terms for 'voiced' and 'voiceless'. As you will remember (from Unit 9 on allophonic variation in voicing), those obstruent consonants that we categorised as being voiced in Unit 2 are often produced without vocal fold vibration – for example, when they are next to silence or a voiceless consonant. So, the term 'lenis' can be used for these sounds instead of 'voiced'. This avoids the problem of saying that 'voiced' consonants are produced without voicing, which can seem rather odd and contradictory. We will not use the terms 'fortis' and lenis' very much in later units, but it is useful for you to know what the terms mean, in case you come across them in your further reading. What is important here is to remember that fortis consonants (for example, [s]) trigger pre-fortis clipping, while lenis consonants do not, even if they are devoiced (for example, [z̊]).

Exercise 12.8 We have said that vowels are shortened when they occur before a voiceless (fortis) consonant in the same syllable, and this shortening is also found for any sonorant consonants. Which sounds are clipped if the words below are said in isolation?

tattoo candid said saint atlas

Comment The /æ/ in 'atlas' is clipped because the voiceless /t/ falls in the same syllable, due to the maximal onset principle. Similarly, in 'saint' /eɪ/ and /n/ are shortened, as they fall in the same syllable as /t/. 'Candid' and 'said' have no clipped sounds as they do not contain voiceless sounds. None of the sounds in 'tattoo' are clipped because both the /t/s form onsets rather than codas, and therefore the vowels are not followed by voiceless sounds within the same syllable.

The diacritic for pre-fortis clipping is [˘], placed above the symbol for the clipped sound. You can find it on your IPA chart (page 281) under 'Suprasegmentals' as 'extra short'. You could show clipping in a parametric diagram by reducing the width of the column for the clipped sounds, but, in practice, this tends not to be done and the diacritic is enough to indicate which allophones are present.

12.5 Additional diacritics for vowels

Looking at the 'Diacritics' section of your IPA chart (page 000), you will notice that there are a number of other diacritics that can help us to describe vowels in detail. These can be added to cardinal vowel symbols, to provide a more precise indication of the quality of the vowel in question. For example, in Unit 6 we said that the English vowel in 'bed' is between cardinals 2 and 3, and we chose to use one of those symbols, /ɛ/, in transcription. A more detailed, narrower, transcription, however, could also add diacritics to indicate the relationship of this vowel to cardinal 3. For example, we can use a diacritic [˔] to say that the tongue is more raised than it is for the cardinal vowel.

We can also use diacritics to show *allophonic* variations of vowels. For example, we can indicate that /u/ is produced with the tongue in a more central position before /j/, and could be narrowly transcribed as [u]̈. We will not focus any more on allophonic variation of vowels here, but will revisit vowel variation when we think more about accent variation in a later unit.

12.6 Diacritics on the IPA chart

Most of the diacritics we have looked at in the last four units are shown in a special section of the IPA chart, which is shown here in Figure 12.3, and on the full chart in Appendix 1 (page 281). A few of the symbols we have used (such as those for labiodental and unaspirated) are not shown here, but come from a related alphabet, known as the extIPA, which provides symbols primarily for transcribing disordered speech. It would be worth highlighting those diacritics that you know on the diacritics section of the main IPA chart, or below, and checking with a good phonetics dictionary, or a teacher, if you would like to know more about those we have not covered.

Diacritics may be placed above a symbol with a descender e.g. ŋ̊

◌̥ Voiceless n̥ d̥	◌̤ Breathy voiced b̤ a̤	◌̪ Dental t̪ d̪
◌̬ Voiced s̬ t̬	◌̰ Creaky voiced b̰ a̰	◌̺ apical t̺ d̺
ʰ Aspirated tʰ dʰ	◌̼ Linguolabial t̼ d̼	◌̻ Laminal t̻ d̻
◌̹ More rounded ɔ̹	ʷ Labialized tʷ dʷ	◌̃ Nasalized ẽ
◌̜ Less rounded ɔ̜	ʲ Palatalized tʲ dʲ	ⁿ Nasal release dⁿ
◌̟ Advanced u̟	ˠ Velarized tˠ dˠ	ˡ Lateral release dˡ
◌̠ Retracted e̠	ˤ Pharyngealized tˤ dˤ	◌̚ No audible release d̚
◌̈ Centralized ë	◌̴ Velarized or pharyngealized ɫ	
◌̽ Mid-centralized e̽	◌̝ Raised e̝ (ɹ̝ = voiced alveolar fricative)	
◌̩ Syllabic n̩	◌̞ Lowered e̞ (β̞ = voiced bilabial approximant)	
◌̯ Non-Syllabic e̯	◌̘ Advanced Tongue Root e̘	
˞ Rhoticity ɚ a˞	◌̙ Retracted Tongue Root e̙	

Figure 12.3 The diacritics section of the IPA chart

12.7 Summary

In this unit, we have looked at nasalisation and pre-fortis clipping of vowels. We have now covered all the major allophones of consonants and vowels in Standard Southern British English, and seen where diacritics appear on the full IPA chart.

12.8 Looking forward

In the next unit, we will consolidate what we have learnt in this section so far, by practising full allophonic transcriptions and drawing parametric diagrams of voicing and velum height.

12.9 Review questions

Have a look at these questions to see if you have understood the main things to learn from this unit.

For vowel nasalisation and pre-fortis clipping, state:

- The diacritic used in allophonic transcription.
- The environment where each occurs.
- How each can be shown in a parametric diagram.

12.10 Review exercises

1 Divide the following words into those with pre-fortis clipping, those with nasalisation, those with both, and those with neither.

list	name	lard	land
panther	notch	bench	mess
Betsy	witch	seed	wobble

2 Find the errors in the parametric diagram and transcription of the word 'paint'.

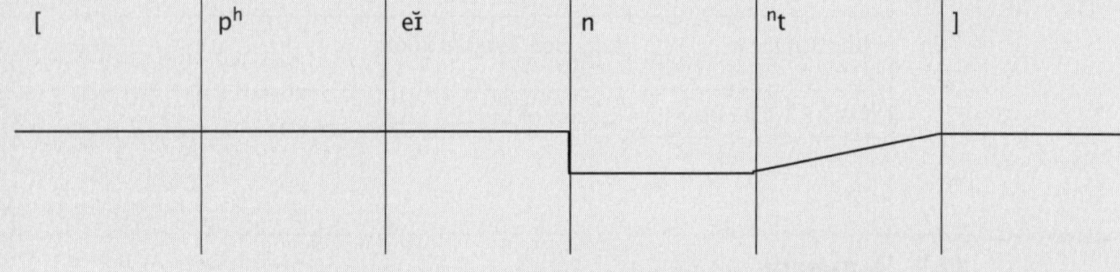

3 The following are lists of the top fifteen most popular baby names for boys and girls in 2008, from the Office for National Statistics in England and Wales. Identify those that have pre-fortis clipping of a vowel. It may help you to transcribe them first, and to remember to apply the maximal onset principle.

Boys: Jack, Oliver, Thomas, Harry, Joshua, Alfie, Charlie, Daniel, James, William, Samuel, George, Joseph, Lewis, Ethan
Girls: Olivia, Ruby, Emily, Grace, Jessica, Chloe, Sophie, Lily, Amelia, Evie, Mia, Ella, Charlotte, Lucy, Megan

UNIT 13 ALLOPHONIC TRANSCRIPTION AND PARAMETRIC DIAGRAMS

13.1 Key learning areas

In this unit we will:

- revise the difference between broad and allophonic levels of transcription
- practise allophonic transcription
- practise drawing parametric diagrams.

13.2 Introduction

In previous units, we have looked in great detail at allophonic variations of voice, place and manner for consonants, and nasalisation and pre-fortis clipping for vowels. In this unit, we will consolidate our understanding of the different levels of transcription, practise allophonic transcription, and learn to draw parametric diagrams.

13.3 Revision about transcription

Exercise 13.1 Without looking back at the previous units, try to define these terms.

phoneme; allophone; coarticulation; broad transcription; allophonic transcription

Comment *Phonemes* are the abstract segments of speech that exist only in our minds. They are the meaningful units of speech, and swapping one for another can make a meaning difference (as we see in minimal pairs). In reality, phonemes are produced in a variety of different forms, and these forms are called *allophones*. The allophone used at any particular time will depend on the environment, and is due largely to *coarticulation*. Segments are not produced in isolation, and the production of one affects, and is affected by, the production of those around it. *Broad transcription*, as we first saw in Unit 9, is a type of transcription in which we ignore allophonic detail and only show the phonemes that are present. *Allophonic transcription* is a more detailed, or narrower, type of transcription, which shows the allophone of a particular phoneme that occurs.

Exercise 13.2 Try to list all the allophonic variations we have considered in the last few units. It may help to consider consonant allophones separately in relation to voice, place and manner, and then move onto allophones relating to vowels.

Once you have made your list, try to add the appropriate diacritics.

Comment

Voice	
Devoicing of obstruents	[˚]
Devoicing of approximants	[˚]
Aspiration	[ʰ]
Unaspiration	[˭]
Voicing of /h/	[ɦ]

Place (primary)	
Retraction of velars	[̠]
Advancement of velars	[̟]
Retraction of alveolars	[̠]
Dental/labiodental	[̪]

Place (secondary)	
Velarisation	[ˠ]
Labialisation	[ʷ]
Palatalisation	[ʲ]

Manner	
Nasalisation	[˜]
Nasal approach/release	[ⁿ]
Lateral approach/release	[ˡ]
Ejective release	[ʼ]
Narrow release	[ˢ ᶻ ᶿ ᶞ] etc.
Inaudible release	[˺]
Unreleased	[˚]

Vowels	
Nasalisation	[˜]
Pre-fortis clipping	[˘]

Remember that a list of these diacritics and the environments in which the allophones occur in SSBE is given in Appendix 3 (page 283).

13.4 Key differences between allophonic and broad transcription

Exercise 13.3 Look at these two transcriptions of the phrase ‘tin of red paint’.

What similarities and differences do you notice?

/ˈtɪn ɒv rɛd ˈpeɪnt/
[ˈt^{h}ĩn ɒ̃v ɹɛd˺ ˈp^{h}ẽĩn̆^{n}t˺]

Comment There are many similarities between these two levels of transcription. After all, they represent the same speech; it is just that the second shows more detail than the first. The allophonic transcription, of course, has a number of diacritics to indicate which allophones of each phoneme occur, so in this way more detail is given. For example, /t/ is only transcribed as /t/ in the broad version, but the precise allophone, be it [t^h] or [^{n}t˺], is given in the allophonic version. Note that both transcriptions mark stressed syllables, so ensure that you do not think of stress as characteristic of allophonic transcription alone.

/r/ is transcribed as [ɹ] in the allophonic transcription. As we have seen already, 'r' on the IPA chart corresponds to a trill. While it is acceptable, and traditional, to use this 'r' symbol to represent an approximant in a *broad transcription*, a narrower transcription requires us to use the [ɹ] symbol for a postalveolar approximant.

In addition, notice that the two types of transcription are enclosed in different sorts of brackets: slash for broad transcription and square for allophonic transcription.

Exercise 13.4 Give an allophonic transcription of the following sentence. Your focus should be on the various allophones of /t/ that occur. Stress is already marked for you.

ˈSteve is ˈtrying to ˈfit the ˈtop onto that ˈbottle.

Comment [ˈst$^=$iv ɪz ˈt̠ɹ̥aĩĩŋ tu ˈfĭt̠^{ð} ðə ˈt^{h}ɒ̆p ɒ̃n ^{n}tu ðæ̆t˺ ˈb̥ɒ̆t^{ɣ}ˈl^ɣ]

Exercise 13.5 Look at the comment on Exercise 13.4. The /t/ in 'to' does not have any diacritics associated with it. What does this mean?

Comment One way to think about allophones with no associated diacritics is that the allophone is very close to the description attributed by default to the phoneme. In this example, it is voiceless and does not have any major voicing effect on the following vowel or approximant, such as strong aspiration or devoicing. Its place of articulation is alveolar and its manner is plosive with wide oral release. It is important to realise that the [t] in 'to' *is* an allophone, just as much as any of the other /t/s that are transcribed with additional diacritics. Being diacritic-free does not mean that it is phoneme /t/, or a 'normal' or 'unchanged' /t/, just that its articulation is similar to that implied by the VPM label for /t/.

Exercise 13.6 Practise your allophonic transcription with the following sentence, which focusses on /p/. Once again, stress has been marked for you.

ˈPete's comˈputer was reˈpaired in ˈSpain by Philip ˈPiper

Comment [ˈp^{h}ĭt^{s}s kə̃mˈ^{n}p^{j}j̊utə wɒz ɹɪˈp^{h}ɛəd ĩn ˈsp$^=$eĩn baɪ fɪlĭp˚ˈp^{h}ăɪpə]

Exercise 13.7 Do you think you need to be able to hear a sentence spoken in order to make an allophonic transcription of it?

Comment When listening to a spoken version of a sentence, it becomes possible to hear allophonic detail with practice. However, this is one of the most difficult tasks in phonetics, as you must work against your instinct, which is to hear all allophones of a phoneme as 'the same'. If you are transcribing SSBE, however, you can make an allophonic transcription *without* hearing a speaker's pronunciation. This is because the allophones to be applied are those set out in the earlier units of the book. As all the allophones are context-dependent and governed by rules, you can easily complete the transcription just by knowing those rules. You would not, however, be able to include any aspects of the pronunciation that are unusual or particular to that speaker, or determine which realisation has been used when there is a choice available (in free allophonic variation). Other accents also have some differences in allophonic realisation.

There will more opportunities for you to practise allophonic transcription in the exercises at the end of this unit, but for now we will move on to think further about parametric diagrams.

13.5 Parametric diagrams

In the last few units, we have looked at parametric diagrams that show details of the articulation of particular stretches of speech.

The following section acts as a tutorial for drawing parametric diagrams of voicing and velum movement. We will start with the example of the word 'temperatures', spoken in isolation in a non-rhotic accent, and with three (rather than four) syllables.

1. First, make a broad transcription of the word or phrase for which you will draw the diagram.

   /ˈtɛmprətʃəz/

2. Now make an allophonic transcription of the same utterance. Remember to turn any /r/s upside down, change the brackets and add diacritics. Stress marks should be retained and these will help you to decide where aspiration and approximant devoicing occur.

   [ˈtʰɛ̃mⁿpɹətʃəz̊]

3. Assign one slot to each of the segments in your transcription, retaining the diacritics. Remember that the lines represent notional beginnings and ends of each segment. Also remember to allow space so you can show what happens before and after the word. (See Figure 13.1.)

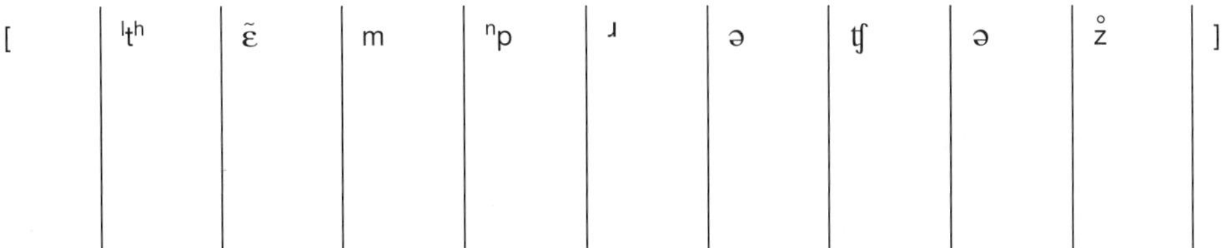

Figure 13.1 Stage 3 of drawing a parametric diagram

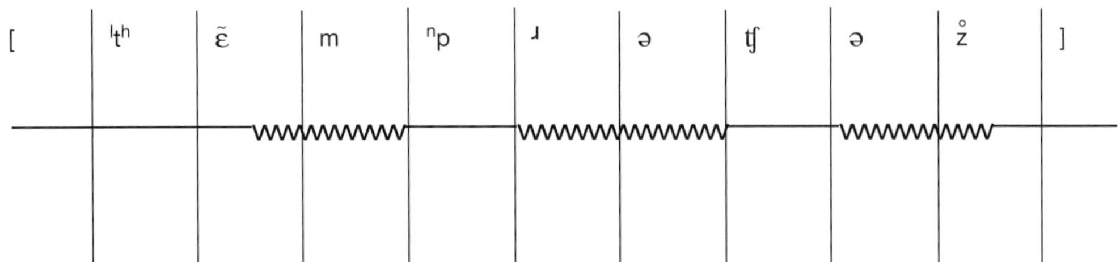

Figure 13.2 Stage 4 of drawing a parametric diagram

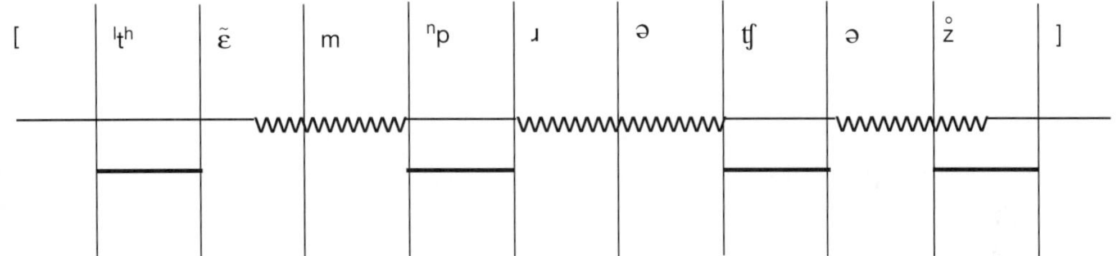

Figure 13.3 Stage 5 of drawing a parametric diagram

4. Now begin to draw the voicing line. Sounds that you categorised as voiced in Unit 2 will have a wiggly line to indicate voicing. Those that you categorised as voiceless will have a straight line. However, you also need to consider the allophonic level of representation. Aspiration will result in a delayed voice onset for the following vowel, and devoicing will mean that sounds are only voiced for part of their duration, as indicated in Unit 9. You should also show that the vocal folds are not vibrating before or after the utterance, by drawing a straight line. (See Figure 13.2.)
5. Now start to work on the velum line. Begin by drawing a high line for all the obstruents, to represent a closed velum. (See Figure 13.3.)
6. Then draw a low line for any nasals, to represent a lowered velum. Remember, if the nasal occurs next to an obstruent, leave enough space for the velum to be raised or lowered during the nasal itself. (See Figure 13.4.)

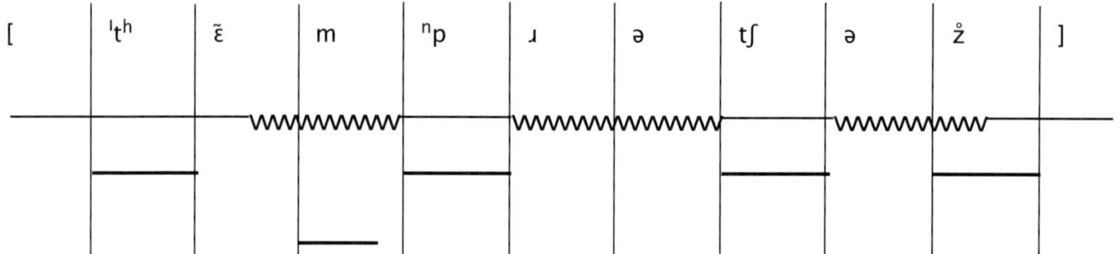

Figure 13.4 Stage 6 of drawing a parametric diagram

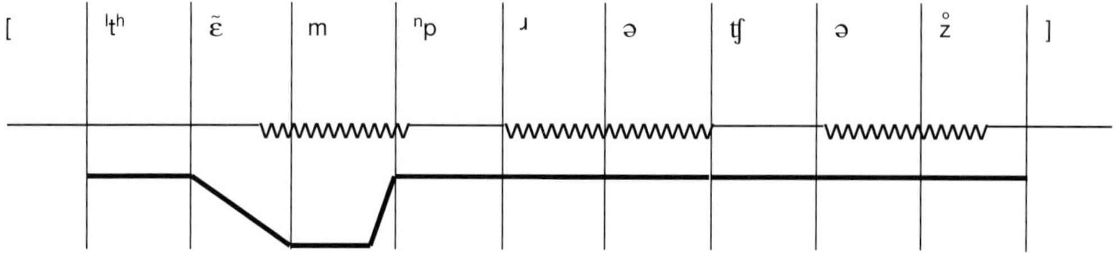

Figure 13.5 Stage 7 of drawing a parametric diagram

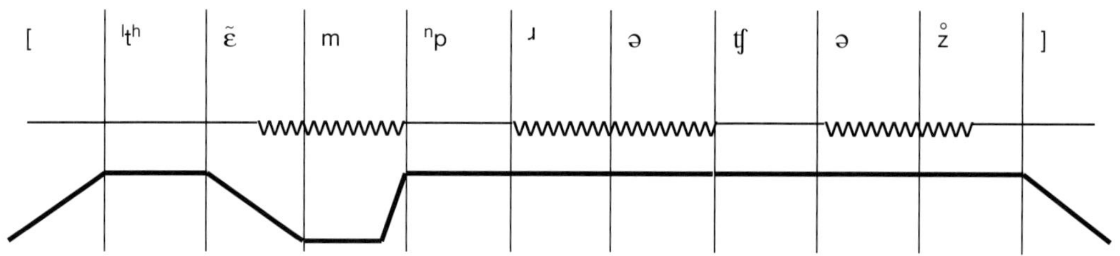

Figure 13.6 Stage 8 of drawing a parametric diagram

7. At this point, approximants and vowels do not have the position of the velum represented. As we know, the velum may be raised or lowered for these sounds, depending on the surrounding sounds. We can work out the position of the velum by simply joining up the lines that we already have in place. Then any nasalised sounds will have a sloping velum line (or a low line if a nasal consonant appears on both sides). (See Figure 13.5.)
8. We then need to show the position of the velum before and after our word. Remember that when we are not speaking, the velum is usually low for normal breathing. If the word starts or ends with a low velum, you simply need to extend this low line past the boundaries of that segment. If, however, the first or final segment has a high line, you need to show it gently sloping to or from a lowered position, as shown in Figure 13.6.

9. In the final step, it is a good idea to check for mistakes. First, check that you show voicelessness and velum movement both before and after the word. Check that the voicing line corresponds to the symbols *and* diacritics in your transcription, and that you have included aspiration and devoicing, as appropriate. Finally, check that the velum is raised for obstruents, lowered for nasals, and is only moving (shown by a sloping line) during nasalised vowels and approximants, and more steeply during nasals themselves when next to obstruents.

Exercise 13.8 Draw parametric diagrams of voicing and velum movement for the following words.

mangoes vaseline impediments gazumping

Comment We have now covered all the major points about allophonic transcription and parametric diagrams. Such diagrams can also be used to show other parameters, like the closure of the lips or tongue. Importantly, they help us to get a feel for speech as a continuous process, where individual segments are influenced by the environment in which they appear.

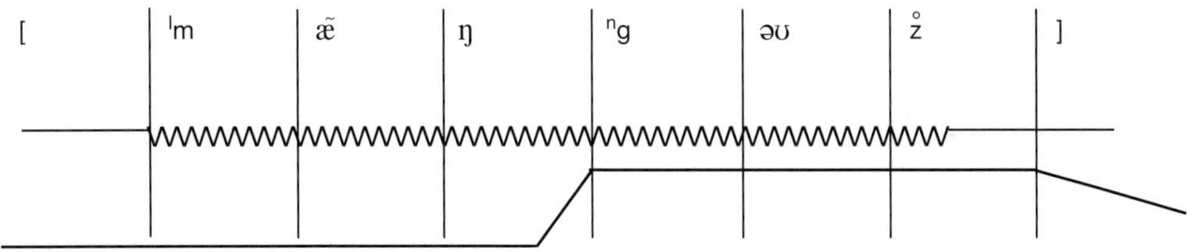

Figure 13.7 Parametric diagram for 'mangoes'

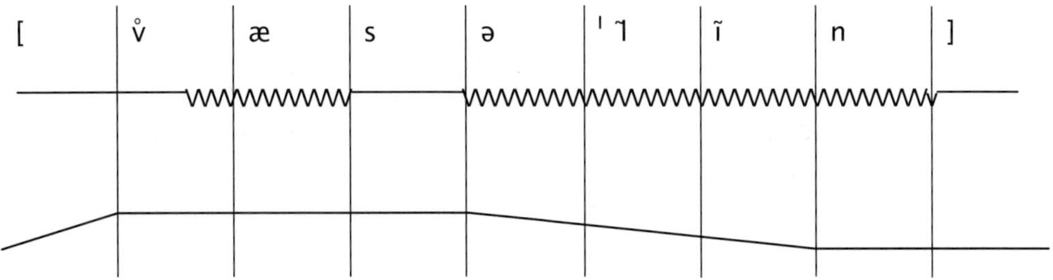

Figure 13.8 Parametric diagram for 'vaseline'

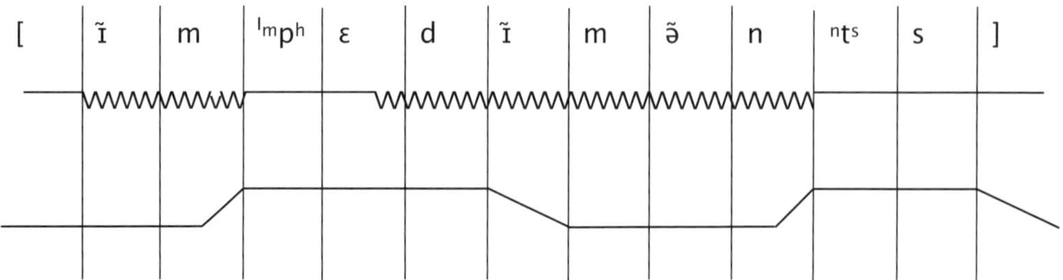

Figure 13.9 Parametric diagram for 'impediments'

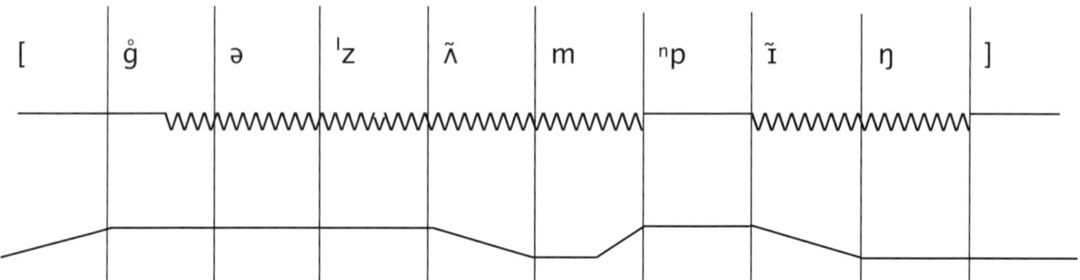

Figure 13.10 Parametric diagram for 'gazumping'

13.6 Summary

Here we have consolidated our knowledge so far by practising allophonic transcriptions of single words. We have also learnt how to show allophonic detail of voicing and velum height by drawing parametric diagrams.

13.7 Looking forward

So far, we have noted that variation occurs in speech, but have mainly focussed on neutral pronunciations in an SSBE accent. In the next unit, we will look more thoroughly at the types of variation that arise in speech.

13.8 Review questions

- What are the major differences between broad and allophonic transcription?
- In a parametric diagram, when does the voicing line differ from the voicing given in a phoneme's VPM label?
- In a parametric diagram, what does it mean if the velum line is sloping, and for which segments can this occur?

13.9 Review exercises

1 Think of some words that could be represented by this parametric diagram.

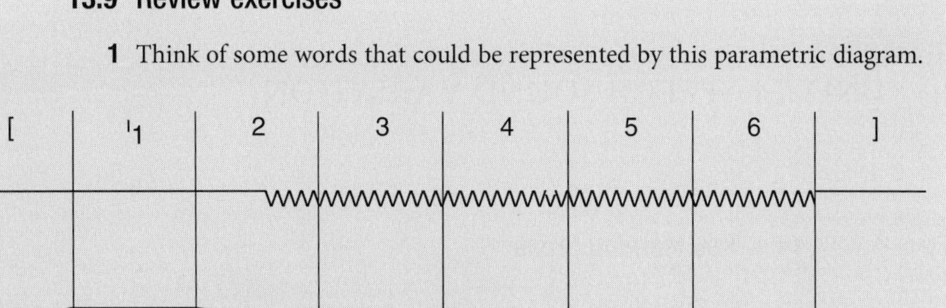

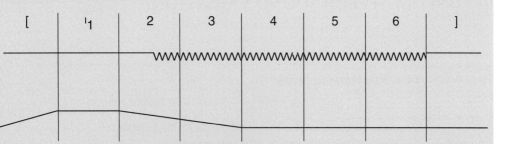

2 Each of the statements below is incomplete. Fill them in, describing which allophone occurs.

e.g. /l/ in 'bell' is dark (or velarised)
/t/ in 'true' is __________
/p/ in 'bump' is __________
/k/ in 'king' is __________
/l/ in 'lead' is __________
/b/ in 'tablet' has __________

3 Make up a sentence containing as many allophones of /k/ as possible. Look at the sentences in Exercises 13.4 and 13.6 for some examples, and go back through your notes to see what the possibilities are for /k/. Do the same for /d/ and /l/.

UNIT 14 SPEECH SOUND VARIATION

14.1 Key learning areas

In this unit we will:

- explore how sounds vary between and within speakers
- investigate why sounds vary in these ways
- explore why some sounds change over time.

14.2 Introduction

In this unit, we will think about how and why the way people speak might vary and change. We will think about why speakers might sound different to one another, and about if, how and why sounds might change over time. We will begin by thinking about what we can tell about a person just from their speech.

14.3 Types of variation

Exercise 14.1 Imagine that you are sitting on a bus, listening to the conversation of the people behind you. What can you tell about the people you are listening to, just from their speech?

Comment You can tell a lot about a person just from their speech, because speech can vary considerably from person to person, and even within a single individual, and particular aspects of a person's speech might be associated with particular characteristics. For example, you might have noted that you would have an idea about the following characteristics: sex/gender, age, where they come from, their social class and their emotional state (for example, whether they are happy or sad). We will take each of these in turn, and think briefly about how and why they are apparent in a person's speech. We will think first about aspects that are relatively constant for a single speaker, but vary between speakers.

14.4 Variation between speakers

14.4.1 Sex/gender

Exercise 14.2 Think again about our hypothetical bus situation in Exercise 14.1. Which factors in a person's speech will tell you about whether they are a man or woman?

Comment One of the most striking and reliable ways in which we judge a person's sex from their voice is pitch. As we have seen in Unit 2, the vocal folds vibrate during voiced sounds. It is the *speed* of these vibrations that gives rise to the pitch we hear, with quicker vibrations sounding higher in pitch than slower vibrations. In turn, the speed of the vibrations is determined by the size, mass and length of the vocal folds. Larger vocal folds produce slower vibrations, which listeners hear as a lower pitch, just as the thicker strings on a guitar produce lower-pitched notes. As a larger person will have larger vocal folds, they will vibrate at a lower frequency and their voices will sound lower in pitch. Since males tend to be larger than females in humans and other animal species, males tend to produce lower sounds, and therefore we can often tell a person's sex from the pitch of their voice. To summarise, men tend to have larger vocal folds, large vocal folds vibrate more slowly, and slower vibrations sound lower in pitch. Therefore, if we hear a low-pitched voice, we often assume the speaker is male.

Exercise 14.3 Do you think that differences in pitch are the only difference between the speech of males and females?

Comment In fact, a difference in the pitch of the voice seems to be only one of a whole host of differences between male and female speech. For example, **pitch range** (the difference between the highest and the lowest pitch) is often wider for women, and their voices may be more breathy, with more air escaping between each closure of the vocal folds. Many linguists have also investigated aspects of language (beyond speech) which differ between the sexes. For example, some authors have suggested that women may apologise more, ask more questions and interrupt less, although it is unclear how much these generalisations really hold. In terms of phonetics, research into languages spoken in western cultures has sometimes suggested that females use more hypercorrect forms. Some evidence from English, for example, suggests that women make bigger differences between short vowels like /ɪ/ and long vowels like /i/ than men do. Also, some studies have suggested that women can be more likely to use prestigious /ɪŋ/ than regional variant /ɪn/ as the progressive form in words like 'running'. Thus, voice pitch is only one of a number of differences between the speech of men and women.

14.4.2 Age

Exercise 14.4 Think about a speaker who is much older than you, whom you speak to regularly. This could be one of your grandparents, for example. (If this is not possible, then think about a much younger speaker.) What are the main differences between this person's speech and yours? Remember to try to focus on phonetic aspects here, rather than particular words or phrases that they use.

Comment Some of the differences you identified between your own speech and that of elderly speakers most likely relate, again, to pitch of voice. Some evidence shows that the pitch of the voice decreases with advancing age in adults, due to thickening of the vocal folds, and possibly also to hormonal changes. In addition, there may be differences in **voice quality** (the way in which the vocal folds vibrate, to produce breathy or creaky voice, for example), the speed of speech, and loudness between older and younger adults. Very young children have high-pitched voices, because of the relatively small size of the larynx and vocal folds. It seems that humans are quite good at estimating a person's age from their speech.

Exercise 14.5 Are there any words that you pronounce differently to your grandparents? Think about the words below. It would be really useful if you could ask an older speaker to produce these words for you, then transcribe their productions and compare them to your own.

ate dissect scallop princess zebra tune

Comment All these words have been identified as potentially differing between speakers of different ages. The results for these words, and many more, can be found in the *Longman Pronunciation Dictionary*, for which a number of pronunciation surveys were carried out in order to establish the differing pronunciations. I provide a short overview of the results here.

'ate' is likely to be pronounced as /ɛt/ by older speakers and /eɪt/ by younger speakers.

'dissect' is likely to be pronounced variably as /dɪˈsɛkt/ or /daɪˈsɛkt/ by older speakers, and more consistently as /daɪˈsɛkt/ by younger speakers.

'scallop' is likely to be pronounced /ˈskɒləp/ by older speakers and /ˈskæləp/ by younger speakers.

'princess' is likely to be produced /prɪnˈsɛs/ by older speakers, whereas younger speakers are split more or less evenly between those saying /ˈprɪnsɛs/ and /prɪnˈsɛs/.

'zebra' is likely to be produced either as /ˈzibrə/ or /ˈzɛbrə/ by older speakers, and more consistently as /ˈzɛbrə/ by younger speakers.

'tune' is likely to be pronounced as /tjun/ by older speakers of British English, and /tʃun/ by younger speakers. Some young speakers may say /tun/ for this word, as do speakers of some regional accents, such as American English, for whom this is by far the more common pronunciation.

Exercise 14.6 Why do you think speakers of different ages pronounce some words differently to each other?

Comment As we will see later on, speech and language change over time; therefore, speakers of different ages have learnt different pronunciations. We will consider the reasons why this happens towards the end of this unit.

14.4.3 Regional variation

Exercise 14.7 What are some of the differences in regional accent that we have identified earlier in this book? Are there any others that you are aware of that we have not mentioned?

Comment Throughout this book, we have talked about several types of differences between accents. We have talked about rhoticity, for example, and the presence vs absence of the /ʌ/ vowel. Depending on your accent, or the accents you are familiar with, you might have thought of some more differences. Many books identify a number of features that distinguish British regional accents, and we will now explore some of the most common.

Exercise 14.8 For each question below, think about which features are found in your own pronunciation.

1. Do you have the /ʌ/ vowel in words like 'cup', or do you use /ʊ/?
2. Are 'witch' and 'which' pronounced the same for you, or does the first sound differ?
3. Do you have the /æ/ vowel in words like 'dance' and 'path'?
4. Do you pronounce the vowel in 'north' and 'force' the same?
5. Do you use an /r/ on the end of the word 'car' when it is spoken in isolation?
6. Do you use /i/ or /ɪ/ at the end of words like 'city' and 'happy'?
7. Do you produce the sound in the middle of words like 'little' as [ʔ]?
8. How much aspiration do you have after voiceless plosives in stressed syllables, such as after /t/ in 'time'?

Comment Obviously the answers you have given will depend on your own regional accent, so here I comment on what different answers reveal about differences between regional accents.

1 and 2 are types of difference known as **systemic variation**. This means that one variety has more or fewer phonemes than another. In 1, Northern and (some) Midland accents lack /ʌ/ altogether, and use /ʊ/ where SSBE would use /ʌ/, as in 'cup'. In 2, Scottish and Irish varieties (and some American varieties) would pronounce 'witch' with /w/ and 'which' with /ʍ/, whereas most other varieties of English use /w/ for both.

3 and 4 are types of **lexical variation**. This is where the sound used for a particular set of words varies between accents. In 3, Northern and Midland varieties use the same vowel in 'dance' and 'bath' as they do in 'trap'. Southern varieties use the vowel that they use in 'palm' for these words. In 4, most varieties of English use the vowel in 'thought' for both 'north' and 'force'. In many types of Scottish English, however, words like 'north' are pronounced with the same vowel as in 'lot' and 'thought', while words like 'force' are pronounced with the vowel in 'goat'.

5 and 6 are examples of **distributional variation**. Here, two varieties have the same phonemes in the system, but use them in different environments. 5 involves rhoticity, which we have revisited many times already. Notably, all accents of English can have /r/ before vowels. Some, however, such as most American accents, Scottish, Irish and West County accents (and some small parts of Lancashire), can also have an /r/ after a vowel, such as in the word 'car'. Likewise, in 6, all accents have /i/ and /ɪ/, but they differ as to which is used at the end of words like 'happy'. Northern English, Scottish and Irish accents tend to use /ɪ/, while most others, including American and Australian, tend to use /i/.

7 and 8 are examples of **realisational differences**. Here, the same phonemes are used in the same environments, but the precise way in which these phonemes are produced and sound varies. Thus, London and Newcastle varieties are likely to have /t/ realised as a glottal stop [ʔ] rather than [t], in the middle of words like 'little'. In addition, the degree of aspiration varies across accents, with Lancashire, Scottish and South African accents having a noticeably shorter voice onset time than other accents of English for voiceless plosives in the same context.

Exercise 14.9 Why do you think people have different regional accents? Where do accents come from, and how are they maintained?

Comment Regional accents have come about due to a number of different factors. England has been subject to many invasions, after which speakers of different languages have settled in different parts of the country, and these languages have affected English accordingly. As we will see shortly, we are all influenced by the speech we hear around us, and decide, consciously or unconsciously, whether we want to fit in with those speakers we hear. Thus, within communities, people tend to speak in a similar manner to their peers.

Exercise 14.10 Are there some regional accents that you feel strongly about? Are there some you love, or hate, or find funny?

Comment It is likely that you hold some opinions about regional accents. However, if you ask your friends the same question, it is perfectly possible that they hold differing opinions, such as loving those accents that you hate, and vice versa. There do not seem to be any particular phonetic characteristics that make an accent likeable or not. However, the media often perpetuates particular stereotypes about accents, suggesting that speakers with a certain accent lack intelligence, are untrustworthy or are more likely to be criminals, for example. So, while it is natural for us to hold some opinions about accents, we should remember that these opinions are usually not based on fact, and, as experts in speech, these may be the sorts of judgements we want to challenge.

14.4.4 Social class

Think back to our exercise at the very start of the unit, where we tried to imagine what we can tell about a speaker solely from their voice. There we commented that social class was something that you might identify in such a situation.

Exercise 14.11 Do you ever think someone is 'posh' or 'common' because of the way they speak? What aspects of their speech make you think that way? Is it related to where they live or where they grew up?

Comment Most of us have an idea about what sounds 'posh' and what sounds 'common'. These ideas might be based on the words that someone uses, or on phonetic features, such as whether someone drops their /h/s or uses glottal stops in the middle of words.

We saw above that a person's speech is influenced by their regional accent. However, there are also differences in accent which arise due to people's social class, rather than the geographical area they come from. So, for example, the RP (Received Pronunciation) accent is thought to be spoken by around 3 per cent of the population of England. Importantly, those 3 per cent do not come from a particular region of the country, but rather share a particular social class (upper class). As with regional accents, however, people are often strongly influenced by the speech they hear around them, and may gravitate towards accent features from another social class if that is what they hear in the environment. For example, people with a non-RP accent may find themselves adopting some aspects of RP if they move to an environment (such as a school or workplace) where this accent is the norm.

14.4.5 Multiple sources of variation

Exercise 14.12 Do you think it is always possible to decide why a particular characteristic of someone's speech occurs? For example, is it always possible to say that a certain pronunciation is due to age or regional accent?

Comment As we have seen, there are multiple factors that may determine the way in which a particular word or sound is pronounced. A potential problem is that many of these factors affect the same sound or set of sounds. For example, pronouncing 'news' as /nuz/ might be more likely if the speaker is American, or if the speaker is female, or if the speaker is young. Thus, in some cases, multiple factors could be responsible for a particular pronunciation.

Some sources of variation are fairly well understood in terms of how they are related. For example, the relationship between social and regional variation in pronunciation is often represented as an equilateral triangle, as illustrated in Figure 14.1. The diagram aims to show that at the very top of the social scale there is very little regional difference in pronunciation, as almost everyone uses RP. At the bottom of the social scale, in contrast, there is large regional variation.

However, the interaction between other sources of variation is more poorly understood. A person's pronunciation will not just be influenced by their regional accent, but also by all the other factors that we have mentioned so far. To complicate matters still further, there are also aspects of speech which differ between individuals, but are not due to any of the factors we have addressed above, as we will see now.

14.4.6 Idiolectal variation and free phonemic variation

Exercise 14.13

a) Have you ever come across a pronunciation variant that is peculiar to just one speaker (that is something that would pick that speaker out for you anywhere, but which does not appear to be related to their age, class or where they grew up)? This variant might affect a single sound, a single word or a whole class of sounds or words.
b) Have you ever had a disagreement with someone about how a word should be pronounced? For example, you might have disagreed about how to say the word 'envelope' or 'either'.

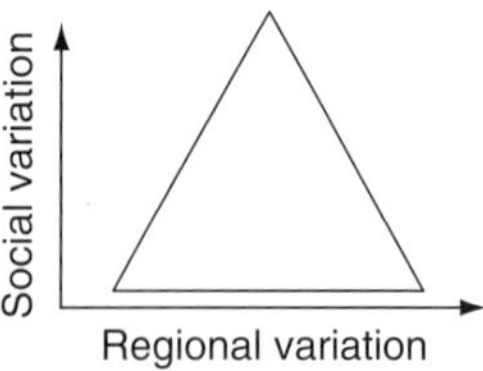

Figure 14.1 Interaction between regional and social variation in pronunciation

Comment a) There are some types of variation between speakers that cannot be attributed to any of the causes we have listed above. For example, labiodental /r/ does not appear to be restricted to a particular age group (although it is increasing among young speakers) or regional accent. In addition, some speakers might produce some of their vowels slightly higher or lower than most other speakers, or slightly nasalise vowels, even when they are not in the vicinity of a nasal consonant. These types of features are termed **idiolectal**. We can also find idiolectal differences at other levels of language, such as vocabulary and syntax. So, while our speech reveals things such as where we grew up, our social class, our age and our sex, some of our speech patterns are idiosyncrasies particular to us, and not attributable to any of these other factors.

b) People tend to be very interested in speech and pronunciation, even if they are not studying phonetics, and they will quite often disagree about the 'correct' pronunciation of a word. In fact, one of my early memories is of my mother and aunt discussing how to say 'garage', and whether or not /ˈgærɪdʒ/ was to be preferred over /gəˈrɑʒ/. Indeed, there are some words where more than one pronunciation can be heard from native speakers, even in isolated form. For example, some SSBE speakers say /ɛnvələʊp/ and others say /ɒnvələʊp/, while some say /aɪðə/, and some say /iðə/, and so forth (situations like this, where there is a choice of phoneme in a word without affecting meaning, are called **free phonemic variation** (FPV)). For these words, the pronunciation an individual chooses does not depend entirely on age, sex, class or regional accent, but is related to individual preference. For example, although the first pronunciation in each of these examples is more common, there is still a large number of people who use the alternative. As experts in speech, we would generally not want to recommend any particular 'correct' pronunciation, but are interested instead in the possible variants and the factors influencing their use.

14.5 Variation within an individual

The factors we have looked at above tend to stay entirely or fairly constant for any individual over time. However, there are also factors affecting pronunciation that can change from moment to moment and lead to variation in the productions of a single individual.

14.5.1 Situational variation

Exercise 14.14 a) Do you think that you speak the same way all the time, or are you affected by the situation?

b) If you listen to your partner, friends or parents on the phone, are you able to tell who they are talking to just by the way they speak?

Comment These two related questions are designed to get you to think about how pronunciation can vary within an individual. Most people are affected to some degree by the situation in which they find themselves. For example, if I am at home speaking informally to my family, I am far more likely to use [ʔ] word-medially than if I am giving a lecture or a conference presentation. The person we are talking to may also make a difference. For example, when I speak to my grandmother, who is hard of hearing, I speak more slowly and carefully. One of the most important influences on a speaker's choice is related to the formality of the situation. So, talking to your lecturer or boss is unlikely to produce the same type of pronunciations as talking to your best friend. The *amount* of change in these situations is very much up to the individual, however. For some, the difference between their most casual and most formal pronunciations is huge, while for others it is very small.

14.5.2 Emotional variation

Exercise 14.15 In Exercise 14.14, you thought about how your speech might be affected by the situation and the person you are talking to. Part of these differences might be due to your mood or emotions in different situations. Can you think how a person's speech changes according to whether they are happy or sad, for example?

Comment As humans, we are generally very good at recognising each other's emotions, even if we are talking on the phone and only have auditory cues to work with. Studies have suggested that pitch might differ when people are happy, perhaps being higher and with a greater pitch range than when they are sad. People may also talk more quickly and loudly when they are interested and excited by what they are saying. It does seem, however, that there may be differences between languages in terms of which phonetic properties signal particular emotions, and our understanding of how humans perceive mood from speech is still not complete.

Exercise 14.16 Do you think that changes an individual makes to their pronunciation are conscious or unconscious?

Comment It seems likely that both apply. Clearly, speakers are consciously altering their pronunciations if they imitate other accents or speakers, for example. In addition, we may make a conscious effort to alter our pronunciations if there is some kind of difficulty in communication. For example, in the case of speaking to my grandmother (mentioned above), I make a particular effort to be loud and clear, as she is hard of hearing. Furthermore, if someone misunderstands us, we may choose to pronounce a word in a different way for clarity.

In most cases however, it is likely that the changes to our pronunciation are largely unconscious. We have different speech styles at our disposal, and fairly unconsciously choose which to use in any given situation. Sometimes the changes to our speech are so unconscious that we do not even realise we are making them – as you will know if anyone has ever asked you why you were talking 'posh' on the telephone when you were not even aware you were speaking differently to normal.

14.6 Pronunciation change over time

Exercise 14.17 What evidence have we seen in this unit that pronunciation (at least of certain words) changes over time?

Comment In the early part of this unit, we talked about some pronunciations being related to age. This provides an indication that pronunciation changes over time. Your grandparents learnt a particular pronunciation for those words we investigated, like 'ate' and 'scallop', and retain that pronunciation today, while the younger generation has learnt and uses a different pronunciation.

Exercise 14.18 Obviously, to make the claim that pronunciation changes over time, we need to know how words used to be pronounced. Can you think of any evidence for how words were pronounced before your grandparents' time? For example, how do we know how words were pronounced in the fourteenth and sixteenth centuries?

Comment If you have read Chaucer or Shakespeare, or heard their works performed in the original pronunciation, you will know that English has changed hugely over time. For example, English used to include sounds such as [x] and [ç], which have now been lost, and vowel sounds were very different to those we hear today. We can use this literature from the past as evidence for previous pronunciations. Of course, recording technology did not exist until relatively recently, so we do not have access to the spoken forms of words, but older pronunciations can be reconstructed from the spellings used, the way words rhymed, and by comparison with related languages.

Exercise 14.19 Why and how do you think languages change?

For example, why might your grandparents say /ɛt/ when you say /eɪt/? And why is the English of Chaucer and Shakespeare so different from that heard today?

How did these changes come about?

Comment It is important to remember that, at any one time, there is a huge amount of variation within the speech we hear around us. We have already seen, in our discussion of age-related variation, that there is variation even within speakers of a single age group. This variation, at any single point in time (called **synchronic** variation), is often responsible for variation *across* time (which is called **diachronic** variation). So, your grandparents may have been living in a world where most of the time they heard /ɛt/, but some of the time they heard /eɪt/. For whatever reason, a large portion of the younger generation adopted the second pronunciation, and this process continued over the generations, until the situation reversed, with most people saying /eɪt/. It is important to remember that, at least for the changing pronunciations we have talked about, it is not the case that 100 per cent of older people have one pronunciation and 100 per cent of younger people have a different pronunciation. There is always some variation within a single speech community, and such variation can lead to language change over time, much as in natural selection, where variations in the gene pool influence the evolution of a species.

Exercise 14.20

a) If there is variation in the production of a particular word at one point in time, what factors do you think are likely to make one variant become more popular than another?
b) Do you think the media can affect which pronunciation of a word becomes the more popular one?

Comment

a) Many different theories have been advanced to explain why certain pronunciations gain a foothold and become the most popular. For example, the choice may be related to ease of effort, with the easiest pronunciations being favoured. In addition, factors such as spelling can influence pronunciation in a literate society, as can analogy with other words.

Social reasons for sound change are currently much discussed. It has often been suggested that we take on the pronunciations of those people whom we wish to emulate. These might be the most highly regarded and successful in society, in which case it could be said that we imitate 'prestige' pronunciations. Alternatively, we might imitate forms with **covert prestige**, such as those used by groups who are admired for other reasons, such as coolness or toughness. Again, though, it is debatable how much of this imitation is conscious and how much is unconscious.

b) It is also debatable how much our pronunciation is influenced by the media, with some experts arguing that pronunciation will only change when speakers can interact with other speakers who have different pronunciations. Some experiments, however, show that we start to imitate precise vowel qualities within a few minutes of hearing them, even if we are only played them over a loud speaker, and have no interaction with the speaker or assumptions about their prestige. This would suggest that we imitate speakers quite quickly and automatically, without necessarily having to interact with them, or worrying about whether we want to be like them.

14.7 Summary

To recap, we have seen that people may speak differently to each other due to sex, age, regional accent, social class or individual preference. In addition, individual speakers may vary their pronunciation according to the situation or their mood. We have learnt that variation exists within the language at any one time and that particular pronunciations may then be adopted by a large number of people, which can lead to change in pronunciation over time. Speakers may adopt other pronunciations, either automatically or due to the prestige of certain individuals. We have now covered a great deal of ground regarding sounds in isolation and when they are grouped together in words.

14.8 Looking forward

In the next section of the book, we will begin to consider longer stretches of speech, and the things that can happen when words occur next to each other, starting with the loss of sounds in connected speech.

14.9 Review questions

Have a look at these questions to see if you have understood the main points to learn from this unit.

- Describe the different ways in which pronunciation varies between speakers.
- What factors might account for different pronunciations by the same speaker?
- What is the relationship between variation in pronunciation at any one time and change in pronunciation over time?

14.10 Review exercises

1 What are some differing pronunciations of the following familiar words? What factors do you think might influence an individual's pronunciation of these words? You may wish to listen out for these words over the course of a month or so, and record what you hear.

cigarette
booth
migraine
schedule
February

2 The following extract is a conversation that takes place between three characters in *Wuthering Heights*, reported by Nellie Dean, the nurse. What aspects of variation in pronunciation is Emily Brontë trying to capture here? In particular, compare the speech of Joseph and Catherine. What do the differences in their speech tell you about their ages, sexes, regional accents and social class? (Note that you can do this exercise whether or not you know the story.)

'She's ill,' said Hindley, taking her wrist; 'I suppose that's the reason she would not go to bed. Damn it! I don't want to be troubled with more sickness here. What took you into the rain?'

'Running after t' lads, as usuald!' croaked Joseph, catching an opportunity from our hesitation to thrust in his evil tongue. 'If I war yah, maister, I'd just slam t' boards i' their faces all on 'em, gentle and simple! Never a day ut yah're off, but yon cat o' Linton comes sneaking hither; and Miss Nelly, shoo's a fine lass! shoo sits watching for ye i' t' kitchen; and as yah're in at one door, he's out at t'other; and, then, wer grand lady goes a-courting of her side! It's bonny behaviour, lurking amang t' fields, after twelve o' t' night, wi' that fahl, flaysome divil of a gipsy, Heathcliff! They think I'm blind; but I'm noan: nowt ut t' soart! – I seed young Linton boath coming and going, and I seed YAH' (directing his discourse to me), 'yah gooid fur nowt, slattenly witch! nip up and bolt into th' house, t' minute yah heard t' maister's horse-fit clatter up t' road.'

'Silence, eavesdropper!' cried Catherine; 'none of your insolence before me! Edgar Linton came yesterday by chance, Hindley; and it was I who told him to be off: because I knew you would not like to have met him as you were.'

[. . .]

'I never saw Heathcliff last night,' answered Catherine, beginning to sob bitterly: 'and if you do turn him out of doors, I'll go with him. But, perhaps, you'll never have an opportunity: perhaps, he's gone.' Here she burst into uncontrollable grief, and the remainder of her words were inarticulate.

3. In which accents would the following pairs of words be homophones, and in which would they sound different?

law lore
what watt
look luck

3 Putting words together

UNIT 15 WEAK FORMS AND ELISION

15.1 Key learning areas

In this unit we will:

- see how sounds can change when words are put together in a sentence
- see how sounds may be lost (elided) when words are put together in a sentence
- explore the unconscious rules for elision of /h/
- explore the unconscious rules for elision of /t/ and /d/.

15.2 Introduction

In this section of the book, we will start to think about what happens when we put words together into longer stretches of speech, such as phrases and sentences. We have already seen that phonemes vary greatly, but predictably, depending on the sounds surrounding them in a word, and will now start to think about what can happen in larger units of linguistic structure, such as sentences. In this unit, we will think about how words change in connected speech, both in terms of their vowels, and in terms of the loss or deletion of sounds. Then, in the following units, we will look at sound addition and sound change.

15.3 Weak forms

Our first job is to think about how the pronunciation of individual words can change when they are put together in a sentence – that is, when they are in **connected speech**.

Exercise 15.1 a) Say the following words in isolation and transcribe them.

for your and of

b) Now say these phrases naturally and fluently, and transcribe the entire phrase.

i. penny for your thoughts
ii. fish and chips
iii. cup of tea

c) Compare the pronunciation of the words in (a) with those same words in (b). What do you notice? What would the phrases sound like if you used the pronunciations in (a) in place of those in (b)?

Comment a) The correct transcriptions are /fɔ/, /jɔ/, /ænd/, /ɒv/.

b) The transcriptions are:

i. /pɛni fə jɔ θɔts/ or /pɛni fə jə θɔts/

ii. /fɪʃ ən tʃɪps/ or 'and' may be /ənd/ /n/ /nd/

iii. /kʌp əv ti/ or /kʌp ə ti/

c) You will notice that the versions in isolation are pronounced differently to the versions included in a sentence. Specifically, the vowels have changed to schwa, and some of the consonants have been deleted. For example, 'and' has been transcribed alternatively as /ən/ and /n/. In both cases, the vowel /æ/ has changed to /ə/, and the /d/ has been deleted in connected speech. Alternatively, the whole syllable can be reduced to just a syllabic nasal.

Such reduced pronunciations are known as **weak forms**, and they tend to occur for function words (such as pronouns and prepositions) in English. It is *possible* to use the pronunciations in (a) in Exercise 15.1 (which are called **strong forms**), instead of those in (b), but they would sound fairly unnatural and disfluent. In particular, weak forms will occur when these words are unstressed, as they tend to be within sentences; therefore, weak forms are related to rhythmic stress (which we looked at briefly in Unit 8). If functions words *are* stressed, however, as they will be in isolation, or if they are stressed in a sentence for emphasis, then the strong form will be used.

The pronunciation of weak forms is often one of the hardest aspects of the language to learn for non-native speakers. A particular problem is that not using weak forms can cause misunderstandings. This is especially the case when the strong forms are homophonous with other **lexical items** (words) in English. For example, 'for' can sound like 'four' and 'to' like 'two', if the weak form isn't used.

15.4 Elision

Elision is simply the deletion or loss of a sound. We have seen some examples of elision in our weak form words above, such as when 'and' is pronounced /n/. Elision does not just occur in weak form words, however. It can occur also occur in content words, and where there is no change of vowel, if certain conditions are met. Again, these conditions are found when we put words together, in connected speech.

15.4.1 Elision of /t/ and /d/

Exercise 15.2 a) Produce the following words in isolation. Can you hear a final /t/ in each case?

next last just

b) Now, produce the following phrases quite quickly and naturally. Listen to the /t/ in each case. Can you hear it being produced?

next day
last week
just so

Comment a) In the isolated versions, you will certainly use a /t/ of some sort (remember from Unit 11 the choice of three allophones of voiceless plosives that occur before a pause).

b) When you produce the phrases, however, the likelihood is that you do not produce the final /t/s at all, so transcriptions of these phrases would be /nɛks deɪ/, /lɑs wik/ and /dʒʌs səʊ/.

Exercise 15.3 Why do you think /t/ can be deleted in these phrases? Do you think /t/ can be deleted anywhere, depending on a speaker's preference?

Comment In fact, there are some quite specific environments in which /t/ can be deleted, depending somewhat on regional accent. It is never deleted in onset position, for example. It would be very confusing and difficult to follow speech if people deleted sounds whenever they wanted to. Instead, accent communities tend to share unconscious rules about where sounds can be deleted; we are going to discover some of those rules now for SSBE.

15.5 Elision of /t/ and /d/

The rules for elision of /t/ and /d/ are actually rather complex. We will discover them one at a time.

Exercise 15.4 To start with, focus on the words below, which end with a /t/ or /d/ when spoken in isolation. Look at the transcriptions and see if the alveolar plosive is elided in each context. Compare the examples in set 1 with those in set 2; then try to work out the environment in which elision can take place.

	Set 1	Set 2
next	/ðə nɛks deɪ/	/ðə nɛkst ɑftənun/
last	/sɪns lɑs wik/	/sɪns lɑst eɪprəl/
just	/ɪt wəz dʒʌs səʊ/	/ɪt wəz dʒʌst aʊt/
wind	/ðɛə wə wɪn tʌnəlz/	/ðɛə wə wɪnd ɪnstrəmənts/
hold	/hi sɛd həʊl faɪə/	/hi sɛd həʊld ɒn/

Comment You will see that /t/ and /d/ are elided in all the phrases in set 1, but not in those in set 2. Hopefully, you will have realised that this is due to the onset of the word following the /t/ or /d/. When the next word starts with a consonant, the /t/ or /d/ is elided, but not when it starts with a vowel. Try saying the phrases on the right with an elided consonant and note that, for many speakers, this sounds rather odd (be careful to *really* elide the /t/, and not just replace it with a glottal stop).

There are, however, more conditions for elision of /t/ and /d/ than simply the following word starting with a consonant.

Exercise 15.5 Again, compare the sentences in set 1, which have elision, to those in set 2, which do not. What rule is being demonstrated?

	Set 1	Set 2
next	/ðə nɛks deɪ/	/ ðə nɛkst hɒlədeɪ /
just	/ɪt wəz dʒʌs səʊ/	/ɪt wəz dʒʌst hɒrɪd/
hold	/hi sɛd həʊl faɪə/	/hi sɛd həʊld hændz/

Comment Although the following word must begin with a consonant for elision to occur, that consonant cannot be /h/.

Exercise 15.6 Does the rule demonstrated in Exercise 15.5 work in your accent of English? Try producing the phrases in set 2 with and without elision, to see if they sound okay.

Comment This rule is fine for SSBE and many closely related accents. For other accents, however, including my own London-Northern hybrid, /t/ and /d/ *can* be deleted when they are followed by an /h/. Experiment, and listen to the speech you hear around you, to find out if this is also the case for your accent.

We now know that in SSBE, /t/ and /d/ can be deleted when they are followed by a word starting with a consonant other than /h/. There are still more conditions for elision to explore, however.

Exercise 15.7 Again, compare the examples in sets 1 and 2, to see what you can discover. There are actually two rules to discover here, one illustrated in the first list of examples, and another in the second. For each rule, you will need to compare the examples in set 1 with those in set 2.

Rule 1:

	Set 1	Set 2
next	/ðə nɛks deɪ/	/ðə raɪt deɪ /
last	/sɪns lɑs wik/	/sɪns mɪd wik/
hold	/hi sɛd həʊl faɪə/	/hi sɛd sɛt faɪə/

Rule 2:

	Set 1	Set 2
wind	/ðɛə wə wɪn tʌnəlz/	/ðɛə wə gɪlt tʌnəlz /
hold	/hi sɛd həʊl faɪə/	/hi sɛd dəʊnt faɪə/
last	/sɪns lɑs wik/	/sɪns rɛnt wik/

Comment The rule 1 examples demonstrate that the /t/ or /d/ must be both preceded *and* followed by a consonant in order to be elided. The rule 2 examples demonstrate that the preceding consonant must agree in voicing with the /t/ or /d/. So, in clusters like /lt/ and /nt/, where the two consonants differ in voicing, the plosive will not be elided (in SSBE), even if all the other conditions are met. As for many of the 'rules' that we have investigated, none of these rules for elision are conscious decisions for a speaker about what it right and what is wrong, but instead represent an unconscious awareness of how things work in their own accent.

Exercise 15.8 We have covered all the rules for elision of /t/ and /d/ in SSBE now. See if you can recap them without looking back in this unit, writing a description of the environment in which they can be elided.

Comment For /t/ or /d/ to be elided in SSBE, they must be in the coda of a syllable, and be preceded by another consonant with the same voicing. Additionally, the following word must start with any consonant except /h/. You can think of the /t/ or /d/ as having to be sandwiched between two other consonants. This rule can also be summarised in Figure 15.1, where C represents a consonant, # is a word (or syllable) boundary and the bold consonant is /t/ or /d/.

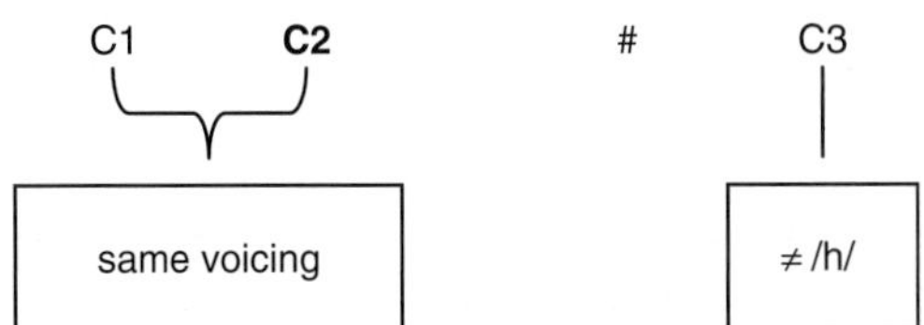

Figure 15.1 Summary of the conditions for elision of /t/ and /d/ in SSBE

15.6 Elision of /h/

Another consonant that is commonly elided in connected speech is /h/. Again, we will discover the rules for /h/ elision in SSBE by working through some example phrases.

Exercise 15.9 What rule is demonstrated below for /h/ elision? Compare the examples in set 1 with those in set 2.

	Set 1	Set 2
his	/ɪts ɪz bɜθdeɪ tədeɪ/	/hɪz bɜθdeɪ ɪz tədeɪ/
he	/ðɛn i wɛnt tə ðə ʃɒps/	/hi wɛnt tə ðə ʃɒps/

Comment Here you can see that /h/ is only elided when it occurs after the beginning of the sentence. If it is at the start of the first word of the sentence, as is the case for the sentences in set 2, then it is not elided. However, there are some more rules we must consider.

Exercise 15.10 Again, compare the examples in sets 1 and 2, to find another condition for /h/ elision.

	Set 1	Set 2
his	/ɪts ɪz ˈbɜθdeɪ təˈdeɪ/	/ɪts ˈhɪz bɜθdeɪ təˈdeɪ/
he	/ˈðɛn i ˈwɛnt tə ðə ˈʃɒps/	/ðɛn ˈhi wɛnt tə ðə ˈʃɒps/

Comment This is a little bit easier than some of the other examples we have looked at. Essentially, /h/ can only be elided when it occurs in an unstressed syllable. When a syllable is stressed, /h/ remains.

Exercise 15.11 Have a look at the final rule for /h/ elision, again, by comparing the examples in sets 1 and 2.

	Set 1	Set 2
his	/ɪts ɪz bɜθdeɪ tədeɪ/	/ɪts hærɪz bɜθdeɪ tədeɪ/
he	/ðɛn i wɛnt tə ðə ˈʃɒps/	/ðɛn hɛnri wɛnt tə ðə ʃɒps/
have	/ðə gɜlz əv gɒn həʊm/	/ðə gɜlz hæv ə həʊm/

Comment In the sentences in set 1, /h/ is elided. All the words from which it is elided are function words. You will have noted that in the final pair, the two 'have's mean different things. In the second sentence, 'have' means 'possess' and is a content word, while in the first, 'have' does not have its own meaning and is therefore a function word.

So, in SSBE, /h/ can only be elided in unstressed function words that do not occur at the start of a sentence. /h/ elision is a common feature of weak form words, as these are function words occurring in unstressed positions, and with phonetic reduction.

Exercise 15.12 Do you think these rules for /h/ elision apply to all accents? Do they work for you?

Comment As for /t/ and /d/ elision, the unconscious rules we have looked at are for SSBE, but may not all apply to other accents. In Cockney, for example, /h/ elision is less restricted and might occur variably in function words, as well as in content words like nouns and verbs.

15.7 Connected speech processes

Elision is an example of a connected speech process (CSP). **Connected speech processes** are changes that occur to sounds when words are put together in groups – that is, when words are in connected form. The way a word sounds when we say it in isolation may be rather unlike the way it sounds in connected speech (as we have already seen when we considered weak forms). There are some important points to remember about connected speech processes:

- They occur at the edges of words, since this is where words 'meet' in sentences.
- Importantly, connected speech processes are optional. Try saying the examples from Exercises 15.7 and 15.11, both with and without elision. Both versions should sound fine, even if the unelided versions sounds a bit more formal and careful.
- We can think of them affecting sounds at the phonemic level rather than the allophonic level. When /t/ or /d/ or /h/ is elided, for example, we do not find that a different allophone occurs; we simply find that the phoneme is lost altogether.
- Because CSPs affect phonemes, they may lead to confusions about meaning (you will remember from Unit 9 that phonemes contribute to meaning, as we see in minimal pairs tests).

Exercise 15.13 Can you think of any examples in which the elision of a consonant might lead to a potential confusion about meaning?

Tip Start by thinking of a word that becomes another word when /t/ /d/ or /h/ is lost.

Comment One example might be the phrase /ðə nɛks rum/. In isolation, you would not know if this is 'the next room' with an elided /t/, or 'the 'necks room' without any elision (particularly if /nɛks/ is stressed). Obviously, context will help you, so it is rare that we even notice potential misunderstandings. We are also likely to go for the most common interpretation, which would be 'the next room' in this particular example. However, you can imagine that, in a doll-making factory, for example, there might be a 'necks room', a 'hands room' and a 'heads room', which would make the phrase more ambiguous.

It is also important to remember that not all elisions will lead to a possible confusion about meaning. For example, 'the last time', spoken with an elided /t/, does not have an ambiguous meaning. It is only the case that CSPs have the *potential* to influence perceived meaning, not that they will always do so.

15.8 Word-internal cases of elision

The examples that we have looked at above are all connected speech examples of elision, as they occur at word boundaries. However, elision can also take place within words.

For example, 'listless' and 'postbox' can be produced with **medial** (in the middle) /t/ in careful speech, but are frequently produced without this consonant. This type of elision follows the same rules as those for between-word elision, except that there is a syllable boundary rather than a word boundary between the second and third consonants in the cluster.

In addition, some sequences of consonants within a single syllable may be prone to elision, as we will now explore.

Exercise 15.14 Produce the words below slowly and carefully and then transcribe them. Now say the same words quickly and casually. What do you notice?

asked fifth clothes

Comment These words contain sequences of consonants that can all be pronounced when the speaker is being slow and careful. When a person is speaking in a normal, casual manner, however, some of the consonants are apt to be elided; these consonants are shown in brackets below.

asked /ɑs(k)t/
fifths /fɪf(θ)s/ or /fɪ(f)θs/
clothes /kləʊ(ð)z/

15.9 Vowel elision

Throughout the book so far, we have seen that words such as 'hidden' and 'bottle' may be pronounced either with a syllabic /n/ or /l/ in the final syllable, as /hɪdn/ and /bɒtl/, or with a schwa before the sonorant consonant, as /hɪdən/ and /bɒtəl/. We have also seen that if the syllabic pronunciation is used, then the /d/ in 'hidden' is nasally released and the /t/ in 'bottle' is laterally released: [hɪd^{n}n] and [bɒtˡl]. One way to explain these cases of syllabic consonants is to say that a person keeps a pronunciation containing /ə/ in their mental lexicon, but that the schwa is elided when they speak, and they produce the version with the syllabic consonant.

Exercise 15.15 Say the words 'hidden' and 'bottle' with and without a schwa in the second syllable. How natural does each one feel and sound to you?

Comment As we saw in Unit 8, this is very much a matter of personal preference, and may also vary according to the situation and who we are talking to, as we explored in Unit 14 when we considered variation. Now that you are quite experienced in phonetics, it would be useful to try to monitor your own pronunciations and those you hear around you, to observe when people do and do not use syllabic consonants.

Schwa might also be deleted word-internally when it is unstressed and comes before a nasal, /r/ or /l/, and then another unstressed vowel (for example, /ənə/, /ərə/ or /ələ/).

Exercise 15.16 Try producing the following words. How many syllables do you produce? Does this vary, depending on how quickly and casually you speak?

camera family traveller battery

Comment For some speakers, these words will all have two syllables (and thus two vowels) in casual speech, such as /kæmrə/, while the middle vowel (or syllabic consonant) will be retained in careful speech, so that the words are produced with three syllables, such as /kæmərə/. The number of syllables produced can also vary according to how frequently a person says a word, with more frequent words being more prone to elision. For other speakers, however, the 'middle' vowel never occurs, even in the most formal speech. In this case, we cannot talk about vowel elision, as there is no sound to be deleted from the entry in the speaker's mental lexicon. This is the case for me, particularly for the word 'camera', which sounds wrong to me when I produce it with three syllables.

The process of elision that occurs in words such as those in Exercise 15.16, is also known as **compression**. There are two alternative pronunciations, and in one of those pronunciations two syllables have been compressed into one.

15.10 Summary

In this unit, we have looked at several situations where consonants and vowels can be deleted, and we have referred to this process as elision. We have seen that /t/, /d/ and /h/ can be elided when they occur in particular environments, and that vowels can change when function words are unstressed and given their weak form.

15.11 Looking forward

In the next unit, we will look at another connected speech process and see that, under some circumstances, sounds that do not exist in individual words can be added when words are put together in sentences.

15.12 Review questions

Have a look at these questions to see if you have understood the main points to learn from this unit.

- How would you define elision?
- Where are the unconscious rules for elision of /t/ and /d/ in SSBE?
- Where are the unconscious rules for elision of /h/ in SSBE?

15.13 Review exercises

1 The paragraph below has been transcribed without any weak forms. Read it through to practise reading transcription, as well as to see how unnatural it sounds. Next, find all the places where a weak form would sound more natural and alter the transcription accordingly. You will mainly be changing vowels to schwa, but you may also need to delete some consonants in weak form words, and should also look for a couple of other examples of elision. The straight lines [| ||] in the transcription represent intonation phrase breaks, which we will think about more towards the end of the book, but, for now, these will help you to read the transcription.

/ aɪ wɒz gəʊɪŋ raʊnd tu maɪ frɛndz haʊz | tu si hɜ nju pʌpi || aɪ kʊd nɒt faɪnd eɪ nʌmbə fɔ eɪ tæksi | səʊ weɪtəd fɔ æn eɪti sɛvən bʌs tu kʌm əlɒŋ || ɪt tʊk lɒŋgə ðæn aɪ hæd θɔt tu əraɪv | ænd baɪ ði taɪm aɪ gɒt ðɛə| pʌpi wɒz əslip ɪn hɪz bɑskɪt||/

2 All of these statements about connected speech processes are false. Correct them so that they are true.

Connected speech processes take place within words.
Connected speech processes affect sounds at the allophonic level.
Connected speech processes can never affect perceived meaning.
Connected speech processes are obligatory.

3 Give a transcription of the following, rather nonsensical, passage, which has been designed to include several examples of elision.

The last time he stayed with her, she put him in a grand guest room in the west wing. They had been the greatest friends for the best part of the past decade. She usually gave him a feast, but it was always fast food and seemed to taste bland sometimes. Most nights he'd eat the least that he could, and hide vast quantities in the waste basket. Then, when the mist was just right, he always crept from the house to hand the basket to a lost traveller, who was trying to fend for himself on the land nearby.

UNIT 16 LIAISON

16.1 Key learning areas

In this unit we will:

- see that liaison is the addition of sounds in connected speech
- explore the unconscious rules for liaison
- identify the difference and similarities between linking /r/ and intrusive /r/.

16.2 Introduction

As we have seen in Unit 15, connected speech processes can delete phonemes when we string words together. This process is called elision. In this unit, we will look at how phonemes can also be added in connected speech.

16.3 The problem of adjacent vowels

Many languages do not like two vowels to occur next to each other, a situation called **hiatus**. For example, if you are familiar with French, you know that special things happen to the definite article when a noun begins with a vowel. So, French speakers say 'la table' and 'le café', but 'l'Angleterre'. Languages use different ways to avoid the problem of hiatus, such as elision in French. The major process for addressing hiatus in English is the addition of a phoneme, which is also known as **liaison**.

16.4 /r/ liaison

In non-rhotic accents of English, the sound that is most commonly added between two vowels is /r/.

Exercise 16.1 a) Transcribe the following words as they would be spoken by a speaker with a non-rhotic accent.

car more fear

b) Now say the following phrases quickly and casually, or ask someone with a non-rhotic accent to say them for you, and then transcribe what you hear.
car aerial
more or less
fear of it

Comment a) You should be familiar by now with the idea that the orthographic <r> in these words is not pronounced by non-rhotic speakers, who only pronounce /r/ before vowels. So we transcribe /kɑ/, /mɔ/ and /fɪə/.

b) When you did the transcriptions of the phrases, you are likely to have found that an /r/ can be inserted between the first two words. By tradition, we add this /r/ to the end of the first word in transcription (and acoustic evidence seems to suggest that it does indeed form the coda of the first syllable). So, we get /kɑr ɛərɪəl/, /mɔr ə lɛs/ and /fɪər əv ɪt/.

16.5 Linking /r/

The phenomenon that we have just investigated is called **linking /r/**. When a word ending in a vowel is followed by a word beginning with a vowel, an /r/ can be inserted between the words. This is perhaps a reinsertion of the /r/ that would have occurred in these words before /r/ was lost in this position in non-rhotic accents (see Unit 1).

It is important to note that, like any connected speech process, linking /r/ is optional. It primarily occurs in rapid casual speech, but *can* be avoided by the speaker, who may well use [ʔ] instead. In contrast, however, the same process also occurs within words, where it is obligatory. A common example of this phenomenon within words is when the progressive suffix '-ing' is added to a word ending in <r> or <re>. So, non-rhotic speakers pronounce 'bore' /bɔ/, but 'boring' is pronounced /bɔrɪŋ/.

16.6 Intrusive /r/

You will have noticed that all the examples above had <r> or <re> in the spelling of the word, and for that reason we have said that, at some point in their history, they would also have contained an /r/ when spoken in isolation, even though that /r/ has now been lost for non-rhotic speakers. However, liaison also occurs when there is no <r> in the spelling, for words that never contained an /r/ when spoken in isolation, and in these instances the process is called **intrusive /r/**.

Exercise 16.2 a) Transcribe the following words.

gnaw baa saw

b) Now transcribe the following phrases when they are said quickly and casually.
gnaw a bone
baa of a sheep
saw a plank

Comment a) These words do not have an /r/ in them in any accent. Speakers pronounce /nɔ/, /bɑ/ and /sɔ/.

b) However, non-rhotic speakers will have found that the words in (a) can all have an /r/ inserted after them when they occur before a word that starts with a vowel, as in (b). So, non-rhotic speakers pronounce /nɔr ə bəʊn/, /bɑr əv ə ʃip/ and /sɔr ə plæŋk/. This is the same process as linking /r/, as can be seen by thinking about homophones of the target words, which all include an /r/ in the spelling (nor, bar and sore). In fact, the joke book title, *Treats for Pets* by Nora Bone, just would not work if it were not for intrusive /r/.

Like linking /r/, intrusive /r/ is an optional process that speakers have some degree of choice over. However, intrusive /r/ is somewhat stigmatised by some non-linguists, and provokes blog posts and letters to newspaper editors, about pronunciations – for example, 'law and order', which may sound like 'Laura Norder' or 'law ran order'. Nevertheless, intrusive /r/ is a typical feature of a great many English speakers' regular pronunciation, and serves as another reminder to us about the differences between speech and spelling.

16.7 Conditions for /r/-liaison

To recap, linking and intrusive /r/ are both types of /r/-liaison, whereby an /r/ is added to separate two otherwise adjacent vowels. However, the situation is not quite as simple as described above, since there are further conditions on what types of vowels lead to /r/-liaison.

Exercise 16.3 a) In all the following phrases, the first word ends in a vowel when produced in isolation and the next word is always 'and', and therefore starts with a vowel. Say the phrases quickly and casually and make a broad transcription, or, if you are a rhotic speaker, ask a friend with a non-rhotic accent to say them for you. Listen particularly for whether /r/-liaison can occur between the first and second words.
cherry and chocolate
banana and toffee

mango and honey
paw paw and yogurt
pear and sugar

b) Now divide the above phrases into two groups: the ones where /r/-liaison occurs, and the ones where it does not. (Do not worry, for now, about whether any instance of liaison is a linking or intrusive /r/; just put them all in one group.)

Comment a) The phrases transcribed in SSBE are: /tʃɛri ən tʃɒklət/, /bənɑnər ən tɒfi/, /mæŋgəʊ ən hʌni/, /pɔ pɔr ən jɒgət/ and /pɛər ən ʃʌgə/. Note that different weak forms of 'and' are possible without affecting our point here.

b) You have probably noticed that the phrases allowing /r/-liaison are the ones that begin with 'banana' /bənɑnə/, 'paw paw' /pɔ pɔ/ and 'pear' /pɛə/. The ones where liaison does not occur are those beginning with 'cherry' /tʃɛri/ and 'mango' /mæŋgəʊ/.

Note that the words where liaison occurs all end in a non-high vowel or a centring diphthong (that is, a diphthong ending in schwa). The words that do not allow liaison end in high vowels or closing diphthongs (that is, diphthongs ending in high vowels). So, if we wanted to summarise the conditions for /r/-liaison, we could say that the first word ends with a non-high vowel and the next word starts with a vowel (which can be of any type). If the first word has an <r> in the spelling, we call this process linking /r/. If there is no orthographic <r> in the first word, the process is known as intrusive /r/. Both linking and intrusive /r/ are types of /r/-liaison.

16.8 /r/-liaison and rhoticity

We have seen that non-rhotic accents use intrusive and linking /r/. However, for rhotic speakers, neither of these processes applies. Firstly, there will be no intrusive /r/ because speakers of these accents only produce /r/ when there is an <r> in the spelling of the word, so never in words like 'gnaw' or 'baa', regardless of what sound follows. Secondly, the words that *do* have an <r> in the spelling (such as 'car' and 'more') will be produced with an /r/, even in isolation, so it is not the case that a linking /r/ will be inserted as part of connected speech.

16.9 Potential meaning confusion

As we have seen in Unit 15, connected speech processes can be thought of as involving change at the phoneme level, and therefore have the potential to affect perceived meaning.

Exercise 16.4 a) How might the phrase 'Did you see her ashes?' be ambiguous in meaning?

b) While on holiday in Cornwall, I came across a shop called 'At your equest', which specialises in horse-riding clothing. How does the name of this shop exploit linking /r/ to give two possible meanings?

Comment a) Out of context, it might be difficult to tell if the final word is 'ashes', with linking /r/, or 'rashes', where the /r/ belongs to the lexical item.

b) If the phrase is produced without a linking /r/, then the final word sounds like 'equest', which refers to horses and the merchandise sold in the shop. If it is pronounced *with* a linking /r/, it will sound like 'request', and the name will suggest good customer service. Therefore, the shop name plays on linking /r/ to highlight two of its most important features: what it sells and how its customers will be treated.

16.10 Newer liaison forms

If you use [ʋ] in lexical items, then you will likely also use this realisation when you produce linking and intrusive /r/. However, it is noticeable that many younger speakers (regardless of whether they use [ʋ] or [ɹ] within words) are now inserting a glottal stop instead of an /r/ when two eligible vowels are adjacent. Listen to yourself and the speakers around you, and see if you can find people using [ʔ], [ʋ] and [ɹ] to separate the vowels of adjacent words.

16.11 Other types of liaison in English

The major liaison type in English is /r/-liaison, as explored above. However, there is another type of liaison, which most speakers are aware of in some form.

Exercise 16.5 Remember back to your schooldays when you were learning to spell. What is the rule about the form of the indefinite article (a/an) when it precedes a noun that starts with a vowel?

Comment As you will probably remember, if a noun starts with a written consonant, we use the indefinite article 'a'. So we write 'a cat', 'a dog' and 'a stegosaurus'. But if a word starts with a written vowel, we use 'an' – for example, 'an owl', 'an elk' and 'an archaeopteryx'.

Of course, when we are learning to spell, we are only thinking about written consonants and vowels, rather than the speech sounds. Although in most cases the two marry up well, there are some exceptions. For example children are warned to pay special attention to words beginning with written <u>. For words like 'umbrella', 'an' must be used, as you would expect from the spelling. For words like 'unicorn', however, 'a' must be used, because the word sounds like it starts with a 'y'. Of course, as phoneticians, we know that this rule is really all about *spoken* vowels and consonants. Words that start with spoken vowels, including the /ʌ/ of 'umbrella', are preceded by 'an'. Those beginning with spoken consonants, including the /j/ in 'unicorn', are preceded by 'a'. This, again, is a type of liaison, as /n/ is used to keep apart vowels that would otherwise be adjacent. For certain words, over the course of time, the /n/ of 'an' has been re-analysed as part of the following noun. Thus 'a newt' was called 'an ewt' in Middle English. The opposite process can also occur, where an /n/ originally belonging to a noun is re-analysed as part of the indefinite article. Thus, 'an apron' was 'a napron' in Middle English.

Exercise 16.6 What about the definite article 'the'? Do you think it changes according to whether the following word starts with a spoken consonant or vowel? (You might remember that we have already considered this briefly in Unit 6.)

Try it out with these pairs, by putting 'the' in front of them and listening to its pronunciation.

ape	monkey
orange	pear
ant	spider

Comment You have likely found that there is a difference in the pronunciation of 'the'. Before words starting with a consonant, the vowel is likely to be a schwa, /ðə/, whereas before words starting with a vowel, the pronunciation is likely to be /ði/. You may have noticed that when we put the /ði/ form next to a word starting with a vowel, we have two vowels adjacent, which is generally the situation that liaison avoids. However, as we have seen in the examples in Exercise 16.3 (such as 'cherry and chocolate'), sequences of vowels are permissible in English when the first vowel is high, like /i/.

16.12 Elision and liaison

It is also possible for elision and liaison to interact. For example, the phrase 'or her sister' might be pronounced as /ɔ hə sɪstə/, or with an elided /h/, as in /ɔ ə sɪstə/, or with an elided /h/ *and* a linking /r/, as in /ɔr ə sɪstə/. Note though that it *cannot* be pronounced with a linking /r/ unless the /h/ is elided too, as the conditions for linking /r/ would not exist (there would not be two adjacent vowels in the utterance). This suggests that there is an ordering of the unconscious rules that we store for connected speech, in that /h/ elision can apply first and provide the conditions for linking /r/ to occur. Of course, it is important to remember that both these processes are optional, so any three of the versions transcribed could be produced.

16.13 Summary

We have seen that sounds that do not occur in isolated words can be added in connected speech if the right conditions exist. Particularly, /r/ can be added to separate adjacent vowels in non-rhotic accents of English; this is called /r/-liaison. If there is an <r> in the spelling of a word, we call the process linking /r/, while it is referred to as intrusive /r/ if there is no <r> in the orthography.

16.14 Looking forward

In the next unit, we will look at the process of assimilation, in which phonemes are not added or deleted, but rather one phoneme changes to sound like another.

16.15 Review questions

You might like to check your understanding of this unit by answering the following.

1. What is liaison?
2. What is the difference between intrusive /r/ and linking /r/?
3. What are the conditions for linking /r/ and intrusive /r/?

16.16 Review exercises

For further practice, you can work through the following exercises.

1 Have a go at transcribing the following phrases broadly, as they would be spoken by a non-rhotic speaker. Next, divide them into three groups, according to whether they can be produced with intrusive /r/, linking /r/ or neither.

fire in the hole
car boot
Arizona and Tennessee
pay on time
in awe of him
a pair of fives

2 Transcribe the following passage as it would be spoken by a speaker with a non-rhotic accent. Identify all the possible instances of intrusive /r/ and all those of linking /r/. Work out how your transcription would differ if the passage were spoken by a rhotic speaker. You may also wish to find places where elision could occur in SSBE, as there are several in this passage.

> Far away from here is the home of a little girl called Clare. Clare is the sister of another little girl called Emma. Emma and Clare like to go shopping for their mum Sarah. One day Sarah asked them to go and buy some fruit from the greengrocer. Clare and Emma got to the store and had a difficult decision to make. Sarah always gave them a shopping list but they'd lost it on the way. They couldn't remember if they were supposed to buy pears or apples or oranges. In the end they decided to go back home to ask their mum, who told them not to worry as they'd all go again the next day.

3 Try to invent a sentence with as many linking and intrusive /r/s as possible. Remember that adjacent words should end with non-high vowels and start with any type of vowel for /r/-liaison to occur. Have a look at the examples in this unit's exercises to get you started.

UNIT 17 ASSIMILATION

17.1 Key learning areas

In this unit we will:

- explore how sounds can change to become allophones of different phonemes (assimilation)
- discover how sounds can change in voice, place or manner
- investigate the unconscious rules for assimilation in English.

17.2 Introduction

In this unit, we will look at the final connected speech process that we will consider for English. We have already investigated elision and liaison, which refer to loss and addition of phonemes, respectively. We will now look at how phonemes can change into other phonemes in connected speech, which is termed **assimilation**.

17.3 Voicing assimilation

Exercise 17.1 Transcribe 'has' and 'have' when they are spoken in isolation.

Now transcribe the phrases 'has to' and 'have to', spoken in a quick and natural style.

Compare the final fricatives of 'has' and 'have' when the words are in isolation to how they sound when they are in the phrases. What do you notice?

Comment The transcriptions for the isolated forms are /hæz/ and /hæv/, with voiced fricatives in the coda. Hopefully, you discovered that, in the phrases, the voiced fricatives are produced as their voiceless counterparts, suggesting we should transcribe /hæs tə/ and /hæf tə/.

Exercise 17.2 Why do you think the voicing of the sounds in Exercise 17.1 might change in connected speech?

Tip Look at the surrounding environment.

Comment In both of the phrases, the voiced fricative is next to a voiceless sound (/t/ in this case). As we saw when we looked at coarticulation, sounds can affect one another. In this case, the voicelessness of the following /t/ affects the voicing of the previous sound; we term this 'anticipatory assimilation of voicing' (you may remember the terms 'anticipatory' and 'perseverative' from when we introduced coarticulation in Unit 9).

Exercise 17.3 a) In the comment on Exercise 17.2, we suggested that assimilation is rather like coarticulation, in that it involves spread, or overlap, of features from one sound to another. If assimilation and coarticulation are rather similar, why do you think we give them different names?

b) A related question is why do you think we transcribe [hæs tu] rather than [hæz̊ tu] in order to show the change in voicing?

Comment a) As we have been saying for the last couple of units, connected speech processes can be thought of as applying to speech sounds at the *phonemic* level. So, for elision and liaison, we talk about adding or deleting phonemes; for assimilation, we are also talking about a difference at the phonemic level. In effect, we are saying that the change is so big that the sound in question sounds like an allophone of a different phoneme.

b) The sound at the end of 'have' is /v/ in the mental lexicon (where the pronunciation in isolation of all words is stored), but it changes so much that it becomes [f] (which is an allophone of /f/) in 'have to'. Evidence for a full phonemic change comes from the duration of the preceding vowel. The vowel in 'has' and 'have' is likely to undergo pre-fortis clipping in 'has to' and 'have to', which, as we saw in Unit 12, happens before consonants classified as voiceless (but not those consonants classified as voiced, even if they are devoiced by coarticulation). Thus, we transcribe this as a change at the phonemic level. Also, these changes can potentially affect meaning, as we will see later.

The view that this is a phonemic change is not taken by all theorists, though, as there are some who say that [s], in this instance, would still be an allophone of /z/, and [f] an allophone of /v/. This debate is outside the scope of this book, however, and we find it quite useful to distinguish variation that can (assimilation) and can not (coarticulation) contribute towards perceived meaning. If you are interested, you can read more about this topic by using the suggestions in the Resources section (page 278).

Exercise 17.4 Have a look at the following phrases and say them quickly and casually. Does voicing assimilation take place here? If not, why not?

has partied   have fought

Comment In these phrases, it is unlikely that assimilation of voicing takes place. It is really important to remember that, in English, voicing assimilation only takes place in set phrases. Set phrases are words that occur together on a very frequent basis, such as 'have to' and 'has to', which we looked at above. Complete devoicing (with a switch from lenis to fortis) certainly is not ubiquitous, and does not occur every time a voiced fricative occurs next to a voiceless sound. For non-set phrases, there *will* be devoicing on an allophonic level, but the sound remains lenis, and the length of the preceding vowel will remain the same. So, our examples above would be /həz ˈpɑtɪd/ [həz̥ ˈpʰɑtɪd̥] and /həz ˈfɔt/ [həz̥ ˈfɔt]. Listen to the speech around you and try to observe which phrases have phonemic devoicing and which do not.

17.4 Place assimilation

One of the most widespread types of assimilation in English is place assimilation. Although it follows particular rules, it is not restricted to set phrases, as voicing assimilation is, and it tends to occur very frequently. Once you know what to listen for, you will likely hear place assimilation anytime you listen to a sample of speech – for example, on the bus or when watching the TV, or even just listening to yourself.

Exercise 17.5 Pronounce and transcribe the word 'tin' as it would be spoken in isolation. Now produce the following phrases quickly and casually, and transcribe what you hear, focussing on the consonant at the end of the word 'tin'.

tin cans
tin pans

Comment You will have noticed that, in isolation, the word 'tin' ends in a voiced alveolar nasal, and thus the word would be transcribed as /tɪn/. In the phrases, however, the place of articulation of the final sound can change. In 'tin cans', the /n/ becomes a velar nasal [ŋ], consistent with the characteristics of the phoneme /ŋ/. In 'tin pans', it becomes a bilabial nasal [m], consistent with the phoneme /m/.

Exercise 17.6 Why do you think /n/ can change to [ŋ] and [m] in the examples in Exercise 17.5? What influences the change, and why does it not change to a different sound, like [k] or [b], for example?

Comment Similarly to what we have seen for coarticulation, the change of place for /n/ is influenced by the following consonant. So, the /n/ has become velar before a velar, and bilabial before a bilabial. Notice that *only* its place of articulation has changed. Its voicing stays the same (that is, it remains voiced) and its manner stays the same (that is, it remains nasal). Place assimilation applies to any alveolar plosive or nasal (that is, oral and nasal stops) before a velar or bilabial sound, and this type of place assimilation is also known as **dealveolarisation**.

Alveolar plosives and nasals can also become bilabial before labial-velar /w/, as in 'right-wing', produced as /raɪp wɪŋ/. In addition, they can become labiodentals before labiodentals (/f/ and /v/). So, in 'cat flap', the /t/ might become [p̪], a labiodental plosive, which is an allophone of /p/, so we could transcribe /kæp flæp/ in broad transcription. This is very similar to the coarticulatory process we saw in Unit 10, where /p b m/ are labiodental before /f v/. Here we consider the process as assimilation, however, as the resulting allophones sound like allophones of different phonemes.

Exercise 17.7 How will the final 'alveolar' sound be pronounced in the following colour terms if dealveolarisation takes place? Remember that place changes to match the next consonant, but voicing and manner stay the same.

white coffee; red wine; green grass; violet cream; emerald forest; chocolate brown; brown bear

Comment Transcriptions are likely to be: /waɪk kɒfi/, /rɛb waɪn/, /griŋ grɑs/, /vaɪələk krim/, /ɛmərəlb fɒrɪst/ or /ɛmrəlb fɒrɪst/, /tʃɒkləp braʊn/ and /braʊm bɛə/.

Note that the /t/s at the end of 'white' and 'chocolate' could be produced as glottal stops at the allophonic level, rather than a phonemic place change occurring. The /d/ in 'emerald' could be elided, since all three conditions for elision are met (see section 15.5, page 193). The choice between connected speech processes is a point we will return to towards the end of the unit.

When looking at the place assimilations, we also need to think back to the idea of 'unreleased plosives', which we first visited in Unit 11. There, we said that in utterances like 'bad day', the first /d/ might have wide oral release, or might be unreleased because it is followed by a homorganic plosive. If it is unreleased, gemination is said to have occurred, and a plosive with a long hold phrase, and single approach and release phases, will be produced. We also noted that the two variants (unreleased and wide oral release) are in free allophonic variation in this environment. The situation is somewhat different, however, when a sequence of homorganic plosives is formed by assimilation, as we will see now.

Exercise 17.8
a) Repeat the following exercise from Unit 11. Produce 'bad day' with an unreleased first plosive, and with wide oral release. Do they both sound okay in your variety of English?
b) Now try the same thing with /waɪk kɒfi/, from Exercise 17.8. Does the first /k/ sound equally fine with wide oral release as it does when it is unreleased?

Comment
a) You should be able to hear that either variant sounds fine, and that the choice between wide oral release and no release is down to the speaker and the situation (a case of free allophonic variation).
b) Here, however, only the unreleased plosive is possible for native English speakers. So, while [waɪk˚ kɒfi] sounds fine, it sounds distinctly odd to say [waɪk kɒfi], with wide oral release of the first plosive. In most varieties of English, then, only the unreleased variant is used when a sequence of homorganic plosives has been formed by assimilation. Therefore, there is no free allophonic variation for plosives in this situation.

Exercise 17.9 What do you think might happen when two (or more) alveolar stops appear in the coda of a syllable and are followed by a velar or bilabial consonant in the next word?

Try it with the alveolar stops in 'can't go' and 'won't move'.

Comment When there are two alveolar stops at the end of a word, and they are followed by a word starting with a bilabial or velar, they can *both* assimilate, so we would transcribe /kɑŋk gəʊ/ and /wəʊmp muv/. This is in line with Unit 8, which dealt with phonotactics, in which we said that a nasal and a voiceless plosive in the coda of a syllable always have the same POA in English.

Exercise 17.10 Alveolar fricatives can also be affected by place assimilation.

Transcribe 'glass' and 'jazz'.

Now transcribe 'glass shavings' and 'jazz shoe', paying particular attention to the final consonant of the first word. What do you notice?

Comment In isolation, 'glass' ends with /s/ and 'jazz' ends with /z/. However, in the phrases, /s/ can become /ʃ/, and /z/ can become /ʒ/. The 'rule' is that alveolar fricatives can become postalveolar fricatives before a postalveolar sound, and also before palatals (/j/).

Exercise 17.11 Transcribe the following sentence, including all place assimilations that could occur.

Those sheriffs surely can't mend my shotgun quickly.

Comment /ðəʊʒ ʃɛrɪfʃ ʃɔli kɑmp mɛmb maɪ ʃɒkgʌŋ kwɪkli/.

Notice that /b/ in 'mend' could also be elided, and that assimilation can also occur within a word, as in 'shotgun' (although here, strictly speaking, it is not a connected speech process).

17.5 Manner assimilation

Assimilation of manner does not really happen in isolation in English, but does happen in combination with place assimilation.

Exercise 17.12 Transcribe the words 'won't', 'did' and 'you' in isolation. Now, saying them quickly and naturally, transcribe the phrases 'won't you' and 'did you'.

Comment In isolation, the words are /wəʊnt/, /dɪd/ and /ju/. However, when the words are combined in connected speech, it is quite likely that you heard /wəʊntʃu/ and /dɪdʒu/.

This process is called **coalescence** and can occur when an alveolar plosive is immediately before /j/. The plosive and /j/ combine to become the single affricate phoneme /tʃ/ or /dʒ/ (depending on the voicing of the plosive). This process has happened word-internally, too, in the history of English. As we saw in our earlier unit on variation (Unit 14), words like 'tune', which you probably pronounce as /tʃun/, were previously produced as /tjun/ in SSBE (and may still have this pronunciation for older speakers). However, they have changed over time, with the coalesced form becoming the most prevalent among younger speakers.

Exercise 17.13 Coalescence can also affect alveolar fricatives. Transcribe 'this year'. Listen closely to the fricative at the end of 'this'. What happens to it in this phrase?

Comment As connected speech processes are always optional, there is the possibility that /s/ remains the same as it is in isolation. If assimilation does occur, there are two possibilities. The first is simple place assimilation, as we have seen above. Here, the /s/ may become /ʃ/, so we have /ðɪʃ jɪə/. However, coalescence may also take place, whereby the /s/ and /j/ combine to become a single /ʃ/ sound, as in /ðɪʃɪə/. Try producing both versions and see which one you are most likely to use.

17.6 Elision and assimilation

As we have seen, we sometimes have situations in which either elision or assimilation can apply. For example, we saw in 'emerald forest' that a speaker could elide the /d/ because the three conditions for its elision, described in Unit 15, are fulfilled (it is in a cluster of three consonants, the one before it agrees in voicing, and the one after is not /h/). So, a speaker of SSBE could say /ɛmərəl fɒrɪst/. However, the /d/ is also in a suitable environment for place assimilation, and therefore could also be produced as [b̥], in which case we would transcribe /ɛmərəlb fɒrɪst/. Since each of these processes is optional, the speaker could also produce /ɛmərəld fɒrɪst/ with no elision or assimilation, or /ɛmrəld fɒrɪst/, if they elide a vowel in 'emerald'. Yet again, we see that speech is subject to a great deal of variation, and that speakers continually make unconscious choices about the forms they use, based on both the situation and personal preference.

So, in some situations, speakers can choose between elision and assimilation. However, elision and assimilation also interact in another way. In some situations, both elision and assimilation can apply at the same time. For example, the word 'handbag' might be produced in full as /hændbæg/. However, the /d/ is in a site where elision is possible, so the phrase could be produced as /hænbæg/. Furthermore, when the /d/ is elided, it leaves /n/ in a position for place assimilation. So, we frequently hear /hæmbæg/. In this final example, we see again that connected speech processes have the potential to influence meaning. Is /hæmbæg/ a rendition of 'handbag' with elision and dealveolarisation, or is it simply 'ham bag'? In real life, the context and knowledge of the speaker's habitual patterns and preferences would help you to decide, and you would probably opt for the most likely meaning. So, in reality, we are rarely confused by CSPs, although they do have the *potential* to cause misunderstandings.

17.7 Summary

We have seen that sometimes sounds change in connected speech so that they sound like allophones of a different phoneme. We have called this process assimilation, and looked at changes of voice, place and manner.

17.8 Looking forward

We have now covered the vast majority of information that we need to know about the consonants and vowels in English. In the upcoming units, we will practise our transcription and think about pitch and intonation in English.

17.9 Review questions

Have a look at the following questions to see if you have understood the main points to learn from this unit.

- What types of assimilation can take place in English?
- What is the most common type of assimilation in English?
- What is the relationship between elision and assimilation?

17.10 Review exercises

1 Imagine that the following phrases were produced with assimilation. The assimilated consonants have been left blank; it is your job is to fill them in.

plant pot	/plɑ□□ pɒt/
mint condition	/mɪ□ □ kəndɪʃən/
lead balloon	/lɛ□ bəlun/
flat pancake	/flæ□ pæŋkeɪk/
food miles	/fu□ maɪlz/
quiz show	/kwɪ□ ʃəʊ/
dress shop	/drɛ□ ʃɒp/

2 Transcribe the following passage, which has been designed to include as many assimilations as possible. Include all the assimilations you can find, while noting that there may be elisions and liaisons too, which can all be checked against the answer in the back of the book.

That garden must surely need plenty of work. You have to keep the grass short, paint fences, shovel sand, plant bulbs, weed borders and water all those shoots. Don't you get bored by all that work, and find you want more hours to appreciate your efforts? If it were up to me, I'd put down gloves and spade, find myself a quiet corner and just relax.

3 Make up some sentences of your own that have as many assimilations as possible. Try to include at least five examples of assimilation in each. Good words to use are those that end in alveolars, as these can assimilate, as well as words that start with bilabials, velars or labiodentals, which trigger assimilation. Have a look at the sentence in Exercise 17.11 to help you get an idea of the sorts of sentences you might produce.

UNIT 18 BROAD TRANSCRIPTION

18.1 Key learning areas

In this unit we will:

- consolidate our knowledge of broad transcription
- practise broad transcription
- think about different types of transcription
- think about some of the potential problems with different types of transcription.

18.2 Introduction

Over the course of this book, we have been discovering more and more about the detail of speech. We have looked at coarticulation and allophones, and various processes of connected speech, such as elision, liaison and assimilation. In this unit we will try to put all of these topics together and also return to some aspects of transcription that students often find difficult.

18.3 Thinking about transcription

Exercise 18.1 Are these statements about transcription true or false?

a) Transcription is the only way to capture what someone says.
b) The type of transcription we use will depend on our purposes and the situation.
c) Transcriptions are an accurate representation of a stretch of speech.
d) There will only ever be one correct transcription for an utterance.

Comment a) Clearly false. We might also make an audio or video recording of a person's speech, or turn it into a parametric diagram. We could write it down in orthography as well.
b) True. At the moment, you know that allophonic transcriptions show more detail than broad transcriptions, and we will look at when you might use each type shortly.

c) This depends very much on the transcription, which, in turn, will depend on the experience and skill of the transcriber, and how difficult the material is to transcribe.

d) It is important to remember that there may be different ways to transcribe the same thing. This is partly due to the purposes for which the transcription is used. For example, both broad and allophonic transcriptions of the same utterance could be correct. Also, it is important to remember that a transcription is not just a recording of an utterance. It represents, in part, the transcriber's analysis of what has been said. Thus, two transcribers could come up with similar, but slightly different, transcriptions, depending on the analysis they have made. For example, the same vowel might be transcribed as [e̞] (lowered cardinal 2) or [ɛ̝] (raised cardinal 3). We will examine some of these points further in this unit.

18.4 Types of transcription

Exercise 18.2 What are the types of transcription you know about so far? Under what circumstances do you think you might use them?

Comment So far, we have concentrated on allophonic and broad transcription. As you know, these can both be used to represent the same stretch of speech. A broad transcription gives us only the detail that might contribute to meaning, and ignores the predictable detail due to the environment and coarticulation. As we saw in Unit 13, an allophonic transcription will include details such as aspiration, devoicing and nasalisation, whereas a broad transcription will not. As we hinted at before, the type of transcription you make will depend on your purposes. In a dictionary, for example, it is likely that only the phonemic level of representation will be considered important. If we want to note subtle details in voicing, then an allophonic transcription will be more appropriate.

18.4.1 Impressionistic and systematic transcription

Both broad and allophonic transcription are types of **systematic transcription**. This means that the transcriber knows what the options are for the speech that is being transcribed. For example, the transcriber of SSBE would know which vowels and consonants are possible in the variety and would pick the appropriate symbol from that limited set. They would also know which connected speech processes operate in that particular variety of English. Likewise, for an allophonic transcription, the transcriber knows what allophones exist in the variety and in which environments they occur. Thus, the transcription follows a system, and is therefore called systematic.

Exercise 18.3 Can you think of any situations in which you would want to transcribe speech, but do not know the system of the variety you are listening to?

Comment There are several situations in which you might not know the system of the speech you are transcribing. For example, if you were working with a language that had not been documented before, you would not have any prior knowledge of the system. Likewise, speech and language therapists working with a client for the first time would not know the system the client used to make meaningful contrasts. If you do not know the system, you are forced into using an **impressionistic transcription**, which means fitting what you hear into all the possible sounds of the IPA, including all the variations indicated by diacritics. In both of these cases, an initial impressionistic transcription would probably be used to develop knowledge of the system, so that systematic broad or allophonic transcriptions could be used in future. In addition, you might choose to use an impressionistic transcription if you wanted to capture individual variation in great detail, or if you wanted to study a variety for which you *think* you know the system, but want to be sure.

Exercise 18.4 What skills do you need to be able to transcribe? Think about the steps that you go through and what you are doing at each stage. For example, as a starting point, you have to be able to hear (or at least imagine) the speech signal to make a transcription.

Comment Transcription is actually an incredibly complex process, using a large number of skills. In some ways, it is like spelling a new unknown word, in that you turn an auditory signal into a set of symbols. However, unlike spelling a new word, for transcription you must also know a special set of IPA symbols, and have representations of the corresponding IPA sounds stored in your head. So, when we transcribe spoken material, we must hear (and see) and attend to the signal. When we transcribe from orthography, we can either say the word out loud, or access a mental representation of it from our minds. In all cases, we must hold the signal, in whole or in part, in our short-term memory, and try to divide it into individual segments. Then, each of these segments must be matched to an IPA sound, and the appropriate symbol accessed and written down.

Exercise 18.5 How important do you think transcription is for a phonetician? Can you get by without it, and are there other things that are more important?

Comment It is important to have good skills in transcription, but just how important will depend on what you want to use phonetics for. In many cases, the listening aspects of phonetics will be more important than the notational aspects. For example, you might not be able to remember that the diacritic for nasalisation is [̃], but this is easily remedied by looking at an IPA chart, and is only a small problem if you can hear that a sound is nasalised and know what this means in terms of articulation. That said, however, if you want to specialise and excel in phonetics, then transcription itself is a very important aspect of the field. It is important, therefore, to be aware of the drawbacks of, and problems with, different types of transcription, which we will now explore.

18.5 Potential problems with transcription

18.5.1 General

We have already alluded to some of the general problems with transcription. One is that there is no single 'right answer', since any transcription will depend on the interpretation of the transcriber. This is particularly the case for impressionistic transcription, where the possible options are so numerous. Another problem is that, when we transcribe, we assume that speech can be broken up into segments. As we have said since the beginning of this book, however, segments may only be a convenient notion that allows us to make sense of a very complex continuous signal. Another possible problem is that some features of speech are extremely difficult to capture by the ear alone; these might include minute differences in voice onset time or the position of the velum. Acoustic measurements or articulatory techniques such as ultrasound can be used to elucidate these aspects of speech, but without them the very fine details may not even be captured by the most skilled transcriber. However, transcription, unlike these acoustic and articulatory techniques, has the added bonus that it is done by a human using ears and brain alone, and these are the very organs that are designed to process speech.

18.5.2 Allophonic

Many students find allophonic transcription difficult. They find it hard to learn and remember the large number of diacritics, and some may wonder why it is even important, when most of the allophonic variation is predictable. If you are to become an expert in speech, however, you really need to be able to hear and understand aspects of it that are not obvious to an untrained person. Knowing about allophonic variation reminds us that speech is continuous, and also trains us to hear features such as aspiration and nasalisation, which any phonetician needs to be aware of for those times when we transcribe less predictable material. It is also worth noting here that allophonic transcriptions frequently leave out a lot of articulatory detail, and even when we include all the variations we have covered in earlier units, we will still not be recording everything about the utterance we are transcribing.

18.5.3 Broad

One controversial issue regarding broad transcription is whether or not we are really transcribing phonemes, which relates to the larger issue of whether phonemes really exist at all. While the full extent of this debate is somewhat outside the scope of this book, it is worth mentioning that some theorists believe that phonemes have no real psychological reality. In addition, there is a question, as we have already mentioned, about whether the changes that occur in connected speech processes really involve sounds changing into allophones of different phonemes. Those phoneticians who favour a different view prefer to think of the sounds resulting from assimilation, for example, as still remaining as allophones of the original phoneme. In this book, we have taken a very traditional view, however, and will therefore maintain the notion of change at the phonemic level. However, if you want to go further in the field, you may well want to explore these issues in more detail, and can find ideas for doing so in the Resources section (page 278).

18.6 Broad transcription practice

In the next couple of exercises, we will recap a few of the basic principles in broad transcription that were covered in earlier sections of the book.

Exercise 18.6 Transcribe the following words, being sure to avoid the tricky letters that are never used as symbols in English broad transcription.

jay Cox icy yacht phoenix cry shy quay

Comment The transcriptions are: /dʒeɪ/, /kɒks/, /aɪsi/, /jɒt/, /finɪks/, /kraɪ/, /ʃaɪ/ and /ki/.

Remember to keep practising your transcription. For example, you might find it useful to write your shopping lists and to-do lists in transcription. New transcribers find they quickly forget symbols if they do not use them frequently. In particular, many novice transcribers struggle to remember their vowel symbols. This is probably because there are lots of them, and they often bear less relationship to spelling than the consonant symbols. The following exercise is designed to help you practise your vowel symbols.

Exercise 18.7 Each of the following sentences contains some of the less common vowels in English. Transcribe each sentence, paying particular attention to the vowels, so that they do not catch you out. Remember, however, to include CSPs wherever they might occur.

They could hear a loud noise somewhere.
Look, that fair bird is near now.
The stern boy cares about the feared wolf.
The idea of bookworms is a rare joy.
The cow put her toy on the rear chair.

Comment /ðeɪ kʊd hɪər ə laʊd nɔɪz sʌmwɛə/
/lʊk ðæp fɛə bɜd ɪz nɪə naʊ/
/ðə stɜm bɔɪ kɛəz əbaʊt ðə fɪəb wʊlf/
/ði aɪdɪer əv bʊk wɜmz ɪz ə rɛə dʒɔɪ/
/ðə kaʊ pʊt hə tɔɪ ɒn ðə rɪə tʃɛə/

If this was difficult, please return to Unit 6 and your flash cards, to practise your symbols for vowels.

This is also a good opportunity to recap our knowledge of where CSPs can occur in SSBE. While some occur in Exercise 18.7, the sentences in the next exercise have been chosen especially to provide examples of weak forms and CSPs, so you should expect to find quite a few.

Exercise 18.8 The sentences below have been transcribed in isolated form, as if each word were given its pronunciation from the mental lexicon. Imagine them spoken in connected speech and add any potential weak forms, elisions, liaisons and assimilations.

a) /ðæt bɑ ɪznt kwaɪt bɪg ɪnʌf/
b) /ðə bɛst frɛnd ʃid mɛnʃənd kʊdənt kʌm/
c) /aɪ kɑnt krɛdɪt jɔ əkaʊnt fɔ ɔl ðæt mʌtʃ/

Comment a) /ðæp bɑr ɪzŋk kwaɪp bɪg ɪnʌf/
b) /ðə bɛs frɛn ʃib mɛnʃəŋ kʊdəŋk kʌm/
c) /aɪ kɑŋk krɛdɪtʃɔr əkaʊmp fər ɔl ðæp mʌtʃ/

Again, please revisit the last three units if this exercise was difficult.

18.7 Summary

In this unit, we have recapped and consolidated our knowledge of different types of transcription, and practised our broad transcription. We have investigated some advantages and disadvantages of each type, and seen for what purposes they might be used.

18.8 Looking forward

In the next units, we will think more about the changing pitch of the voice, which is called intonation.

18.9 Review questions

- What is meant by broad and narrow transcription?
- What is meant by impressionistic and systematic transcription?
- What are some problems with different types of transcription?

18.10 Review exercises

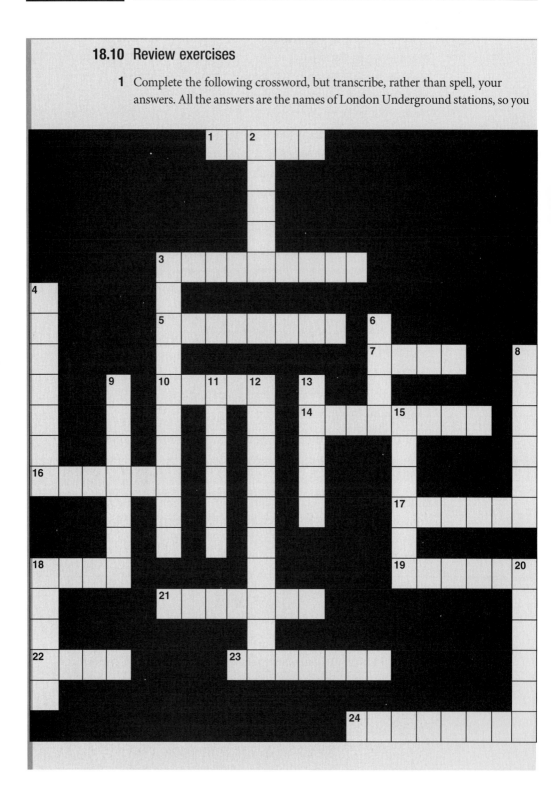

1 Complete the following crossword, but transcribe, rather than spell, your answers. All the answers are the names of London Underground stations, so you may wish to consult a list of these on the web, for example. You may also need to do a bit of searching to answer the clues, some of which are factual, and some of which are cryptic. In addition, you will need to transcribe elision and assimilation wherever they can apply in SSBE or you will not be able to complete the crossword.

Across:

1. Alight here for the British Museum (7)
3. Immediately before and after Heathrow (6, 5)
5. Perhaps 007 lives here? (4, 6)
7. Not down on the leg joint (5)
10. A place for storing weapons (7)
14. Where you would get off to see West Ham play football (5, 4)
16. Laurel's first name, and then some (8)
17. Poet Laureate 1689–92 (8)
18. Keep your money here (4)
19. Place of worship (6)
21. Not a green way to cross a river (9)
22. An ellipse (4)
23. *Where* is the border to this street? (8, 4)
24. A famous bridge and concert venue (11)

Down:

2. Home to the insane, or dogs, perhaps? (7)
3. Home to the Constitution Arch (4, 4, 6)
4. Like 3 across, but fresher (3, 5)
6 London is divided up into thirty-two of these (7)
8. A make of car (8)
9. Like 14 across, but the colour you would expect (5, 4)
11. Where the leg joints live? (7)
12. It is falling down (6, 6)
13. There is also a Bridge and a Green station in this part of London (6)
15. An 'earthy tube' on the Isle of Dogs (8)
18. The street where you might expect to hear the 'Great Bell' from the Oranges and Lemons nursery rhyme (3, 4)
20. The 'walk' made famous in the musical *Me and My Girl* (7)

Lengths of words in orthography are given in the clues, but do not forget that you need to *transcribe* your answers to fill in the crossword.

2 Find twenty-five errors in the following, assuming that it is spoken in SSBE. Errors may be in lexical stress, vowels or consonants. CSPs and weak forms are present and should not be considered errors. Remember that the symbols | and || represent intonation boundaries, which you do not need to worry about for now, although they may help you to read the transcription.

Mr. Bennet was so odd a mixture of quick parts, sarcastic humour, reserve, and caprice, that the experience of three and twenty years had been insufficient to make his wife understand his character. *Her* mind was less difficult to develop. She was a woman of mean understanding, little information, and uncertain temper. When she was discontented, she fancied herself nervous. The business of her life was to get her daughters married; its solace was visiting and news.

/mɪstər ˈbɛnɪp wəz ˈsəʊ ˈɒdd ə ˈmɪxstʃə əv ˈquɪk ˈpɑts | ˈsɑkæstɪk ˈhumə | rɪˈzɜv |əŋ kəˈpris | ðət ðə ɛkˈspɪərɪəns əf ˈthri ən ˈtwɛnty ˈjɪəz| həb bin ˈɪnsəfɪʃənt to meɪk hɪz ˈwaɪf ʌndəˈstænd hɪz ˈchærɪktə || ˈhɜ mɪnd wəz lɛss ˈdɪfikəlt tə dəvɛ ˈləp || ʃi wəz ə ˈwomən əv ˈmin ʌndəˈstændɪng | ˈlɪttəl ɪnfəˈmeɪʃən | ənd ʌnˈcɜtən ˈtɛmpə ||ˈ wɛn ʃi wəz ˈdɪskəntɛntɪd | ʃi ˈfansɪd həsɛlf ˈnɜvəs || ðə ˈbuɪsnəs əv hə ˈlaɪf wəz tə ˈgɛt hə ˈdɔtəz ˈmærrɪd | ɪts ˈsɒlɪse wəz ˈvɪsətɪŋ ən ˈnjus/

3 Transcribe the following as if spoken in a fairly natural, casual style. Remember to mark stress and include any possible weak forms and connected speech processes.

One of Sherlock Holmes's defects – if, indeed, one may call it a defect – was that he was exceedingly loath to communicate his full plans to any other person until the instant of their fulfilment. Partly it came no doubt from his own masterful nature, which loved to dominate and surprise those who were around him. Partly also from his professional caution, which urged him never to take any chances. The result, however, was very trying for those who were acting as his agents and assistants. I had often suffered under it, but never more so than during that long drive in the darkness. The great ordeal was in front of us; at last we were about to make our final effort, and yet Holmes had said nothing, and I could only surmise what his course of action would be. My nerves thrilled with anticipation when at last the cold wind upon our faces and the dark, void spaces on either side of the narrow road told me that we were back upon the moor once again. Every stride of the horses and every turn of the wheels was taking us nearer to our supreme adventure.

UNIT 19 INTONATION

19.1 Key learning areas

In this unit we will:

- see how intonation relates to the changing pitch of the voice
- discover how we can transcribe intonation in different ways
- explore the form of SSBE intonation.

19.2 Introduction

In this unit, we will look at intonation, which refers to the changing pitch of the voice as we speak. In some ways, intonation is like music or singing: first, because it involves changes in pitch, and, second, because the same vowels and consonants can be produced with a variety of different pitches.

19.3 The production of intonation

Exercise 19.1 Take a single vowel, such as [ɑ]. Try to say/sing it on a very high pitch, and then on a very low pitch. What aspects of your articulation do you think are responsible for the change in pitch?

Comment You may remember that we briefly summarised how different pitches are produced in Unit 14, when we talked about speech variation. It is the voiced segments of speech, such as our vowel [ɑ] in the exercise above, that carry changes in pitch. When a sound is voiced, the vocal folds always vibrate, but they vibrate at different speeds, depending on their size and stiffness. While different people might have different-sized vocal folds (due to their sex or age), speakers can also vary the length and stiffness of the folds by using muscles in the larynx. This will alter the speed at which the folds vibrate; in turn, the speed at which they vibrate determines the pitch of what we hear. Just as with all vibrations, a high frequency of vibration causes us to hear a high pitch, and a low frequency of vibration causes us to hear a low pitch. So, in the exercise above, the high-pitched sound has quicker vocal fold vibration than the lower-pitched sound. Notably, however, other aspects of its articulation do not change. The tongue and lips are in the same position in each case, and, if they vary at all, it is only to accommodate the slight changes in the position of the larynx which might occur with very high and very low pitches.

In our example in Exercise 19.1, we changed pitch on a single sound. In normal speech, we string these changes in pitch together over the course of an utterance; these changes are known as **intonation**. Because different sounds and words can be produced with different pitches, segments (vowels and consonants) and intonation are thought of as being somewhat independent. Thus, intonation is often described as being **suprasegmental** or **autosegmental**, meaning above, or independent of, the segmental level.

Exercise 19.2 Try saying the word 'arm' on two different pitches, as you did for the vowel [ɑ] in Exercise 19.1. Does the word mean something different at a high and low pitch, or does it mean 'arm' in each case?

Comment The pitch of the word does not affect the meaning of the word at all. 'arm' means 'arm' whether it is said at a high pitch, a low pitch, somewhere in the middle, or even with an elaborate pitch movement that rises and falls and rises again. This is not the case in all languages, however. As we will see below, there are many languages, called **tone languages**, which *do* make word-meaning differences by using changes in pitch.

19.4 Tone languages

Many of the languages of Africa and Asia, as well as the indigenous languages of North America, are tone languages. In these languages, the pitch on which a word is produced can change its meaning. Here are two examples from Asian languages, taken from the illustrations of these languages, in the IPA handbook, a reference for which is given in the Resources section (page 278). (Note that I am ignoring complicated notations of tone here, as there are quite a few different systems in use, which are not important for our current purposes.)

	Cantonese	Thai
	/si/	/k^{h}a/
High tone	silk	to engage in trade
Mid tone	to try	to get stuck
Low tone	matter	galangal (a ginger-like root)

Exercise 19.3 Try producing the Cantonese and Thai words above, using the appropriate tone.

Comment This exercise is a good test of your phonetic production skills, as you do not have any lexical knowledge to rely on (unless you speak these languages, of course). In fact, these same vowels and consonants (/si/ and /k^{h}a/) actually have even more different meanings in these languages which are distinguished by pitch movements such as rises and falls, not exemplified here.

19.5 Intonation

Up to this point, we have said that intonation relates to the changing pitch of the voice, and that the pitch can be changed by changing the frequency of vibration of the vocal folds. We have also seen that pitch does not change word meaning in English, as it does in other languages. We will now briefly investigate what effects pitch *does* have in English, and will return to this in much greater detail in Unit 20.

Exercise 19.4 Try producing a sentence using just one pitch. For example, try producing 'Twinkle, twinkle, little star' on a monotone. What does it sound like?

Comment To speak without using pitch variations sounds very unnatural, and possibly artificial or robotic. Intonation adds a great deal to the naturalness of our speech. If people lose the ability to use intonation – for example, if they have had certain types of strokes or throat cancers – it can be very difficult for them to sound natural, and sometimes difficult for them to be understood.

As we have learnt, in English and the vast majority of European languages, pitch does not distinguish the meaning of individual words. It does make our speech sound natural and coherent, however, and contributes to our understanding of the meaning of longer utterances (by signalling aspects such as emotion and the difference between questions and statements), as we will see in Unit 20. For now, we are going to concentrate on the form (rather than the function) of intonation and the ways in which we might transcribe it.

19.6 Systems of intonation notation 1

Exercise 19.5 Thinking back over the rest of the book, have you seen anything that we could use to transcribe the pitch of the voice? If not, or if you can not remember, what might be a good system?

Comment In this book so far, we have concentrated on transcribing vowels and consonants, and have not really suggested any system that might be useful for pitch. There are, however, quite a few different ways of noting down the pitch of the voice. The most intuitive system is rather like musical notation, and is capable of giving quite a precise description of changing pitch. We will work with this system for now, and think about other ways of notating pitch later.

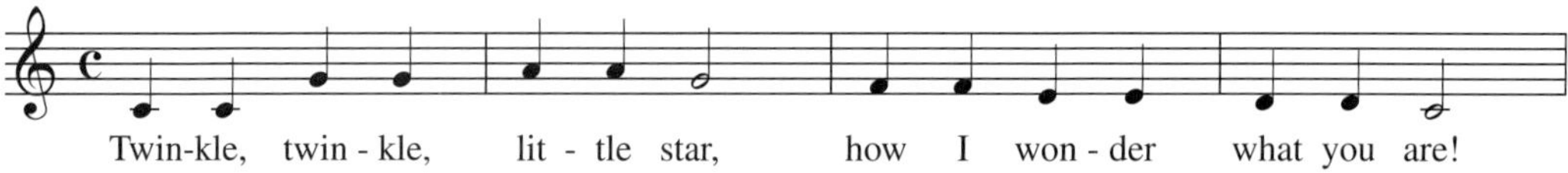

Figure 19.1 A musical score for a simple tune to the first line of 'Twinkle, Twinkle, Little Star'

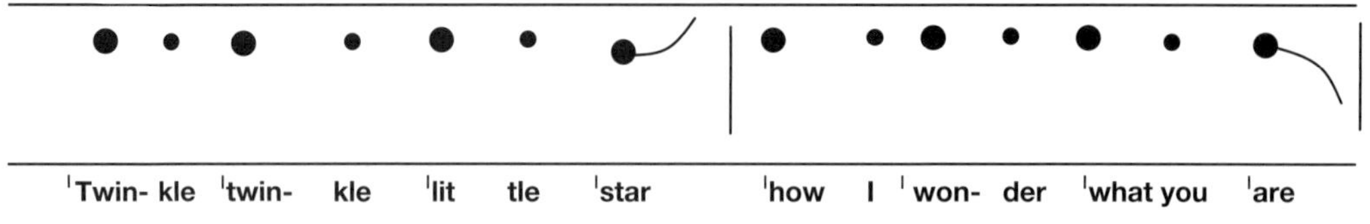

Figure 19.2 An interlinear diagram for the first line of 'Twinkle, Twinkle, Little Star'

In the musical notation in Figure 19.1, there are notes for each syllable, and different types of notes (minims and crotchets) for notes of different lengths. Importantly, these notes are placed at different heights within the stave to indicate their pitch. Notes at the bottom are low in pitch, while notes at the top are high in pitch.

We can use a similar notation to describe intonation. Figure 19.2 shows an **interlinear diagram** of one way in which a person might say (rather than sing or play) the first line of the same nursery rhyme. There are, in fact, many different forms of intonation we could use when producing this sentence (and, indeed, any other), a point that we will return to later on. Figure 19.2 represents a fairly neutral way to say the sentence.

Note that the top line represents the highest normal pitch of the voice for any particular speaker, and the bottom line represents the lowest. The difference between the highest and lowest pitches can be called the pitch range.

Exercise 19.6 Compare the musical and the interlinear notations in Figure 19.2. What are the similarities and differences between the two?

Comment Firstly, you see that in the interlinear diagram there is a dot for each syllable, in a similar way to a *note* representing each syllable in the musical stave. The interlinear diagram also has different types of dots, although these differ merely by size (rather than colour, as in the musical stave), with larger dots representing stressed syllables and smaller ones representing unstressed syllables. There are divisions in both the interlinear notation and the score, but these are different in character: where there are four bars in the score, the interlinear diagram divides into two sections. These sections are called intonation phrases, and boundaries between them are notated using single (|) or double lines (||). These two intonation phrases, coincidentally, have seven syllables each, due to the structure of the poem, but they could have any number, as we will see shortly.

Finally, in our interlinear diagram we have two dots with tails, rather like tadpoles (in fact, this type of representation is sometimes referred to informally as a 'tadpole' diagram for this reason). These tails indicate a change in pitch on a single syllable, which would be rather similar to a slur in music, none of which are shown in the stave above.

19.7 Intonation phrases

In music, we know that a bar is well formed if it contains the right number of beats. In common, or 4/4, time, all the bars must have four beats, which are made up of notes and rests. In music, then, the basic unit is the bar, but in intonation, the basic unit is the **intonation phrase**. The two separate sections of 'Twinkle, twinkle, little star' in our interlinear diagram are both intonation phrases. In an interlinear diagram we can divide intonation phrases using straight lines, as shown in Figure 19.2. Double bars usually occur at the end of an utterance, and indicate that there will be a definite pause before any following material. Single lines may also be used to indicate that the words in the first phrase are closely related in grammatical terms to the words in the second phrase. So, the next line of the nursery rhyme could be produced as:

how I wonder | what you are?||

Here you see that we can also use the bars to indicate phrase breaks in orthography.

As we will see in Unit 20, speakers also have a choice over how they divide spoken material into intonation phrases, and may choose different patterns according to the meanings they wish to convey. Importantly, an intonation phrase can contain any number of syllables, so it is not constrained by size or length in the same way as a musical bar. It does have to contain certain elements, however, which we will now investigate. We are going to start by looking at intonation phrases that contain only one syllable and examine the various patterns that are possible.

Exercise 19.7 Consider the word 'no'. How many different ways can you say it, by varying just the pitch of your voice?

Comment You have probably thought of lots of different ways, including keeping the pitch quite level or rising and falling in pitch. You may have had difficulty deciding how to group and classify these different pitch changes, however, and therefore may have had difficulty counting the different patterns you produced. Specifically, you may have been uncertain as to which productions were sufficiently different to count as separate patterns.

19.7.1 Nuclear tones

In the British school of intonation, as applied to SSBE and related accents, there are considered to be seven pitch patterns that can occur when there is only a single syllable in an intonation phrase. So, although you may have produced more than seven types in Exercise 19.7, some of these would be considered to be versions of the same pattern, based on whether or not they seem to make a substantial difference to meaning (we will look further at intonational meaning in Unit 20). The basic seven patterns, called **nuclear tones**, are shown in Figure 19.3.

High falls start towards the top of a speaker's range and fall to the bottom. Low falls are similar, except that they start from the middle of the range. Rise-falls have a more complicated pattern. They start from a mid-pitch, rise almost to the top of the range, and then fall to the bottom of the speaker's range.

There is a similar distinction between the rises. High rises start at a mid-level and rise to the top of the range, while low rises start low and rise to the middle of the range. Fall-rises are more complicated, falling to the bottom of the range before rising slightly again.

Finally, mid-level tones start in the middle of the range, and the pitch continues on this level, with no appreciable movement.

Exercise 19.8 Try to produce the word 'no' using each of the different tones.

Consider if the different tones give different interpretations to the word 'no'.

Comment For some speakers, it is rather difficult to produce intonation to order like this. If this is the case for you, try to begin by being able to produce high and low pitches on cue, and then work up to producing the patterns above. You may notice that the different tones give different interpretations to the word 'no'. The falls may sound more definite, and the rises more hesitant, or questioning, for example. We will consider these different interpretations and the uses of intonation in Unit 20.

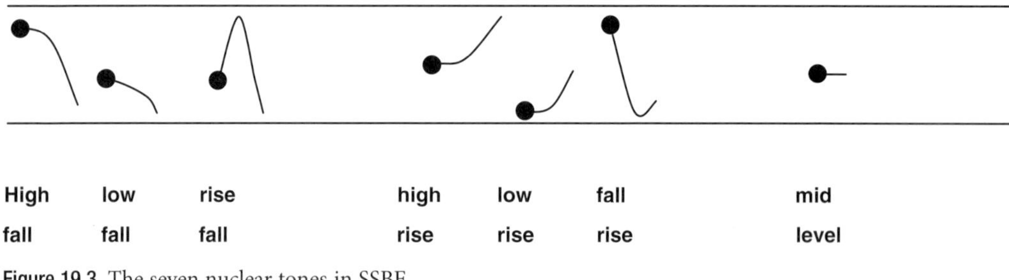

Figure 19.3 The seven nuclear tones in SSBE

19.7.2 Tails

Above, we have only looked at single-syllable intonation phrases, but there is a multitude of different types of intonation phrase that contain more than a single syllable. We will now try to build up several different types of intonation phrase, considering the various intonation options for each one. We will begin with two-syllable utterances, where the stress is on the first syllable, such as in the word 'no one'.

Exercise 19.9 Compare the patterns on the two-syllable utterances in Figure 19.4 with the patterns on one-syllable utterances in Figure 19.3.

What do you notice? (Remember that the large dots represent stressed syllables and the smaller dots represent unstressed syllables.)

Comment You should notice that the basic pattern in the one syllable utterance now spreads out over the two-syllable utterance. The stressed syllable where the pitch movement starts is known as the **nucleus**, and we will return to this definition shortly. Another part of the intonation phrase is the tail. The syllable or syllables after the nucleus make up the **tail**. Note that 'tail' does not refer to the movement lines in the interlinear diagram (the tails of the 'tadpoles'), as these simply indicate where pitch moves on a single syllable.

Exercise 19.10 What do you think these pitch patterns might look like if there were more syllables in the tail. What would 'nobody' and 'nobody can' sound like when produced with a high fall, for example? How would these look in an interlinear diagram?

Comment As we have hinted at above, the pitch in the tail will continue with the same pattern. So, for example, after high and low falls, the syllables in the tail stay low and level, regardless of the number of syllables. After high and low rises, the pitch in the tail keeps on rising, regardless of the number of syllables that follow.

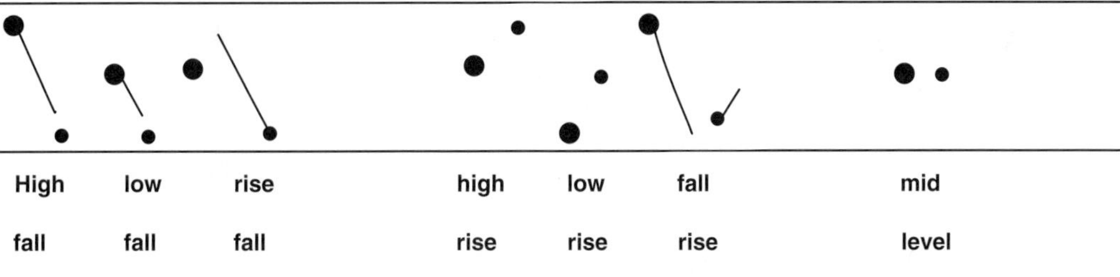

Figure 19.4 The seven nuclear tones produced with a one-syllable tail

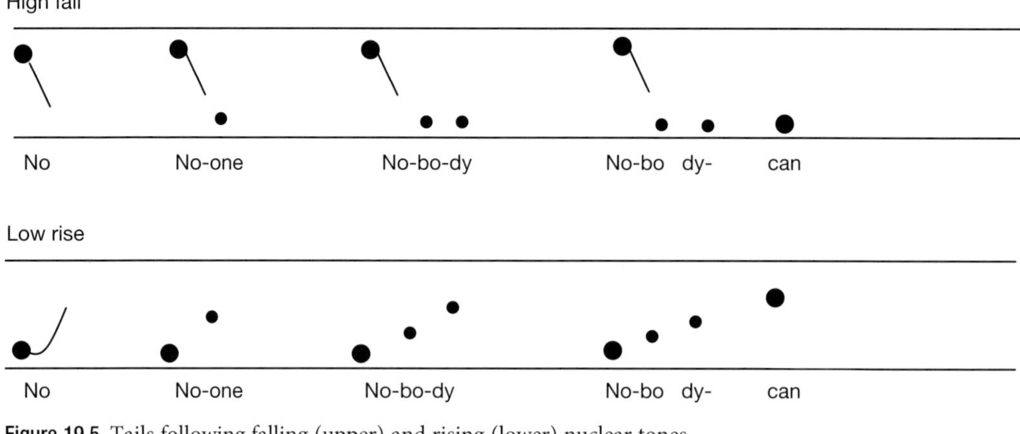

Figure 19.5 Tails following falling (upper) and rising (lower) nuclear tones

19.8 Stress and accent

Exercise 19.11 Look at 'nobody can' in the two interlinear diagrams above in Figure 19.5 . What is different about the tail in this phrase in comparison to the other tails?

Comment For 'nobody can', there is a stressed syllable in the tail (represented by a large dot), which is different to the other tails we have looked at. However, it is perfectly permissible to have a stressed syllable in the tail of an intonation phrase.

At this point, we need to remind ourselves what we know about stress, and then introduce a new term, 'accent'.

Exercise 19.12 Remind yourself about some facts to do with stress by answering the following questions.

a) What are the characteristics of a stressed syllable?
b) What are two types of stress dealing with words and connected speech, respectively?
c) Can we predict with certainty which syllables will be stressed in a new word or in a sentence?

Comment a) In Unit 8, we said that stressed syllables are longer and louder than unstressed syllables.
b) We looked at both lexical and rhythmic stress. We said that lexical stress is the stress pattern a word has when it is pronounced in isolation, whereas rhythmic stress refers to stress patterns within a stretch of speech.

c) In English, lexical stress can go on any syllable within a word, so, when we learn a new English word, we have to learn its stress pattern too, unlike in other languages, where stress might be fixed on the first or final syllable, for example. Likewise, in an utterance, it is not possible to say with certainty which words will be stressed, but those that are will usually carry stress on their lexically stressed syllable (except in cases such as stress shift).

In addition to stressed syllables being louder and longer, we also learnt in Unit 8 that stressed syllables might be associated with pitch prominence. This is what we will explore now, and it is this pitch movement that is relevant for the distinction between 'stress' and 'accent'. When we talk about intonation, **accents** are stressed syllables that are also made prominent by pitch. So, accents are always stressed syllables and are louder and longer than unstressed and unaccented syllables. In addition, they have a pitch movement associated with them, or are higher or lower in pitch than the syllables adjacent to them.

Exercise 19.13 Given the definition of 'accent' above, look back at the interlinear diagram for the high fall pronunciation of 'nobody can' in Figure 19.5. For each syllable, say whether it is stressed, unstressed or accented.

Comment 'no' is accented because it has a pitch movement within it. 'bo' and 'dy' are unstressed and unaccented. While 'bo' has jumped down in pitch from the syllable before it, we know it can not be accented because it is not stressed, and just represents the end of the falling movement on 'no'. 'can' is stressed, but not accented, because it is not associated with a change in pitch, and will simply be louder and longer than the unstressed syllables.

Exercise 19.14 Both the terms 'accent' and 'nucleus' are important for describing intonation. You have seen them both before in this book. Do you think these terms mean the same as they did in the previous units?

Comment You've heard the term 'nucleus' in relation to the compulsory part of the syllable, and the term 'accent' in relation to regional and social variation. The terms do not mean the same thing in this unit, as you will have noted from the definitions we have given.

The term 'nucleus' in intonation, however, does have something in common with the 'nucleus' which refers to the centre of the syllable. If you remember, the minimum syllable is just a nucleus, represented by a word like 'eye', for example. The nucleus in intonation, similarly, is the only compulsory part of the intonation phrase. So, in our examples of 'no', above, we have an intonation phrase consisting of just a nucleus, while in the latter examples we have a nucleus plus a tail.

The nucleus, however, is more than simply the only compulsory part of the intonation phrase. In fact, the nucleus is the *final accent* within an intonation phrase. So, if there is more than one accent in the phrase, the nucleus will be the last one. We have seen that nuclear patterns spread out over the tail; therefore, all intonation phrases, whatever their length, will end with one of our seven patterns from above.

Exercise 19.15 We now know that an intonation phrase must contain a nucleus, which is the last accented syllable, and can contain a tail if there are syllables occurring after the nucleus. What else do we need to do to describe an entire intonation phrase?

Comment If you have been following so far, you will realise that we have only described intonation phrases with a single accented syllable, which might be followed by more unaccented syllables (the tail). We have not described what can happen before the nucleus and will now do that by describing heads and pre-heads.

19.9 Heads

As we have said above, intonation phrases can contain more than one accented syllable. When there are two or more accented syllables in an intonation phrase, the first accent marks the start of a unit called the **head**.

Exercise 19.16 Produce these film titles in a fairly natural way and try to listen to your pitch as you do so. First of all, work out where you put the nucleus (the final accented syllable), and then work out if you can hear any other accents within each title.

a) A Fistful of Dollars
b) For a Few Dollars More

Comment First of all, we should bear in mind that intonation can vary greatly, even when the same sentence is produced by the same speaker. This is why we have used these well-known film titles, which people are more likely to produce in the same way than less familiar phrases. However, even in these familiar items there could be variation, a topic we will revisit in Unit 20. For now, we will assume that all are spoken as a single intonation phrase, and I will give a plausible intonation pattern for each phrase below.

a) It is likely that the nucleus in on 'do-', and that it is a high or low fall. There is also likely to be a jump up in pitch on 'fist', so this syllable is also an accent, and the start of the head. (See Figure 19.6.)

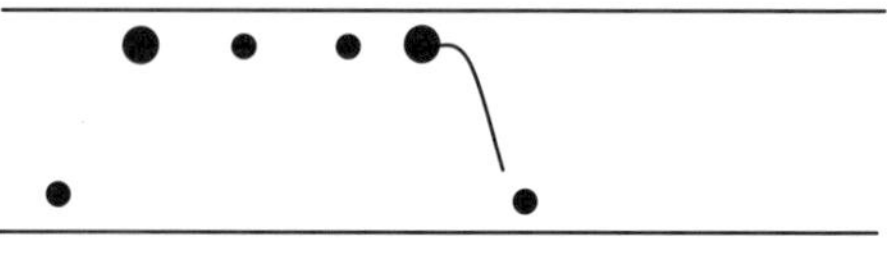

Figure 19.6 A possible intonation pattern for 'A fistful of dollars'

b) The pattern is very similar, with the first accent on 'few', which begins the head, and a high fall nucleus on 'more'. But now we have two syllables before the first accent, which we will investigate shortly, when we come to pre-heads. (See Figure 19.7.)

In each case, the head starts from the first accented syllable and comprises all the syllables up to, but not including, the nucleus.

Exercise 19.17 Thinking back to the film titles in Exercise 19.16, why do you think particular words/syllables are accented?

Comment As we keep hinting, intonation is not entirely predictable. There are some general rules, however, that do allow us to predict which patterns might be used. Firstly, accents can only go onto stressed syllables. So when the word 'dollars' is stressed in the first film title, its first, rather than its second, syllable will be stressed, as this is the lexically stressed syllable. It will also attract the accent.

You will also notice that accents tend to go onto content words rather than function words, as these are usually more important for getting our message across. Accents help to focus our attention on various parts of the sentence that are most important for meaning, as we will see in Unit 20.

We have seen that the nucleus can have seven different tones associated with it. The head can also have a variety of patterns. We will look at four basic types here. They are low level, high level, falling and rising (see Figures 19.8, 19.9, 19.10 and 19.11, respectively).

Exercise 19.18 a) Try to produce the various patterns shown in Figures 19.8 to 19.11.

b) From what you can see so far, does the type of head determine the type of nucleus?

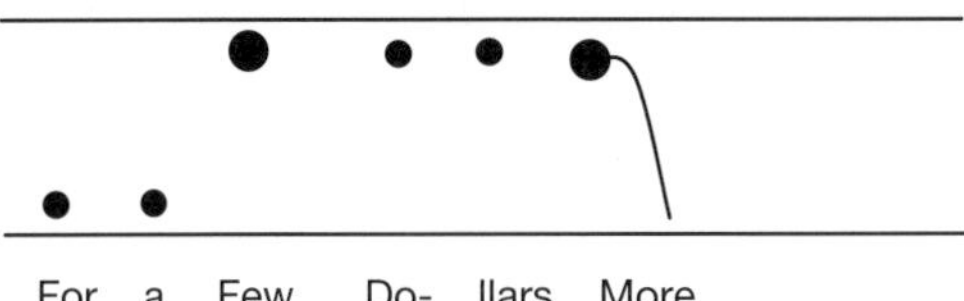
For a Few Do- llars More

Figure 19.7 A possible intonation pattern for 'For a few dollars more'

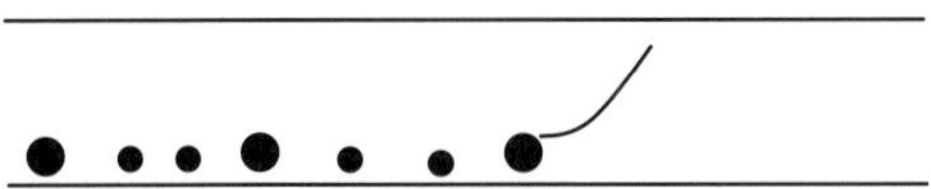
Can't we just stay here instead?

Figure 19.8 An example of a low-level head

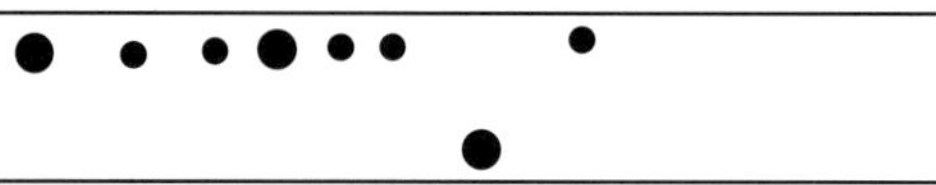

When can we go to the pictures?

Figure 19.9 An example of a high-level head

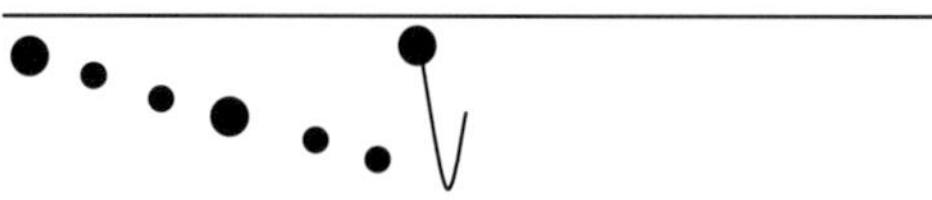

Surely we mustn't do that.

Figure 19.10 An example of a falling head

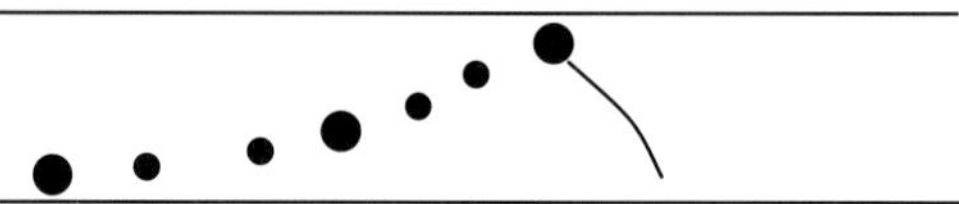

How could she end up like that?

Figure 19.11 An example of a rising head

Comment

a) Even if it is difficult to produce these patterns, do persevere, and seek help from a phonetics teacher if possible. Try to get the high and low accents right first, and then add in the others.

b) If you compare the sentences for high-level and low-level heads, you will see that they both combine with low-rise nuclear tones, demonstrating that there is no one-to-one correspondence between the type of head and the type of nucleus.

Heads and nuclei are rather separate entities, but some authors describe particular restrictions in the way they can combine, such as low heads occurring most commonly with low rises, falling heads with fall-rises, and rising heads with high falls. The high head frequently occurs with many different types of nuclear tone. We will not investigate this further here, but you might like to listen out for the various head + nucleus pairings that can be heard.

19.10 Pre-heads

We now come to the final part of the intonation phrase in our discussion, which is actually the very first part of an intonation phrase to be produced, because it occurs (optionally) at the start of an utterance. The **pre-head** is defined as any unstressed syllables that occur before the head, as we saw in our film titles above. In the vast majority of cases, the pre-head is low in pitch, and lower than – or on the same level as – the syllables at the start of the head. Such pre-heads are called low pre-heads.

Occasionally, a high pre-head occurs, which is above the pitch level of the first accent (or on the same level as the start of a high fall). These are much rarer than low pre-heads, however, and are generally associated with emphasis or liveliness on the part of the speaker.

Exercise 19.19 Look back at the sentences above which demonstrate the different types of head, in Figures 19.8 to 19.11. Try to produce each sentence with a pre-head by putting the word 'but' in front of it. Try this first with a low pre-head, and then, if you can manage that easily, with a high pre-head.

Comment Hopefully, you found that the low pre-head sounded more neutral in each case. In the interlinear diagrams in Figure 19.12, low pre-heads are shown with the usual filled circle. High pre-heads are at a level around that of the start of a high fall, and towards the top of the speaker's pitch range. These are illustrated here

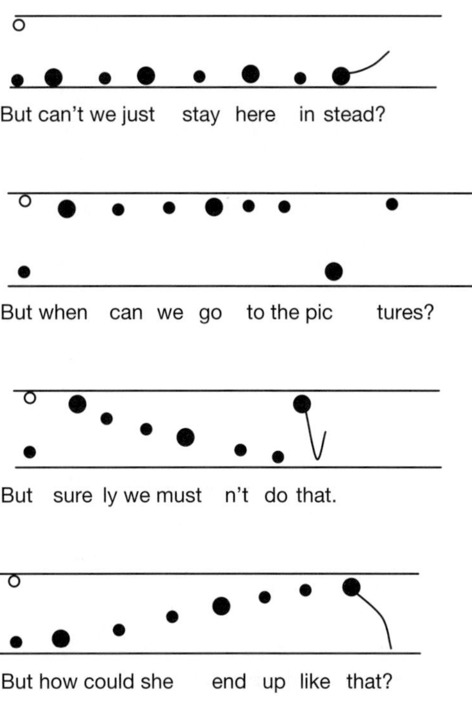

Figure 19.12 Examples of pre-heads

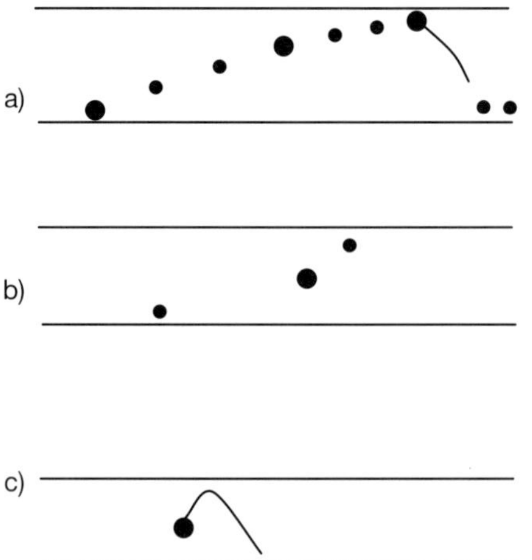

Figure 19.13 Interlinear diagrams for interpretation

with an open circle, but this is only so the two types of pre-head can be compared. Usually they are shown with a filled circle, just as for all other syllables.

19.11 Complete intonation patterns

As we said earlier, intonation phrases only need to have a nucleus, meaning that all the other parts are optional. So, a nucleus can come in combination with some, any or none of the other parts, such as pre-head, head and tail.

Exercise 19.20 In the diagrams in Figure 19.13, see if you can work out which units of intonation are present, and what the pitch pattern is in the nucleus and any other constituents.

Comment In (a) there is no pre-head, a rising head, a high fall nucleus and two syllables in the tail. In (b) there is a low pre-head, a high rise nucleus, and one syllable in the tail. In (c) there is just a rise-fall nucleus; none of the other elements are present.

19.12 Systems of intonation notation 2

Exercise 19.21 What are the advantages and disadvantages of the interlinear diagram for transcribing intonation?

Comment One advantage is that the system is closely linked to our perception, so it is not arbitrary and takes almost no time to learn. It may be difficult for some people to *hear* rises and falls, but this is not inherent to the system of transcription, and once you can hear them it is easy to notate them. One disadvantage is that it is rather hard to combine interlinear diagrams with transcription of segments, as you have to do two separate tasks: an IPA transcription of the vowels and consonants, and a separate transcription of pitch. Something that may be an advantage or a disadvantage, depending on your point of view, is that the transcription has the potential to be very detailed. You can show tiny differences in pitch (as long as you can hear them), even if these do not make a contribution towards meaning. Note that the two systems described below disregard some of this detail and give a broader transcription, aimed primarily at capturing different meanings or interpretations rather than minute details.

19.12.1 In-text notation

Many phoneticians use the same system of analysis as that described above (comprising nuclear tones, heads, and so on), but use a system of distinct symbols to mark up the nucleus and other accents on an orthographic or phonetic transcription, instead of showing pitch movement in an interlinear diagram. This system is quite detailed in full, with separate marks for different types of heads and to indicate the difference between stressed and accented syllables. Here, I simply give the symbols for the different type of nuclear tones. The nucleus can also be indicated by underlining the appropriate syllable.

High rise: ˊno
Low rise: ˏno
Fall-rise: ˇno
High fall ˋno
Low fall ˎno
Rise-fall ˆno
Mid level ˃no

Exercise 19.22 Can you see why these symbols were chosen to represent these tones? Do you think they are easy to remember and interpret?

Comment The direction of the pitch movement is indicated by the shape of the symbol, reading from left to right. The starting height of the pitch movement is shown by the symbol's position in relation to the word – that is, high or low in the line of text. In this way, the symbols are quite easy to remember and interpret, and this system is quite useful and popular, as it captures some of the iconic nature of the pitch movements, while combining the system with an orthographic or phonetic transcription. Note that this system *does not* show high and low versions of fall-rises, rise-falls and levels, because there are not considered to be appreciable differences in meaning between high and low realisations of these tones in English.

19.12.2 Highs and lows

While the seven nuclear tones model described above has been very influential in Britain, many teachers in North America use a different system, which is based on pitch levels, and is referred to as the **autosegmental metrical** (AM) model. This system has also come to dominate research into intonation in many different languages.

This system uses 'high' and 'low', as basic categories to indicate pitch levels at particular moments in time, rather than 'rises' and 'falls'. What follows is a very brief and simplified introduction to this system.

Exercise 19.23 How would you describe a fall in terms of high and low pitch levels? What about a rise?

Comment A fall can be thought of as a high level followed by a low level, and a rise as a low level followed by a high level, as shown in Figure 19.14. When we want to describe a rise or fall, therefore, we can use the letters H (for high) and L (for low), in various combinations. So, we can use HL for a fall, and LH for a rise.

Exercise 19.24 How might you indicate a fall-rise or a rise-fall?

Comment We can simply add another letter to our label, to show that there is another important pitch level: HLH is a fall-rise and a rise-fall is LHL.

Exercise 19.25 How do you think you might indicate the difference between a high rise and a low rise?

Comment As a high rise starts high, it can be notated as HH; a low rise will be LH, indicating that is starts low and then rises.

Exercise 19.26 Can you think of any advantages or disadvantages of this system, compared to a system of rises and falls?

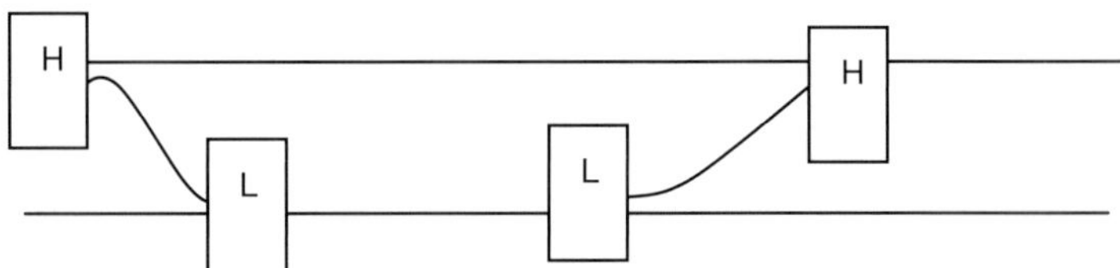

Figure 19.14 A fall and rise described in terms of high and low pitch levels

Comment The system is very powerful for describing the phonetics and phonology of intonation in English and other languages. It uses a simple set of two labels to describe all accents, including the four types of head, and seven types of nuclear tone in the British tradition. For some people, however, the system of high and low levels and the non-iconic symbols used are off-putting.

You may like to read more about the AM system of intonation by looking at the suggestions in the Resources section (page 278). In this book we will continue to use the seven nuclear tones from the British tradition, as they are still more commonly taught in the UK, are perhaps a little more intuitive, and more is written about them in terms of how they help to convey meaning, which is the focus of Unit 20.

19.13 Summary

In this unit, we have looked at the form of intonation in English and how we can describe the component parts of intonation and the options within those parts. We have seen that intonation phrases must contain a nucleus, and, optionally, a pre-head, head and tail. We have described seven options for nuclear tones and tails, four different types of head, and two types of pre-head. We have also looked briefly at AM forms of notation.

19.14 Looking forward

In the next unit, we will look at how we can change the meaning and interpretation of utterances by varying the length of the intonation phrase, the position and type of the nuclear tone, and the overall pitch of the voice.

19.15 Review questions

Have a look at these questions to see if you have understood the main points to learn from this unit.

- How many types of nuclear tone are there in the British tradition of intonation description?
- Other than the nucleus, what are the other possible units of an intonation phrase called?
- Falls and rises are one way of describing intonation. What is another way?

19.16 Review exercises

1 Answer true or false to the following statements and then correct the false ones.

a) An accented syllable must also be a stressed syllable.
b) An intonation phrase must contain a nucleus.
c) Intonation phrases with a pre-head must also have a head.
d) The nuclear tone can take seven different forms in SSBE.
e) Rising tones are followed by rising tails.
f) Falling tones are followed by falling tails.
g) The nucleus is the last stressed syllable in an intonation phrase.

2 For the following utterance, describe the intonation pattern as fully as possible. Does it have a pre-head, head and/or tail? If so, which syllables make up these units, and what are the pitch patterns inside these units? Which syllable is the nucleus, and what is the nuclear tone?

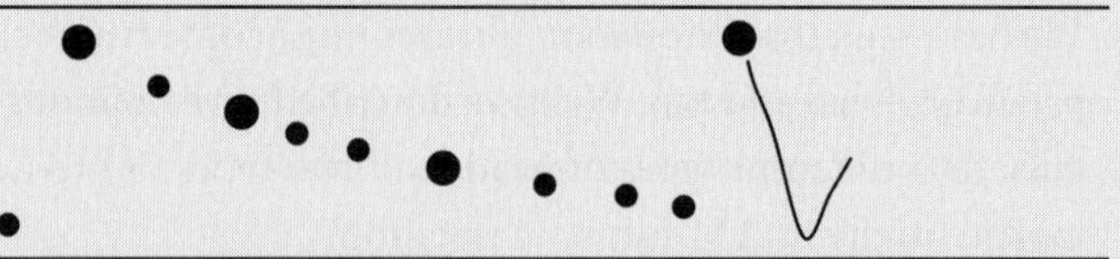

I hope he'll wa-ter the plants while I'm a -way

3 Draw an interlinear diagram for the sentence, 'She can't seem to pass her exam'. Draw a low pre-head on 'she', a high head starting on 'can't', and a low rise nucleus on the stressed syllable of 'exam'.

Now alter the diagram to illustrate the sentence, 'She can't seem to pass her driving test'. Keep everything the same, but put the nucleus on 'drive'.

UNIT 20 FUNCTIONS OF INTONATION

20.1 Key learning areas

In this unit we will:

- identify how various features of intonation can contribute to the meaning or interpretation of an utterance
- learn how intonation can affect meanings related to focus, attitude, grammar and discourse.

20.2 Introduction

In the previous unit, we have seen various ways to describe intonation. In this unit, we will look at how intonation functions and how it can affect the meaning of an utterance.

20.3 Recap about intonational meaning

Exercise 20.1 What have we already said about the meaning of tone and intonation in Unit 19? Can the pitch of the voice change the meaning of individual words?

Comment In Unit 19, we decided that pitch does not affect the meaning of individual words in English. Saying any particular word with a rise, fall or fall-rise, for example, does not affect the meaning of that word. Therefore, 'dog' still means 'dog', regardless of the pitch on which it is produced. In tone languages, however, pitch can and does change the meaning of individual words, just as changing a vowel or consonant can do so in English.

20.4 Intonational meaning in English

Having established that intonation does not affect the meanings of individual words, we must now turn to the effect of intonation on longer stretches of speech. Here we will find that intonation does indeed influence meaning.

Exercise 20.2 Using what you learnt in Unit 19, imagine how the following words could be spoken with a variety of intonation patterns. Think about which aspects of intonation you might vary and the different meanings that are then created. Note that the material does not have any punctuation and is not necessarily spoken as a single intonation phrase or by a single individual.

I'll get the shopping tonight

Comment No doubt you have come up with many different ways in which the sentence might be produced. You may have chosen to break it into two intonation phrases, for example, with the first four words spoken by one person and 'tonight' by another person. You can also vary the position of the nucleus (and other accents), depending on which words you want to make important; and you can vary the nuclear tone to any one of the seven we discussed in Unit 19. Or, you might have used a very wide or narrow pitch range. All of these alterations will have some effect on the intended and perceived meanings of the utterance. We will now take each type of change in turn and think about each one in a bit more detail.

In what follows we will look at four different ways in which intonation might contribute to the perceived meaning of an utterance. These concern (a) how the speaker breaks their speech into intonation phrases, (b) the choice of accent position, (c) the choice of nuclear tone and (d) the choice of key or register. For each of these, we will look at the default, or neutral, pattern, and at how alternative meanings are created by using patterns other than the default.

In particular, the meanings we will consider are of four main types (although many subdivisions and extra meanings are possible).

- **Focus** – here we can change meanings by altering what is emphasised in a sentence.
- **Attitude** – here we can signal our attitude to the utterance or to the listener, or we can signal our emotional state.
- **Grammar** – here we can use intonation to mark out particular structures, and to indicate different types of utterance, such as statements and questions.
- **Discourse** – here we use intonation to show where we are in our talk, such as whether we are planning to carry on speaking or are ready to let someone else speak.

20.5 Intonation phrases

As we saw in Unit 19, the basic unit of intonation is the intonation phrase, which must have a nucleus and can optionally contain a pre-head, head and tail. The material in an intonation phrase may relate quite closely to what comes next, in which case it is demarcated in notation with a single bar (|), or it may be less closely related, and concluded with a pause, which is indicated by a double bar (||). One of the decisions that we make (largely unconsciously) when we talk is how to divide what we want to say into intonation phrases.

The default, or most neutral situation, is for there to be a single unit of information per intonation phrase. So, the most neutral version of our sentence above might be:

A: I'll get the shopping ||
B: Tonight? ||

where the dialogue is shared between two speakers and each intonation phrase contains one unit of meaning.
Alternatively, another neutral version, spoken by a single speaker might be:

A: I'll get the shopping tonight ||

where all the information is put together into one intonation phrase.
Other, less neutral, versions are also possible, as we will now explore.

Exercise 20.3 What meaning would you attribute to the same sentence spoken as follows by a single speaker? (Remember that the bars illustrate intonation phrase breaks and the marks illustrate the nuclear tones, as shown in Unit 19.)

ˏI'll | get the ˏshopping | toˋnight ||

Comment Here, the single sentence is broken up into three intonation phrases. Combined with the position of the nuclei and the choice of nuclear tones, this may have the effect of sounding rather pedantic and definite. You could imagine, for example, that it might be said at the end of a somewhat heated conversation about whose turn it is to do the weekly shop. So here, the division into intonation phrases (as well as other aspects of the intonation) has an attitudinal function, as it shows how the speaker is feeling.

Exercise 20.4 Look at the following sentences. They are both written without any punctuation. Can you find two different meanings for each and decide how intonation boundaries might help us decide between the alternatives when they are spoken out loud?

a) The dogs who had bones were content
b) There was chocolate and coffee cake

Tip Try adding commas to create the different meanings.

Comment a) The first sentence might mean that all the dogs had bones and were therefore content, as follows:

The dogs | who had bones | were content ||

Or the sentence could mean that only some of them had bones, but the ones that did were content.

The dogs who had bones were content ||

Put the nucleus on 'had' if you need help imagining how this might sound. (Note that for some speakers this option cannot work, as 'dogs' should be referred to with the impersonal pronoun 'that' rather than 'who'.)

b) Turning to the second sentence, this might mean that there were blocks of chocolate, as well as some cake flavoured with coffee:

   There was chocolate | and coffee cake||

   Or the sentence could mean that there was cake flavoured with both chocolate and coffee:

   There was chocolate and coffee cake||

In each of these utterances, the intonation breaks help us to decide which units of information belong together. In (a) the presence of a boundary after 'dogs' sets apart the relative clause, almost as though it were in brackets. In (b) the break after chocolate tells us that, semantically, the chocolate and coffee relate to different objects, and that, syntactically, they belong to different noun phrases.

These decisions relating to intonation phrases relate largely to the grammatical function of intonation, as they help us to decide which parts of the utterance belong together.

20.6 Accent position

Another important feature of intonation for meaning is the position of the accents in the intonation phrase, chiefly the location of the nucleus. As you may remember from Unit 19, the nucleus can in fact go onto any syllable in the phrase, although some positions are more likely and more common than others.

Exercise 20.5 If our sentence is spoken as a single intonation phrase, where do you think the nucleus is most likely to go in a very neutral production?

I'll get the shopping tonight.

Comment A very neutral production might well be

I'll get the shopping to<u>night</u>.

where the nucleus falls on the final syllable.

Exercise 20.6 Try the following sentences by reading them in a neutral fashion. Where do you think the nucleus is most likely to fall in each case? Can you spot a general pattern?

a) He doesn't really care for it.
b) Can you feed the animals?
c) Can you feed the giraffe?
d) She needs to water the plants.
e) He forgot the spider plant.
f) What about the spider?

Comment It is likely that you placed the nucleus as follows:

a) He doesn't really care for it.
b) Can you feed the animals?
c) Can you feed the giraffe?
d) She needs to water the plants.
e) He forgot the spider plant.
f) What about the spider?

When the production is neutral, the nucleus is most likely to fall on the lexically stressed syllable of the final content word. Note that in (a) 'for' and 'it' are both function words and 'care' is the last content word. In both (b) and (c), the final word is a content word and carries the nucleus, but in (b) the nucleus is not on the final syllable, because 'animals' is lexically stressed on the *first* syllable. In (e) the nucleus goes on the first syllable of 'spider', just as in (f). This may seem odd, and perhaps you would expect the pattern to resemble that in (d), with the nucleus on 'plant'. However, 'spider plant' is a **compound** (made up of two other words) and treated very much as a single lexical item; consequently, the nucleus (and the lexical stress) occurs on the first syllable. This works for other compounds, too, like 'peace-lily' and 'blackbird'.

By some estimates, around 80 per cent of intonation phrases have their nucleus on the stressed syllable of the final content word. It is possible, however, to change the position of the nucleus from this neutral or default setting in order to affect meaning.

Exercise 20.7 Try to produce our earlier example sentence with a nucleus in each of the underlined positions. Try to keep the same nuclear tone (such as a high fall) in each case. What different meanings do you create? Also, try to think of an appropriate context for each version of the sentence.

a) I'll get the shopping tonight
b) I'll get the shopping tonight
c) I'll get the shopping tonight
d) I'll get the shopping tonight

Comment Putting the nucleus on a syllable other than the default draws our attention to that syllable and suggests it is important. For example, (b) might mean that the speaker will get the shopping, while the listener should get something else, like the dry-cleaning. Likewise, (d) might mean that the speaker is insisting that he or she, rather than the listener, will pick up the shopping. Note, here, that the nucleus can be as early as the first syllable in the phrase, if that is what the speaker wishes to highlight. The remainder of the intonation phrase will then comprise the tail. (c) is harder to account for, as 'get' is quite an unusual place for the nucleus. However, it might be said in irritation, or in contrast to 'not get'. (a) is our default pattern, but, depending on the tone, it may also be said contrastively, to indicate 'tonight', as opposed to 'tomorrow' or 'on Saturday', for example.

The main function associated with the position of the nucleus, then, is focus. A nucleus in the default position is said to give the intonation phrase **broad focus**, focussing our attention on the *entire* phrase. However, we may also move the nucleus to another syllable, which will then become the focus of the listener's attention, a situation called **narrow focus**. We may choose to focus on words or syllables because they are new to the discussion. We also unfocus information that has already been mentioned or implied (which is sometimes called **given** information). This is achieved by not accenting given information, a process called **deaccenting**. For example, the response in (d) in Exercise 20.7 might come about if the previous utterance has been, 'I don't think I'll have time to get the shopping tonight', in which 'shopping' and 'tonight' are both explicitly mentioned. Alternatively, it may be a response to 'I don't think I'll have time to go to the supermarket after work'. In this case, 'shopping' and 'tonight' have only been implied, but nevertheless are deaccented in the response. In fact, it sounds rather odd to put the nucleus on items that have recently been mentioned, as we will now investigate.

Exercise 20.8 Try to produce the following sentences in response to the prompt, 'I don't think I can get the shopping tonight'.

Which sounds natural and which sounds decidedly odd?

a) I'll get the shopping tonight.
b) I'll get the shopping tonight.
c) I'll get the shopping tonight.

Comment You will probably find that only (a) is really acceptable. In English (and in many Germanic languages), it sounds odd to assign the nucleus to items that have already been mentioned or implied. This is not the case in all languages, however. In many Romance languages, for example, the nucleus cannot move around so freely; therefore, given information can readily be accented. In such languages, focus can be placed on new information by changing the word order of the utterance.

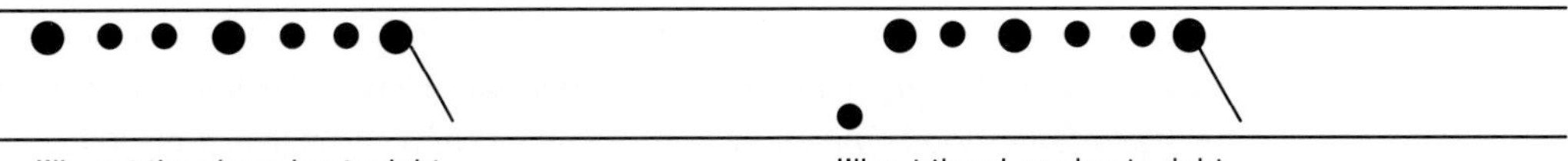

Figure 20.1 Interlinear diagrams for 'I'll get the shopping tonight', with the head starting on 'I'll' (left) and 'get' (right)

As mentioned above, the position of accents other than the nucleus can also affect meaning. As we already know, the head starts with the first accent, and the position of this accent, along with the position of the nucleus, can add to the meaning that is understood.

Exercise 20.9 Imagine our earlier sentence with the nucleus on 'night', as in our neutral version. What would be the difference in meaning between the head beginning on 'I'll', and the head beginning on 'get' with a pre-head on 'I'll'?

Comment Similarly to the effect of the location of the nucleus, the location of the other accents also focusses our attention on the words with which they are associated. Interlinear diagrams are shown in Figure 20.1. So, a head starting on 'I'll' or 'get' will focus our attention on these items, but usually less strongly than the focussing effect of the nucleus.

So, the position of the nucleus and other accents relates largely to the focussing effect of intonation, and draws the listener's attention to those parts of the utterance that the speaker wishes to highlight.

20.7 Nuclear tone

The choice of nuclear tone is perhaps the aspect of intonation that most obviously affects meaning for non-experts, even if they do not have the terminology to describe what they have heard.

Exercise 20.10 Again, think about our original sentence, with the nucleus in the default position on 'night'.

a) How would it sound with different types of fall, such as a low fall or a rise-fall?
b) How would it sound with a rise?
c) Can you identify different meanings for these tones?

Comment (a), (b) and (c) The falling tones may sound like statements, and also as though the speaker is being definite, while the rising tones may sound like questions or suggestions, or as if the speaker is unsure. In fact, the division between rise and fall is one of the most basic ones in intonation analysis.

However, the common belief that questions 'go up' in pitch and statements 'go down', while being quite useful, is not entirely accurate, as this depends on the type of question being asked (and also the variety of English a person speaks), a topic we will now investigate.

Exercise 20.11 Imagine the following questions spoken with the nucleus on the first syllable of 'pasta'. Do they both sound right with a rising tone, or is one more neutral and natural with a fall?

a) Do you want the pasta?
b) When do you want the pasta?

Comment Hopefully, it is clear that (a) sounds more neutral with some sort of rise, while (b) sounds more neutral with a falling tone. Therefore, we must make a distinction between **yes-no questions**, like (a), where only a yes or no answer is needed, and **wh-questions**, like (b), where a fuller response is required. Yes-no questions frequently have rising nuclei, while wh-questions frequently have falling nuclei. This is especially the case when there is nothing in the choice of words to signal whether the speech is a question or a statement. Imagine, for example, how the word 'pasta' would be pronounced on its own, in order to ask a person if they would like some.

It is difficult to state what default or neutral tones are, and to do so we at least need to know the type of material that is being produced (question, statement, command, and so on). While it is rather difficult to generalise the meaning of different tones, we can basically say that the default tones for yes-no questions are rising nuclei, while wh-questions, statements, exclamations and commands usually have falling nuclei. This aspect of tone variation relates to the grammatical function of intonation. We will see later that different *types* of rises and falls can also affect meaning.

In addition, when we are considering a dialogue, or when there is more than one intonation phrase in an utterance, the tone of the nucleus may also have a discourse function, as we will see in Exercise 20.12.

Exercise 20.12 Imagine the following sentence spoken in two different ways, as shown below. What meaning do you think is implied by each one?

a) You can do ˏlanguages | or ˏliterature
b) You can do ˏlanguages | or ˋliterature

Comment In (a) the rising tone on 'literature' seems to suggest that there are more options to come, like 'humanities', for example, whereas the fall in (b) suggests that the speaker is finished and that these are the only two options available.

Exercise 20.13 Imagine our 'shopping' sentence spoken as a single intonation phrase, with a rise on 'tonight'.

I'll get the shopping to<u>night</u>

Does the rise suggest that there might be more to come, or that the speaker is finished?
Do the same exercise with a fall on 'to<u>night</u>'.

Comment The rise is more likely to suggest that the speaker will carry on, and perhaps say, 'and then I'll go to the pub' or 'and then I'll have time to go out tomorrow'. Similarly, the mid-level tone, which we have not yet discussed, also carries an indication that the speaker has not yet finished and is preparing to produce another intonation phrase. Conversely, the fall may mean that the speaker has finished and is ready for the other person to speak. This type of usage is related to the discourse function of intonation.

So far, we have seen that the choice of nuclear tone can have a grammatical and a discourse function. The choice of tone is also largely responsible for how we signal our emotions and attitudes.

Exercise 20.14 Imagine our 'shopping' sentence spoken with the following falling tones on 'tonight'. What do you think they tell the listener about the speaker's emotions and attitudes?

a) I'll get the shopping to\night.
b) I'll get the shopping to ˎnight.
c) I'll get the shopping to^night.

Comment All the falling tones in (a), (b) and (c) are likely to indicate some sort of statement or declaration, as we discussed above, and this choice of a fall over a rise is a grammatical use of tone. However, the choice of the *type* of fall may tell us about how the speaker feels in general (that is, his or her emotional state), or how the speaker feels about the words spoken, or how the speaker feels about the listener (his or her attitude towards this person). The difference between a high fall (a) and a low fall (b) often tells us about the degree of enthusiasm the speaker feels, with a high fall sounding enthusiastic, and a low fall sounding bored or disengaged. The rise-fall (c) has a more **marked** or unusual meaning, and is often associated with the speaker either being impressed or challenging something. These two potential meanings for the same tone illustrate the lack of a one-to-one relationship between intonation and meaning. Used with the sentence in the exercise, a rise-fall might mean that the speaker is being self-congratulatory, or that he or she is being somewhat obstinate with the listener.

Exercise 20.15 Now try Exercise 20.14 again, but this time with the rises. What do the different tones tell you about the emotions and attitudes of the speaker?

a) I'll get the shopping to ˊnight.
b) I'll get the shopping to ˏnight.
c) I'll get the shopping to ˇnight.

Comment Here, the choice of any of the rises in (a), (b) and (c) perhaps suggests some kind of uncertainty or questioning, as opposed to the falls, which, as we have seen, are more definite and associated with statements. The choice of a *particular* rise, however, may indicate the speaker's emotion or attitude to what they are saying. Similarly to what we said about falling tones, the differences between the high (a) and low (b) versions of rising tones may reflect the speaker's interest or involvement, with the low rise sounding less engaged than the high rise. So, the choice of tone may also have an attitudinal function. The fall-rise (c) often has a special meaning, which might be that of reserve, or leaving something unsaid. Here, for example, the speaker might be avoiding saying 'but actually I was hoping to just stay in and watch TV' or 'but I'm really hoping you'll get it next week'. Hearing this tone will often lead the listener to ask about what is being unsaid. For example, some people would say, 'I can hear there's a *but* coming', in response to a sentence with a fall-rise nucleus. In addition, mid-level tones may also indicate that more is to come and that a further intonation phrase will follow.

We have seen that the choice of nuclear tone may signal a number of different meanings. Fans of *The Wire* may remember the scene from 'Old Cases' in season one, where Bunk and McNulty try to recreate the events surrounding an old murder. The scene consists of multiple repetitions of the same one-syllable swear-word, produced with a variety of nuclear tones. This single word is manipulated so that, along with their gestures (and other aspects, such as speed of delivery and loudness), the viewers can follow their train of thought and understand the feelings they express.

20.8 Key and register

Another feature of intonation that we have not really considered so far is the key of the voice. **Key** refers to the pitch range of a particular intonation phrase. Changes in key normally involve a difference in the upper part of the pitch range, while the lower end of the scale stays at the same level as in a default key. So, in a high key, the high accents are higher, while syllables produced on a low pitch are at their normal level, as shown in Figure 20.2. You will remember from the previous unit that the lines represent the top and bottom of the pitch range.

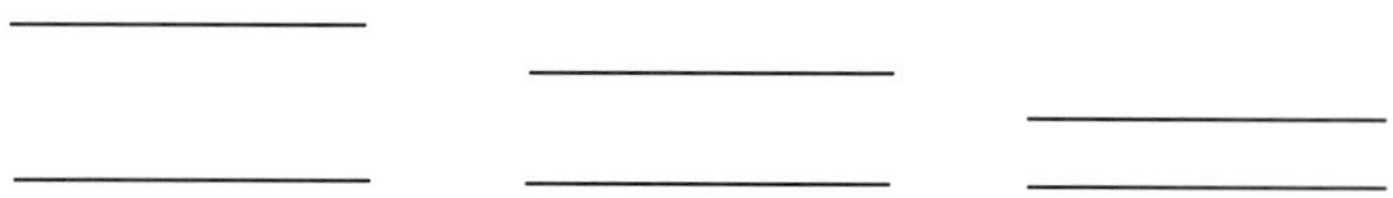

Figure 20.2 High (left), neutral or default (middle) and low (right) key

Exercise 20.16 Think back to one of the sentences we looked at in Exercise 20.4: 'The dogs who had bones were content'. There we said that one possible way of chunking this sentence was to divide it into three intonation phrases, as if the 'who had bones' part was in brackets, as follows:

The dogs | who had bones | were content ||

Try saying this sentence chunked in this way. Can you hear any difference between the key you use in the different intonation phrases?

Comment You may have noted that the middle intonation phrase sounds quite natural if it is produced using a lower key than the intonation phrases on either side. One main use of low key is to signal that some section of the spoken material is offset, or separate, from the main utterance. Similarly, when you listen to adverts on the radio, the 'terms and conditions' part at the end is often in a low key (and spoken quickly and quietly) compared to the main body of the advert. This use of low key, then, is a discourse function of intonation.

Another main use of changes in key is to be found in TV and radio news reports.

Exercise 20.17 The following text is based on a extract from a spoken round-up of the news headlines from the BBC. Imagine how the entire extract might be spoken by a newsreader. What use might be made of changes in key?

> Unemployment's risen again | with nearly two and a half million people out of work | in the three months to December || The number of sixteen-to twenty-four-year-olds looking for work | rose to nine hundred and sixty five thousand ||
>
> The bank of England | has downgraded its growth forecast for the UK | and hinted at an interest rise in May || It says the rate of inflation | will probably reach almost five percent | before falling to the target of two percent | in 2012 ||
>
> Prince William | and Kate Middleton | will make their first official overseas trip | as a married couple | to Canada || According to officials there | they'll travel around the country | for around two weeks | in the summer ||

Comment You may have noted that the intonation phrases at the start of new topics will be in a higher key than those at the end of topics. There is a general tendency in many languages for pitch to drift down, both within an intonation phrase and across intonation phrases within a single topic (**declination**). So, an intonation phrase in a high key might signal to the listener that the speaker has changed topics, which, again, is a discourse feature of intonation. This use of key is very clear in most spoken news reports: try to spot it the next time you are watching TV or listening to the radio

Exercise 20.18 Look at the following extract from the *Friends* episode 'The One Where Underdog Gets Away' (season one, episode 9). The group have just returned from the roof, where they were watching an escaped balloon, but have found themselves locked out of Monica's apartment, where Thanksgiving dinner is burning in the oven. They start to argue about whose responsibility it was to remember the key to the door.

MONICA: Isn't it enough that I'm making Thanksgiving dinner for everyone? You know, everyone wants a different kind of potatoes, so I'm making different kinds of potatoes. Does anybody care what kind of potatoes I want? Nooooo, no, no! (starting to cry) Just as long as Phoebe gets her peas and onions, and Mario gets his tots, and it's my first Thanksgiving, and it's all burned, and, and I. . . I. . .

CHANDLER: Ok, Monica, only dogs can hear you now

a) How might Monica's pitch sound, given that she is starting to cry and is very upset?
b) What does Chandler mean by his comment?

Comment It would be useful to see if you can locate a copy of this clip, especially as we will consider another from the same episode in the review exercises.

a) Monica's pitch becomes higher and squeakier as she gets more and more upset. In fact, it is not just the top of her pitch range that rises, but also the bottom of her pitch range. When both the top and the bottom of the pitch range change, we say that this is a change in **register** (rather than a change in key, where only the top of the range changes). A high register, such as the one Monica uses here, tends to be associated with extreme emotion or stress, and is thus an attitudinal function of intonation.
b) Chandler's comment implies that Monica's speech is now so high in pitch that it is outside the range of human perception. Dogs can generally hear much higher pitches than humans, which is why they can hear dog whistles, and humans generally can not.

20.9 Multiple meanings

As you will have realised from the discussions above, there is no single meaning for any particular tone, or for any particular nucleus placement, or for any particular way of chunking a sentence into intonation phrases, or even for any particular key. Even if we just consider a rising nuclear tone, this may mean that the speaker is uncertain (a matter of attitude), or is asking a question (a matter or grammar), or is about to say more (a matter of discourse).

Exercise 20.19 How do you think a listener tells the difference between all of these possible meanings?

Comment Some of the meaning of intonation is related to the form of words that are used, so the form of the words and the intonation must operate together to produce a meaning. For example, changing our utterance slightly to 'shall I get the shopping tonight' would tell us definitively that this was a yes-no question. However, if a speaker starts a topic with 'if I get the shopping tonight', this strongly indicates that they are going to add something else, regardless of their intonation. Thus, intonation cannot stand on its own to create meaning, but must also be interpreted in the light of the words and structure of the sentence, and the ongoing events.

In this unit, we have only talked about a few ways in which intonation might contribute to meaning. We have not considered the effect of different types of head and pre-head, or considered how factors such as speed, tempo, voice quality and a whole host of other considerations might interact with intonation to influence perceived meaning and help a listener to understand what is intended. The way in which intonation contributes to meaning is very rich, but is still not fully understood scientifically, even though speakers and listeners do it every day, usually with no problems.

20.10 Variation and change in intonation

So far, we have described intonation very much as though it is a single, fixed system. However, this is far from being the case. In fact, what we have described is only a small part of the intonation of Standard Southern British English. Just as for vowels and consonants, there is a considerable amount of variation in intonation, which can be attributed to a person's regional accent, sex and age, and/or the style in which they are speaking.

Exercise 20.20 Think of some other regional accents that you know well. Can you think of any particular features of their intonation which differ from those described here, or from the intonation you use yourself?

Comment Often, one of the most striking differences between accents is their intonation, even if we are not always able to put our finger on exactly what those differences are. One of the differences that attracts rather a lot of attention, however, is the more frequent use of rising tones in some accents, such as Australian, Welsh and some northern varieties of English. Similarly to variation in segments across accents (recall our discussion of the differences between regional accents in Unit 14), intonation can vary in different ways. For example, accents may have the same meaningful tones, but realise them differently (for example, by starting at a higher or lower pitch), or may use different basic nuclear tones. However, it is rather difficult to compare different systems of intonation, largely due to the lack of a one-to-one relationship between intonation and meaning.

Exercise 20.21 What do you consider to be the main differences between intonation in male and female speakers?

Comment As we discussed in Unit 14, women's voices are more highly pitched than men's, and this is largely due to the fact that the vocal folds are smaller and lighter in women. As we have seen, however, it is possible for all of us to vary the pitch at which we speak within the range that is physically determined by the size of our vocal folds. It has been observed that in some languages and cultures, there is a greater difference between the pitch of male and female voices than in others. These differences between languages are not related to biology, but rather to cultural norms, with women speaking in a higher register, possibly in order to sound feminine, and males in a lower register, possibly to sound more masculine. Thus, the natural biological difference in size of the vocal folds can be exploited for cultural reasons. We see similar behaviours in other animals too. While larger animals naturally produce deeper-sounding calls, animals can also *make* themselves sound larger, and therefore potentially more dominant, by producing deeper calls.

As well as the overall pitch of the voice and the register used, there may also be a difference in the tones chosen by male and female speakers. Studies with English have shown that rises may be used more frequently by female speakers, which relates to our observation in Unit 14, that women may ask questions more often than men do.

Exercise 20.22 Have you noticed any differences in the intonation of younger and older speakers?

Comment The use of rising tones appears to be on the increase for younger speakers. Often, younger speakers use rises even when there is no question or continuation implied, and it has been suggested that these rises may serve as a means of checking that the listener is following what is being said. Nevertheless, some listeners seem to find the frequent use of rises quite irritating, as they think they are continually being asked for a response. This phenomenon has entered the public consciousness to some degree, and has been mentioned on TV shows such as *QI*, *The Weakest Link* and *Top Gear*. The use of an increased number of rises, in places where we would not normally expect them, is referred to variously as **Australian question intonation** (as rises are also more common in Australian English), **high rising terminals**, or **uptalk**.

20.11 Summary

In this unit, we have seen that the choices a speaker makes about their intonation can affect the meaning and interpretation of an utterance. We have seen that choices regarding intonation phrases, nucleus placement, nuclear tones, and key and register can all affect meaning. In particular, intonation can have effects of focus, attitude, grammar and discourse.

We have now completed all the units in the book. You should take some time to reflect on how much you have learnt since you first started with Unit 1. We have looked at consonants, vowels, airstream mechanisms, allophones of voice, place and manner, and allophones of vowels, elision, liaison and assimilation, syllables, stress, broad and allophonic transcription, speech sound variation, and the form and function of intonation. Well done!

20.12 Looking forward

Hopefully, you have found that your knowledge and interest in phonetics have increased during your reading of this coursebook. The following pages provide some charts and tables that you might find useful, and ideas for further study. If you keep listening to speech around you, you will never be bored and will continue to learn about and be fascinated by phonetics.

20.13 Review questions

Have a look at the following questions to see if you have understood the main points to learn from this unit.

- What are the different ways in which intonation can vary in order to influence meaning?
- Is there a strict one-to-one correspondence between a particular intonation pattern and a particular meaning?
- What types of meaning can be created by intonation?

20.14 Review exercises

1 Consider the following sequence of words. As we have done throughout this unit, explore how differences in intonation can help to create different meanings using the same words. Try to come up with different meanings for three different ways of chunking the words into intonation phrases, three different positions of the nucleus, and three different nuclear tones. Note that the material is not punctuated and is not necessarily all spoken by a single individual.

I can't talk to her when she's on a night out

2 Think about the intonation you typically use when you give someone your phone number. What aspects of intonation phrase boundaries, nucleus placement and tone are likely to be shared by all speakers? Take a phone number you know well and then produce it as you might if you were giving it over the phone to a stranger. Note the intonation pattern you use, and try to work out why you have made the choices you have made.

3 The following is an extract from the Friends episode 'The One Where Underdog Gets Away' (season one, episode 9), which we looked at earlier in the unit. This part of the episode is when the group first realise that they are locked out of Monica's apartment. Look at the reoccurring word 'keys' (or 'key', in one instance) and try to work out what the appropriate intonation pattern is each time. For each occurrence, consider if 'keys' is likely to be the nucleus of the phrase, and, if so, what tone is likely to be used. If 'keys' is not the nucleus, explain which syllable might be, and why. This is American English, but you can still apply the types of analysis that we have used in this unit.

You might also like to watch the episode, to help you determine the intonational features of the exchange, and to watch Rachel and Monica's hand gestures, which go along with their intonation patterns.

MONICA: Okay, right about now the turkey should be crispy on the outside, juicy on the inside. Why are we standing here?
RACHEL: We're waiting for you to open the door. You got the keys[1].
MONICA: No I don't.
RACHEL: Yes, you do. When we left, you said, "got the keys[2]."
MONICA: No I didn't. I asked, "got the ke-eys[3]?"
RACHEL: No, no, no, you said, "got the keys[4]".
CHANDLER: Do either of you have the keys[5]?
[. . .]
JOEY: Wait, wait, we have a copy of your key[6].
MONICA: Well then get it, get it!

ANSWERS TO REVIEW EXERCISES

Unit 1

1 'high' and 'hay' each have two sounds. 'door' and 'four' have two sounds for non-rhotic speakers and three sounds for rhotic speakers. 'Case', 'ball', 'loan' and 'mail' have three sounds, and 'gold', 'hand', 'disk' and 'list' have four sounds.

2 'Think' should be CVCC, as <th> represents one sound. 'Union' is CVCVVC or CVCCVC (depending on whether you pronounce this word with three or two syllables), as the first sound is a consonant. 'Finch' is CVCC, as <ch> represents only one sound. 'Summit' is CVCVC, as double <m> represents only one sound. 'Five' is CVC, as the final <e> is not pronounced. 'Metre' is CVCV for non-rhotic speakers or CVCVC for rhotic speakers. 'Knave' is CVC, as <k> and <e> are silent.

3

CVC	thought
CVCC	bank
CCVCVC	music
CVCV	cover
CCCVCC	stripes
CCVCCVC	trumpet
CVCVC	catches
CVCVCV	eulogy

Unit 2

1 All except 'Cardiff' start with voiced sounds.

2 'hat', 'cap', 'back', 'cliff' and 'heath' all end in voiceless sounds, so will be pluralised with voiceless /s/. The others end in voiced sounds and will be pluralised with /z/.

3

both	/bVθ/
bother	/bVðə/
kitty	/kVtV/

kitten	/kVtVn/
hit	/hVt/
hid	/hVd/
foal	/fVl/
vole	/vVl/

Unit 3

1

/p/	bilabial
/z/	alveolar
/f/	labiodental
/ð/	dental
/tʃ/	postalveolar
[ʔ]	glottal
/j/	palatal
/ŋ/	velar

2 In (a), /p/ is bilabial, while the others are alveolar. In (b), /z/ is voiced, while the others are voiceless. In (c), /f/ is voiceless, while the others are voiced. In (d), /p/ is bilabial, while the others are postalveolar.

3 In (a), words that fit are 'pan', 'ban' and 'man'. In (b), words that fit are 'mate', 'made', 'mace', 'maze', 'main' and 'mail'. In (c), words that fit are 'tuck', 'tug' and 'tongue'.

Unit 4

1

lentil	/l/ is a lateral approximant
fish	/f/ is a fricative
mayonnaise	/m/ is a nasal
bagel	/b/ is a plosive
rice	/r/ is a (median) approximant
pasta	/p/ is a plosive
cheese	/tʃ/ is an affricate
noodles	/n/ is a nasal
yogurt	/j/ is a (median) approximant
jam	/dʒ/ is an affricate
sausage	/s/ is a fricative
lemon	/l/ is a lateral approximant

2 a) /p/ is voiceless, the others are voiced.

b) /g/ is velar, the others are alveolar.

c) /w/ is approximant, the others are fricatives.

d) /d/ is obstruent, the others are sonorant.

3 a) This is false because the velum is raised for /g/, as for all plosives.

b) This is true.

c) This is false because some voiced sounds are obstruents, such as /b v dʒ/.

d) This is true.

e) This is false because the air flows over the midline of the tongue, as /j/ is a median approximant. It only flows over the sides of the tongue for lateral sounds such as /l/.

Unit 5

1 a) quick /kwVk/

[q] = voiceless uvular plosive
[c] = voiceless palatal plosive

b) ring /rVŋ/

[R] = voiced uvular trill
[N] = voiced uvular nasal
[G] =voiced uvular plosive

c) box /bVks/

[B] = voiced bilabial trill
[x] = voiceless velar fricative

2 Voiced labiodental fricative

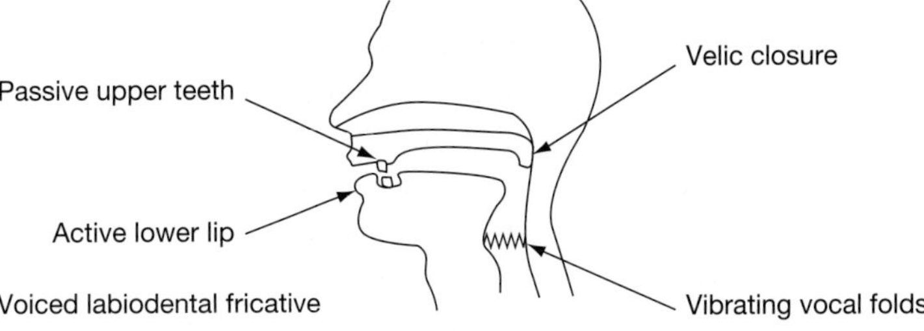

3

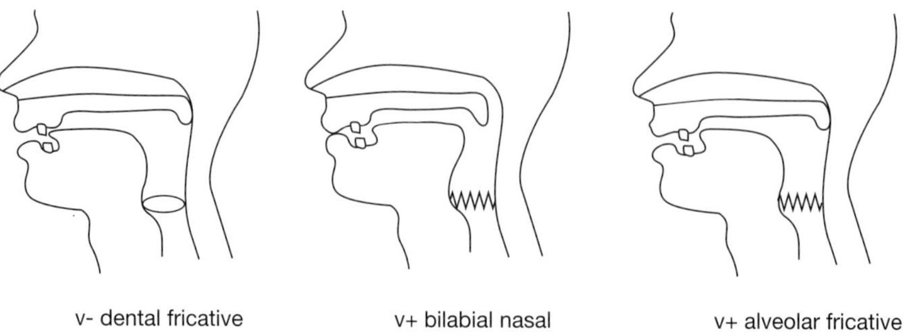

Unit 6

1 /ɪə/ hear
/ɑ/ part
/ɛə/ hair
/u/ plume
/æ/ mass
/ɪ/ gin
/ɔɪ/ boy
/aʊ/ cow

2 **a** /ɔ/ as in thought

b /ə/ as in comma

c /i/ as in fleece

d /æ/ as in trap

e /ɑ/ as in palm

f /aʊ/ as in mouth

g /eɪ/ as in face

h /ʊə/ as in cure, or maybe not in any words, depending on your accent

3 Please see website (www.cambridge.org/knight) for longest sentences submitted by readers.

Unit 7

1

Initiator direction	Pulmonic	Glottalic	Velaric
Ingressive	Used instead of egressive ASM to indicate surprise in some languages	Implosives	Clicks
Egressive	Most speech sounds	Ejectives	Reverse clicks (no known languages)

2 [kʘ] voiceless bilabial click
[ɗ] voiced alveolar implosive
[gǁ] voiced alveolar lateral click
[p'] voiceless bilabial ejective plosive
[ŋǀ] voiced nasal dental click

3 Voiced velar implosive

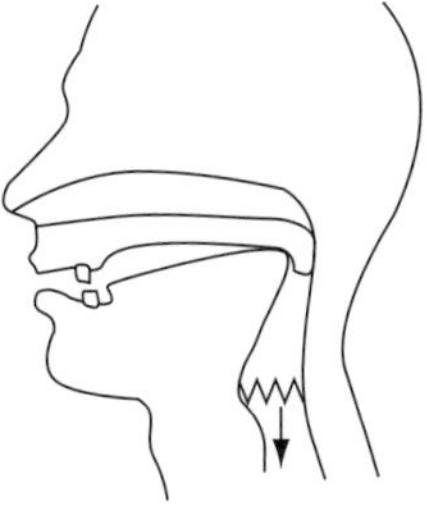

Voiceless dental click

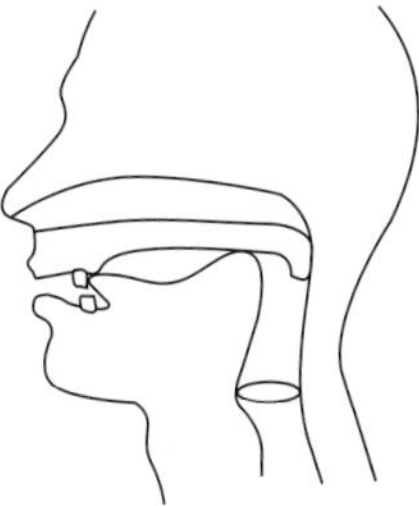

Voiceless dental ejective plosive

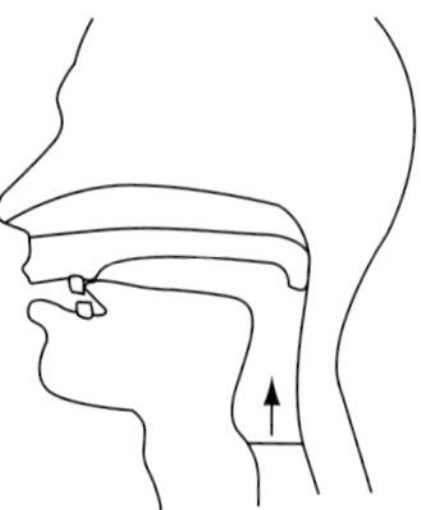

Unit 8

1 1st syllable stress: trumpet, piccolo, triangle, harpsichord, cello, tuba
2nd syllable stress: guitar, recorder, bassoon, trombone, viola
3rd syllable stress: clarinet, violin

2

kiwi	CV.CV
guava	CCV.CV
grapes	CCVCC
melon	CV.CVC
apple	V.CVC
coconut	CV.CV.CVC
pineapple	CV.CV.CVC
orange	V.CVCC
lime	CVC
raspberry	CVC.CCV
pear	CV
plum	CCVC
apricot	V.CCV.CVC
mango	CVC.CV
strawberry	CCCV.CCV

3 ˈphotograph phoˈtography photoˈgraphic ˈphotographed reˈphotographed ˈphotographing

The suffixes '-y' and '-ic' have triggered a change in stress location from that in 'photograph'. The others have not affected this pattern.

Unit 9

1 Aspirated consonants are those in ‘appendix’, ‘kidney’ and ‘pancreas’. The /t/ in ‘stomach’ is unaspirated. The second /t/ in ‘intestines’ and the /t/ in ‘uterus’ are weakly aspirated, as they do not occur in stressed syllables.

2 ‘Bladder’, ‘brain’ and ‘vein’ all have devoiced obstruents at the start if they are spoken in isolation. The /r/ in ‘prostate’ is devoiced, while ‘heart’ and ‘lung’ do not contain any devoiced consonants.

3 [əˈpʰɛndɪks] [ˈkʰɪdni] [ˈst˭ʌmək] [ɪnˈtʰɛstɪnz̊] [ˈjutəɹəs] [ˈpʰæŋkriəs] [ˈb̊lædə] [ˈb̊ɹeɪn] [ˈpɹ̊ɒsteɪt] [v̊eɪn] [hɑt] [lʌŋ]

Unit 10

1

retraction	[̠]
advancement	[̟]
dental/labiodental	[̪]
labialisation	[ʷ]
palatalisation	[ʲ]
velarisation	[ˠ]

2

corners	[ˈk̠ ʰʷɔnəz̊]
huge	[ˈhʲjud̊ʒ]
twitch	[ˈtʷẘɪtʃ]
eleventh	[ɪˈlɛvən̪θ]
bold	[ˈb̊əʊlˠd̊]
trance	[ˈt̠ɹ̊ɑns]

Most of these are similar across English accents, but ‘corners’ is [ˈk̠ʰʷɔɹnəɹz̊] for rhotic accents, and ‘trance’ is [ˈt̠ɹ̊æns] for Northern accents.

3 In ‘million’, the /l/ should be clear, as it occurs between two vowels. In ‘cupid’, the /k/ should be advanced, as velars are never palatalised before palatals, but rather their POA is advanced. In ‘green’, the /g/ should not be retracted; velars are only retracted before back vowels and /k/ (alveolars *are* retracted before /r/).

Unit 11

1

‘broaden’	nasal release	[dⁿ]
‘yodel’	lateral release	[dˡ]
‘odds’	narrow release	[dᶻ]
‘dreadful’	inaudible release	[d˺]
‘bread dough’	unreleased	[d˚]

2 The velum should be low most of the way through [n], as it is a nasal. It must be raised throughout [t], as it is a plosive and needs the velum to be raised for pressure to build. Therefore, the position of the velum should change rapidly between the two. As [ɪ] is nasalised, the velum will not be raised throughout. In this case, the velum will lower during [ɪ], in preparation for the upcoming nasal.

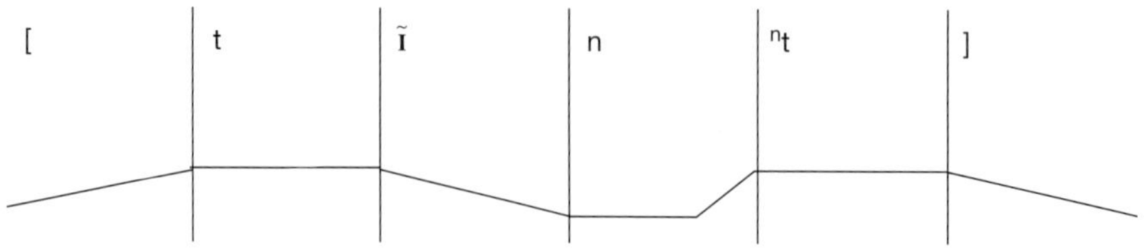

3 Please see the website (www.cambridge.org/knight) for answers submitted by readers.

Unit 12

1

Nasalisation	Pre-fortis	Both	Neither
land	Betsy	bench	seed
panther	witch	notch	lard
name	list	mess	wobble

2 There are a number of difficulties with the diagram. In the transcription, the vowel is clipped, but the nasal should be transcribed as clipped too. In addition, the vowel should be nasalised. In the diagram, the velum line should start and end low for normal breathing. In addition, it should slope through the vowel, indicating nasalisation, and should rise rapidly between /n/ and /t/, as the velum must be fully closed for the obstruent.

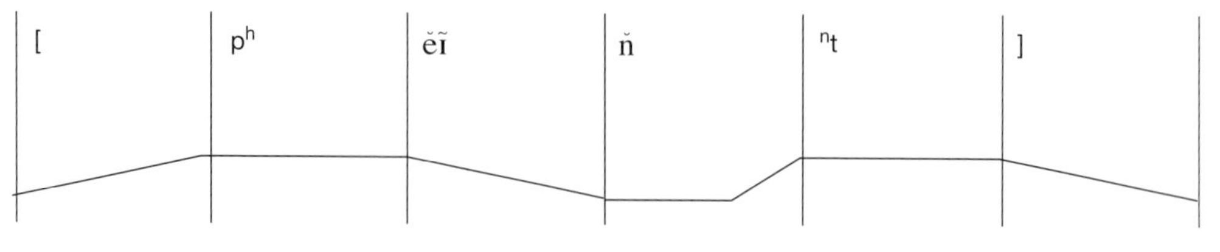

3 **Boys:** Jack, Thomas (second vowel), Joshua (first vowel), Joseph (second vowel) and Lewis (second vowel) all have pre-fortis clipping. The others do not. Alfie, for example, has the /f/ in the onset of the second syllable, rather than in the coda of the first.

Girls: Only Grace and Charlotte (second vowel) have pre-fortis clipping. The /s/ in Jessica and Lucy forms the onset to the second syllable in each, as does the /f/ in Sophie.

Unit 13

1 The first thing to notice is that the word has six segments, with stress on the first syllable. The first sound is a voiceless obstruent because the velum is raised and the vocal folds are not vibrating. The second sound is either devoiced or aspirated, and also nasalised, so it must be an approximant or a vowel. This implies that the first sound is a plosive, as devoicing and aspiration do not occur after the other obstruents (that is, fricatives or affricates) in English. The third sound is also nasalised. Sound four is a nasal, as it is the first sound for which the velum is fully lowered. The final two sounds are both voiced and either nasal or nasalised. Example words might be 'planning', 'training' or 'tollman'.

2 /t/ in 'true' is retracted.
/p/ in 'bump' is nasally approached.
/k/ in 'king' is aspirated and advanced.
/l/ in 'lead' is clear.
/b/ in 'tablet' has wide oral release.

3 Please see the website (www.cambridge.org/knight) for sentences submitted by readers.

Unit 14

1 'cigarette' is likely to be stressed on the third syllable by speakers of British English, but on the first by speakers of American English.

'booth' normally has a voiced dental fricative for the final consonant in England, but is more likely to have a voiceless dental fricative in Wales and Scotland.

The first vowel in 'migraine' is usually /i/ for older speakers, compared to /aɪ/ for younger speakers.

'schedule' normally starts with /ʃ/ for older speakers, but may begin with /sk/ for younger speakers of British English, which is also the typical American English pronunciation. In addition, the middle of the word may be pronounced as /dj/ or /dʒ/.

'February' has a number of different pronunciations, based on regional accent and age. American speakers are more likely to say /fɛbjuɛri/, while British speakers are more likely to say /fɛbruəri/. However, younger speakers with both accents appear to be moving towards the /ju/ pronunciation. One final variation is that the word may be spoken with only three syllables, with deletion of the medial /ə/. Use of this pronunciation may depend on the individual or the situation.

2 Catherine and Hindley are from the upper classes and are relatively young. Their pronunciations look fairly standard in contrast to Joseph's. Joseph is older, male and a servant, and his speech is represented with many regional pronunciations, such as 't'' for 'the' and 'yah' for 'you'. It seems that Emily Brontë intended to link lower social class with regional accents, which is especially interesting, as the book is concerned throughout with the issues of social class and mobility.

3 You may recall that this is very similar to an exercise we did at the start of the book, before we knew much about phonetics. At that point, we simply tried to decide if the words in each pair were homophones. Now, however, we can say much more about them. Pair 1 will be homophones in non-rhotic accents, but 'lore' will have an /r/ in the coda for rhotic accents. Pair 2 will be homophones for many speakers, but some Scottish and American accents, for example, use [ʍ] at the start of 'what'. Pair 3 are homophones for many Northern accents of English, where they both have the 'foot' vowel [ʊ]. Southern varieties are likely to use the 'strut' vowel [ʌ] in 'luck', however, whereas some Lancashire varieties may use the 'goose' vowel [u] in 'look'.

Unit 15

1 / aɪ wəz gəʊɪŋ raʊn tə maɪ frɛnz haʊs | tə si ə nju pʌpi || aɪ kʊdnt faɪnd ə nʌmbə fə ə tæksi | səʊ weɪtəd fə ən eɪti sɛvən bʌs tə kʌm əlɒŋ || ɪt tʊk lɒŋgə ðən aɪd θɔt tə əraɪv| ən baɪ ðə taɪm aɪ gɒt ðɛə| pʌpi wəz əslip ɪn ɪz bɑskɪt/

'And' can take several forms, so /ənd/, /ən/ and /n/ are all appropriate. Other examples of elision can be seen in 'round' and 'friends'. You may feel that an /r/ is needed between 'for' and 'a', and between 'for' and 'an'. This is a process called liaison, which we will return to in a later unit.

2 Connected speech processes take place at word boundaries.
Connected speech processes affect sounds at the phonemic level.
Connected speech processes can potentially affect perceived meaning.
Connected speech processes are optional.

3 /ðə lɑs taɪm i steɪd wɪð ə | ʃi pʊt ɪm ɪn ə græn gɛs rum ɪn ðə wɛs wɪŋ || ðeɪd bin ðə greɪtɪs frɛnz fə ðə bɛs pɑt əv ðə pɑs dɛkeɪd|| ʃi juʒəli geɪv ɪm ə fis | bʌt ɪt wəz ɔweɪz fɑs fud | ən sim tə teɪs blæn sʌmtaɪmz || məʊs naɪts id it ðə lis ðət i kʊd | ən haɪd vɑs kwɒntətɪz ɪn ðə weɪs bɑskɪt || ðɛn | wɛn ðə mɪs wəs dʒʌs raɪt | hi ɔweɪz krɛp frəm ðə haʊs | tə hæn ðə bɑskɪt tu ə lɒs trævlə | hu wəz traɪɪŋ tə fɛn fə hɪmsɛlf | ɒn ðə læn nɪəbaɪ||/

Unit 16

1 Linking /r/:

/faɪər ɪn ðə həʊl/
/ə pɛər əv faɪvz/

'fire' and 'pear' both end with a non-high vowel, and the next word starts with a vowel, so we get /r/-liaison. Because both words have an orthographic /r/, we call this process linking /r/.

Intrusive /r/:

/ærɪzəʊnər ənd tɛnəsi/
/ɪn ɔr əv hɪm/

'Arizona' and 'awe' both end with a non-high vowel, and the next word starts with a vowel, so we get /r/-liaison. Because these words do not contain an orthographic 'r' (at the end), we call this process intrusive /r/.

Neither process:

/kɑ but/
/peɪ ɒn taɪm/

Although 'car' ends with a vowel, the following word does not start with a vowel, so the conditions for /r/-liaison are not met. 'Pay' ends in a vowel and is followed by a word starting with a vowel, but the vowel at the end of 'pay' ends high, so, again, the conditions for /r/-liaison are not met.

2 /fɑr əweɪ frəm hɪər ɪz ðə həʊm əv ə lɪtəl gɜl kɔl klɛə || klɛər ɪz ðə sɪstər əv ən ʌðə lɪtəl gɜl kɔld ɛmə || ɛmər ənd klɛə laɪk tə gəʊ ʃɒpɪŋ fə ðɛə mʌm sɛərə || wʌn deɪ | sɛərər ɑsk ðəm tə gəʊ ənd baɪ səm frut frəm ðə griŋgrəʊsə || klɛər ənd ɛmə gɒt tə ðə stɔr | ənd hæd ə dɪfɪkəlt dɪsɪʒən tə meɪk || sɛərər ɔlweɪz geɪv ðəm ə ʃɒpɪŋ lɪs |bʌt ðeɪd lɒst ɪt ɒn ðə weɪ || ðeɪ kʊdnt rɪmɛmbər ɪf ðeɪ wə səpəʊs tə baɪ pɛəz | ɔr æpəlz | ɔr ɒrɪndʒɪz || ɪn ði ɛn | ðeɪ dɪsaɪdɪd tə gəʊ bæk həʊm tu ɑsk ðɛə mʌm | hu təʊl ðəm nɒt tə wʌri | əz ðeɪd ɔl gəʊ əgɛn ðə nɛks deɪ ||/

There are eight examples of potential linking /r/: 'Far away', 'here is', 'Clare is', 'sister of', 'Clare and', 'store and', 'remember if', 'or apples' and 'or oranges'.

There are three examples of potential intrusive /r/: 'Emma and', 'Sarah asked' and 'Sarah always'.

Points that might have caused confusion are 'to ask' and 'go again', but in each case the first vowel is high, so liaison will not take place.

Rhotic speakers would not produce any linking /r/s. They would produce /r/s in the same place as non-rhotic speakers produce linking /r/s; however, the /r/s would not be inserted as a form of connected speech, since they would also occur in the isolated version of the words.

There are also examples of potential elision in 'called Clare', 'asked them', 'list but', 'supposed to', 'end they', 'told them' and 'next day'.

3 Please see the website (www.cambridge.org/knight) for sentences submitted by readers.

Unit 17

1

plant pot	/plɑmp pɒt/
mint condition	/mɪŋk kəndɪʃən/
lead balloon	/lɛb bəlun/
flat pancake	/flæp pæŋkeɪk/
food miles	/fub maɪlz/
quiz show	/kwɪʒ ʃəʊ/
dress shop	/drɛʃ ʃɒp/

2 /ðæk gɑdəm mʌʃ ʃɔli nib plɛnti əv wɜk || ju hæf tə kip ðə grɑʃ ʃɔp | peɪmp fɛnsəʒ | ʃʌvəl sæmb | plɑmp bʌlbz | wib bɔdəz | əm wɔtər ɔl ðəʊʒ ʃuts || dəʊntʃu gɛp bɔb baɪ ɔl ðæp wɜk | əm faɪndʒu wɒmp mɔr aʊəz tu əpriʃieɪtʃɔr ɛfəts || ɪf ɪp wər ʌp tə mi | aɪb pʌt daʊŋ glʌvz ən speɪb | faɪm maɪsɛlf ə kwaɪək kɔnər | ən dʒʌs rɪlæks/

Note that if a CSP occurs across a phrase boundary (as in 'corner and'), it strongly implies that there is no pause.

3 Please see the website (www.cambridge.org/knight) for answers submitted by readers.

Unit 18

1

							h	əʊ	b	ə	n									
									ɑ											
									k											
									ɪ											
					h	æ	t	ə	ŋ	k	r	ɒ	S							
n					aɪ															
j					b	ɒ	n	s	t	r	i	t		b						
u					p									ʌ	p	n	i			v
k			g		ɑ	s	n	ə	l		p			r						ɒ
r			r		k		i		ʌ		ʌ	p	t	ə	m	p	ɑ	k		k
ɒ			i		k		z		n		t				ʌ					s
s	t	æ	m	m	ɔ		d		d		n				d					ɔ
			p		n		ə		ə		i				ʃ	æ	b	w	ɛ	l
			ɑ		ə		n		m						u					
b	æ	ŋ	k						b						t	ɛ	m	p	ə	l
əʊ					r	ɛ	b	b	r	ɪ	dʒ									æ
r									ɪ											m
əʊ	v	ə	l					ɛ	dʒ	w	ɛə	r	əʊ	d						b
d																				ə
													h	æ	m	ə	s	m	ɪ	θ

2 /**mɪstə** ˈbɛnɪp wəz ˈsəʊ ˈ**ɒd** ə ˈ**mɪkstʃə** əv ˈ**kwɪk** ˈpɑts | sɑˈ**kæstɪk** ˈ**hjumə** | rɪˈzɜv | əŋ kəˈpris | ðət **ði** ɛkˈspɪərɪəns **əv** ˈ**θri** ən ˈ**twɛnti** ˈjɪəz| həb bin ɪnsəˈ**fɪʃənt** tə meɪk hɪzˈwaɪf ʌndəˈstænd hɪz ˈ**kærɪktə** || ˈhɜ **maɪnd** wəz **lɛs** ˈdɪfikʌlt tə dəˈ**vɛləp** || ʃi wəz əˈ**wʊmən** əv ˈmin ʌndəˈ**stændɪŋ** | ˈ**lɪtəl** ɪnfəˈmeɪʃən | ənd ʌnˈ**sɜtən** ˈtɛmpə ||ˈ wɛn ʃi wəzdɪskənˈ**tɛntɪd** | ʃi ˈ**fænsɪd** həsɛlf ˈnɜvəs || ðə ˈ**bɪznəs** əv hə ˈlaɪf wəz tə ˈgɛt hə ˈdɔtəzˈ**mærɪd** | ɪts ˈ**sɒlɪs** wəz ˈ**vɪzətɪŋ** ən ˈ**njuz**/

3 /ˈwʌn əv ˈʃɜlɒk həʊmz ˈdifɛks | ˈɪf | ɪnˈdib | wʌm meɪ ˈkɔl ɪt ə ˈdifɛk | wəz ðət hi wəz ɛkˈsidɪŋli ˈləʊθ tə kəˈmjunɪkeɪt hɪz ˈfʊl ˈplænz tu ˈɛni ˈʌðə ˈpɜsən | ʌnˈtɪl ði ˈɪnstənt əv ðɛə fʊlˈfilmənt || ˈpɑtli ɪk ˈkeɪm | nəʊ ˈdaʊt | frəm hɪz əʊm ˈmɑstəfəl ˈneɪtʃə | wɪtʃˈ lʌvd tə ˈdɒmineɪt ən səˈpraɪz ðəʊz hu wər əˈraʊnd hɪm || ˈpɑtli ˈɔlsəʊ frəm hɪz prəˈfɛʃənəl ˈkɔʃən | wɪtʃ ˈɜdʒd hɪm ˈnɛvə tə ˈtɛɪk ɛni ˈtʃɑnsɪz || ðə rɪˈzʌlt | haʊˈɛvə |wəz ˈvɛri ˈtraɪɪŋ fə ˈðəʊz hu wɜr ˈæktɪŋ əz hɪz ˈeɪdʒənts ənd əˈsɪstənts || ˈaɪ hədˈɒftən ˈsʌfəd ʌndər ɪt | bʌt nɛvə ˈmɔ səʊ ðən ˈdʒɔrɪŋ ðæt ˈlɒŋ ˈdraɪv ɪn ðə ˈdɑknəs ||ðə ˈgreɪt ɔˈdɪəl wəz ɪm ˈfrʌnt əv əs || ət ˈlɑs wi wər əˈbaʊt tə ˈmeɪk aʊə ˈfaɪnəl ˈɛfət |əndʒɛt ˈhəʊmz həd sɛd ˈnʌθɪŋ| ən aɪ kʊd ˈəʊnli səˈmaɪz wɒt hɪz ˈkɔs əv ˈækʃəm wʊbˈbi || maɪ nɜvz ˈθrɪld wɪð æntɪsɪˈpeɪʃən wɛn | ət ˈlɑs | ðə ˈkəʊl ˈwɪnd əpɒn aʊə ˈfeɪsɪz| ən ðə ˈdɑk ˈvɔɪd ˈspeɪsɪz ɒn iðə ˈsɑɪd əv ðə ˈnærəʊ ˈrəʊd | ˈtəʊlb mi ðəp wi wə ˈbæk əˈpɒn ðə ˈmɔ wʌns əˈgɛn | ɛvri ˈstraɪd əv ðə ˈhɔsɪz | ənd ɛvri ˈtɜn əv ðə ˈwil | wəz ˈteɪkɪŋ əs ˈnɪərə tu aʊə suˈprim ədˈvɛntʃə/

Unit 19

1 **a)** True.

b) True.

c) False. An intonation phrase must have a nucleus, but all the other constituents can occur in any combination.

d) True.

e) True.

f) False. Falling tones are followed by low and level tails.

g) False. The nucleus is the last accented syllable in an intonation phrase.

2 There is a fall-rise nucleus on '-way' and no tail. There is a falling head from 'hope' to 'a-', with stress on 'wat-' and 'plants' . There is a low pre-head on 'I'.

3

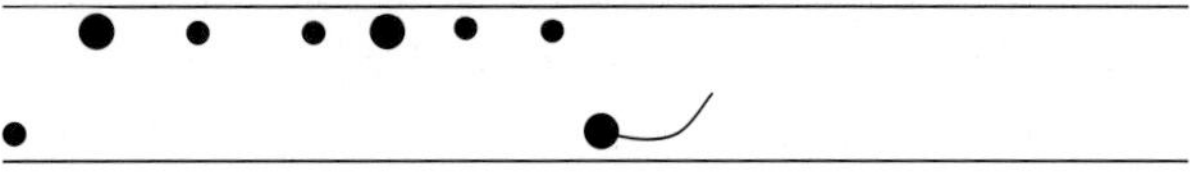

She can't seem to pass her ex-am

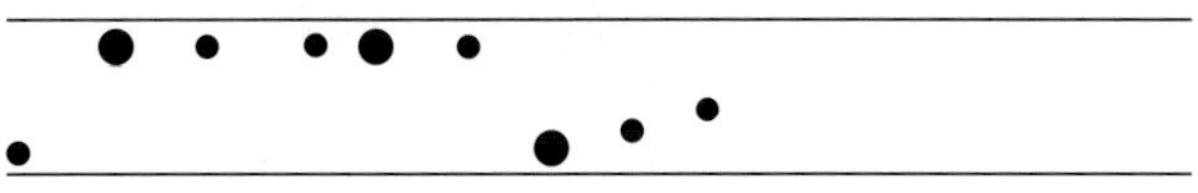

She can't seem to pass her driv-ing test

Unit 20

1 We can split the phrase up into *intonation phrases* in a number of ways.

a I can't | talk to her | when she's on a night out||

b I can't talk to her || when she's on a night out||

In both of these examples, intonation phrases may alternate between two speakers, as in a conversation, or all be said by a single speaker.

c I can't talk to her when she's on a night out||

In this third example, the phrase is spoken by one person as a single intonation phrase.

If spoken by a single speaker in a single intonation phrase, the *nucleus* may occur in various positions.

a I can't talk to her when she's on a night out.

This is perhaps the default nucleus position, assuming the night out has not been mentioned before, and the speaker does not wish to emphasise any other points.

b I can't talk to her when she's on a night out.

Here the speaker may wish to draw a contrast with other activities, such as dancing or drinking, or be deaccenting 'on a night out', as it is given information.

c I can't talk to her when she's on a night out.

Here the speaker may be able to talk to other people, but not to 'her'.

The *nuclear tone* can also vary, of course, and create different meanings. Here I keep the default position of the nucleus and vary only the tone

a I can't talk to her when she's on a night ˊout.

This may be a question about whether or not this is an appropriate action to take, or the speaker may be about to continue and say something else.

b I can't talk to her when she's on a night ˋout.

This may be an emphatic statement that this is not possible.

c I can't talk to her when she's on a night ˇout.

This may be implying that the speaker feels there is another time to talk to her that would be more appropriate, so might be followed by something like, 'but I could catch her tomorrow morning before work'.

2 Firstly, we tend to use boundaries to break up telephone numbers into easily remembered sections. So, using the main phone number for my university as an example, I would do the following:

020 | 7040 | 5060 ||

This practice also has the effect of grouping together the different parts of the number, which, here, are the area code, the number shared by all parts of the university, and then the extension. Notice that each falls into a separate intonation phrase.

Interestingly, some people group the '7' in London numbers with the area code, producing 0207 | 040 |. However, grouping the 7 (in speech or writing) with the 020 area code can cause a problem, because the area code can be omitted if you are dialling from within the same area. So, grouping the 7 with the area code may lead the listener to believe, erroneously, that it is unnecessary if dialling from within London. This is an illustration of how intonation can affect meaning in a practical way.

In intonation phrases for most phone numbers, the nucleus probably goes on the final digit of each phrase (using the default pattern).

020 | 7040 | 5060||

However, for this phone number, I often say 7040 in the middle phrase instead, to mark out the contrast between '70' at the beginning of the second phrase, and '40' at the end, and because the repetition of '0' causes it to be deaccented.

The first two nuclei are usually some sort of rise, to indicate continuation, while the final one is a fall, to indicate finality.

02ˊ0 | 70ˊ40 | 50ˋ60

3 In (1) and (2), 'key' is the nucleus, with a high fall nuclear tone. It is not deaccented the second time, as Rachel is repeating verbatim something she claims Monica said earlier, where the intonation was especially important for meaning and thus needs to be repeated exactly. In (3) and (4), the characters play with the idea that the same words can be a statement or a question, depending on the nuclear tone. In (3) Monica uses an exaggerated high rising tone, with matching hand gestures, and in (4), Rachel responds with another high fall, also showing the intonation pattern with gesture. In (5), Chandler moves the nucleus to 'have', because the word 'keys' has been repeated so many times, and he now wishes to focus the attention on whether anyone actually has a set with them. He could have put the nucleus on 'either', but it would not have sounded natural on 'keys'. He uses a rising tone, with an exaggerated rising tail, partly imitating Monica's tone in (3). In (6), Joey shifts the nucleus to 'we' and uses a fall-rise nuclear tone, with 'key' part of a rising tail. Here the nucleus is on 'we', reflecting the fact that neither of the *women* (you) has the key. He could also have put the nucleus on 'copy', but, again, it would not have sounded natural on 'key'. The fall-rise tone may leave something unsaid, perhaps that he can go and get it.

RESOURCES

The following materials can be used to extend your study of phonetics. I have included both paper-based and online resources, with a brief summary.

Books

Abercrombie, D. (1967) *Elements of General Phonetics*, Edinburgh University Press.
A classic introduction to general phonetics, which has formed the inspiration for much of the material in this book.

Ashby, P. (2005) *Speech Sounds*, London: Routledge.
Lots of exercises for practice and a very friendly and accessible style.

Ashby, M. and Maidment, J. (2005) *Introducing Phonetic Science*, Cambridge University Press.
Very clear explanations and diagrams, and successfully links acoustic and articulatory aspects of phonetics.

Catford, J. C. (2001) *A Practical Introduction to Phonetics*. Oxford University Press.
An excellent resource for learning to produce the sounds of the world's languages, as well as a good general introduction to phonetics.

Collins, B. and Mees, M. (2003) *Practical Phonetics and Phonology: A Resource Book for Students* (Routledge English Language Introductions), London: Routledge.
Lots of practical exercises, including those from an audio CD. Covers accents and pronunciation change, as well as basic concepts in phonetics and phonology.

Cruttenden, A. (1997) *Intonation*, Cambridge University Press.
Covers form and function of intonation, including the system presented in this book and alternatives.

Cruttenden, A. (2008) *Gimson's Pronunciation of English*, 7th edn, London: Hodder Arnold.
This book deals with much that has been covered in this text, including intonation. The newer editions also include acoustic information.

Garcia Lecumberri, M. L. and Maidment, J. A. (2000) *English Transcription Course*, London: Arnold.
Includes lots of practice exercises, concentrating particularly on broad transcription. It also includes short and clear explanations of connected speech processes.

International Phonetic Association (1999) *Handbook of the International Phonetic Association: A Guide to the Use of the International Phonetic Alphabet*, Cambridge University Press.
The definitive guide to the IPA, including illustrations for lots of languages, examples from which have been used throughout this text.

Ladefoged, P. (2001) *A Course in Phonetics*, 4th edn, Belmont, CA: Thomas Learning.
Generally considered to be the best general phonetics textbook for beginners, it is most comprehensive and covers articulatory and acoustic phonetics, as well as providing many practice exercises.

Lodge, K. (2009) *A Critical Introduction to Phonetics*, London: Continuum.
Covers acoustics, articulatory phonetics and varieties of English, while encouraging the reader to think critically and go beyond introductory concepts. This is a perfect text for when you are ready to deal with some of the more advanced topics in phonetics.

Trask, R. L. (1996). *A Dictionary of Phonetics and Phonology*, London: Routledge.
Covers just about every term you will need when studying phonetics and phonology, often with references for further information, and always with a transcription letting you know how to pronounce the term.

Trudgill, P., Hughes, A. and Watt, D. (2005) *English Accents and Dialects: An Introduction to Social and Regional Varieties of English in the British Isles*, London: Hodder.
Covers variation across many different varieties of British English, going well beyond what we have covered in this text.

Wells, J. (1982) *Accents of English*, 3 vols., Cambridge University Press.
The most comprehensive study of English accents worldwide, and responsible for the lexical set words that we used throughout this book.

Wells, J. (2008) *Longman Pronunciation Dictionary*, Harlow: Longman.
An indispensible reference for checking transcriptions of individual words, and can therefore be used for daily transcription practice of individual words. Also covers definitions of phonetic terms, and information about pronunciation change.

Online

Clickable IPA charts

Charts which let you hear the sounds of the IPA, including ultrasound images showing the tongue positions for English consonants:

www.cetl.org.uk/learning/phonetic/index.html

www.yorku.ca/earmstro/ipa

www.cog.jhu.edu/courses/325-F2004/ladefoged/course/chapter1/chapter1.html

http://web.uvic.ca/ling/resources/ipa/charts/IPAlab/IPAlab.htm

http://jbdowse.com/ipa

Phonetics blogs

For keeping up your interest in phonetics on a daily basis:

http://blogjam.name (John Maidment)

http://phonetic-blog.blogspot.com (John Wells)

www.yek.me.uk/Blog.html (Jack Windsor Lewis)

http://languagelog.ldc.upenn.edu (Language Log, with many linguists contributing)

Other online resources

The original cardinal vowel recordings by Daniel Jones:
www.let.uu.nl/~audiufon/data/e_cardinal_vowels.html

A number of excellent tutorials from UCL, including practice for transcription, symbols and intonation:
www.phon.ucl.ac.uk/resource/tutorials.html

An online dictionary of phonetics terminology by John Maidment and colleagues:
www.phon.ucl.ac.uk/home/johnm/sid/sidhome.htm

APPENDIX 1 IPA CHART

Courtesy of International Phonetic Association
(Department of Theoretical and Applied Linguistics, School of English, Aristotle University of Thessaloniki, Thessaloniki 54124, GREECE).

THE INTERNATIONAL PHONETIC ALPHABET (revised to 2005)

CONSONANTS (PULMONIC)

	Bilabial	Labiodental	Dental	Alveolar	Postalveolar	Retroflex	Palatal	Velar	Uvular	Pharyngeal	Glottal
Plosive	p b			t d		ʈ ɖ	c ɟ	k ɡ	q ɢ		ʔ
Nasal	m	ɱ		n		ɳ	ɲ	ŋ	ɴ		
Trill	ʙ			r					ʀ		
Tap or Flap		ⱱ		ɾ		ɽ					
Fricative	ɸ β	f v	θ ð	s z	ʃ ʒ	ʂ ʐ	ç ʝ	x ɣ	χ ʁ	ħ ʕ	h ɦ
Lateral fricative				ɬ ɮ							
Approximant		ʋ		ɹ		ɻ	j	ɰ			
Lateral approximant				l		ɭ	ʎ	ʟ			

Where symbols appear in pairs, the one to the right represents a voiced consonant. Shaded areas denote articulations judged impossible.

CONSONANTS (NON-PULMONIC)

Clicks		Voiced implosives		Ejectives	
ʘ	Bilabial	ɓ	Bilabial	ʼ	Examples:
ǀ	Dental	ɗ	Dental/alveolar	pʼ	Bilabial
ǃ	(Post)alveolar	ʄ	Palatal	tʼ	Dental/alveolar
ǂ	Palatoalveolar	ɠ	Velar	kʼ	Velar
ǁ	Alveolar lateral	ʛ	Uvular	sʼ	Alveolar fricative

VOWELS

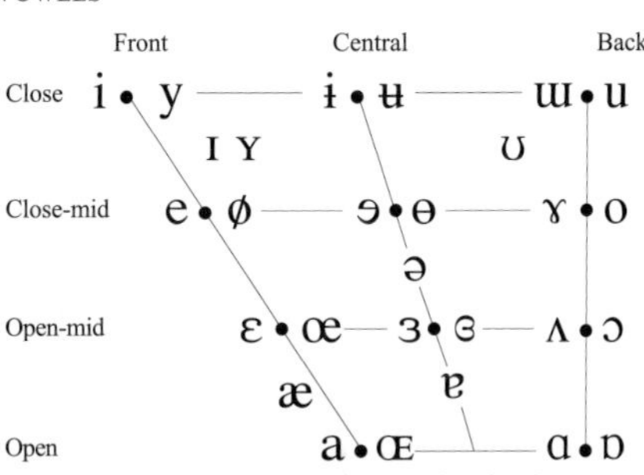

Where symbols appear in pairs, the one to the right represents a rounded vowel.

OTHER SYMBOLS

ʍ Voiceless labial-velar fricative
w Voiced labial-velar approximant
ɥ Voiced labial-palatal approximant
ʜ Voiceless epiglottal fricative
ʢ Voiced epiglottal fricative
ʡ Epiglottal plosive
ɕ ʑ Alveolo-palatal fricatives
ɺ Voiced alveolar lateral flap
ɧ Simultaneous ʃ and x

Affricates and double articulations can be represented by two symbols joined by a tie bar if necessary. k͡p t͜s

SUPRASEGMENTALS

ˈ Primary stress
ˌ Secondary stress ˌfoʊnəˈtɪʃən
ː Long eː
ˑ Half-long eˑ
◌̆ Extra-short ĕ
| Minor (foot) group
‖ Major (intonation) group
. Syllable break ɹi.ækt
‿ Linking (absence of a break)

DIACRITICS Diacritics may be placed above a symbol with a descender, e.g. ŋ̊

◌̥	Voiceless	n̥ d̥	◌̤	Breathy voiced	b̤ a̤	◌̪	Dental	t̪ d̪
◌̬	Voiced	s̬ t̬	◌̰	Creaky voiced	b̰ a̰	◌̺	Apical	t̺ d̺
ʰ	Aspirated	tʰ dʰ	◌̼	Linguolabial	t̼ d̼	◌̻	Laminal	t̻ d̻
◌̹	More rounded	ɔ̹	ʷ	Labialized	tʷ dʷ	◌̃	Nasalized	ẽ
◌̜	Less rounded	ɔ̜	ʲ	Palatalized	tʲ dʲ	ⁿ	Nasal release	dⁿ
◌̟	Advanced	u̟	ˠ	Velarized	tˠ dˠ	ˡ	Lateral release	dˡ
◌̠	Retracted	e̠	ˤ	Pharyngealized	tˤ dˤ	◌̚	No audible release	d̚
◌̈	Centralized	ë	◌̴	Velarized or pharyngealized	ɫ			
◌̽	Mid-centralized	e̽	◌̝	Raised	e̝		(ɹ̝ = voiced alveolar fricative)	
◌̩	Syllabic	n̩	◌̞	Lowered	e̞		(β̞ = voiced bilabial approximant)	
◌̯	Non-syllabic	e̯	◌̘	Advanced Tongue Root	e̘			
˞	Rhoticity	ɚ a˞	◌̙	Retracted Tongue Root	e̙			

TONES AND WORD ACCENTS

LEVEL			CONTOUR		
e̋ or	˥	Extra high	ě or	˩˥	Rising
é	˦	High	ê	˥˩	Falling
ē	˧	Mid	e᷄	˦˥	High rising
è	˨	Low	e᷅	˩˨	Low rising
ȅ	˩	Extra low	e᷈	˧˦˧	Rising-falling
ꜜ		Downstep	↗		Global rise
ꜛ		Upstep	↘		Global fall

APPENDIX 2
LIST OF VPM LABELS FOR SSBE CONSONANTS

/p/ as in pig	Voiceless	Bilabial	Plosive
/b/ as in bent	Voiced	Bilabial	Plosive
/t/ as in tank	Voiceless	Alveolar	Plosive
/d/ as in dale	Voiced	Alveolar	Plosive
/k/ as in kind	Voiceless	Velar	Plosive
/g/ as in grind	Voiced	Velar	Plosive
/f/ as in fun	Voiceless	Labiodental	Fricative
/v/ as in vole	Voiced	Labiodental	Fricative
/θ/ as in theory	Voiceless	Dental	Fricative
/ð/ as in they	Voiced	Dental	Fricative
/s/ as in soon	Voiceless	Alveolar	Fricative
/z/ as in Zen	Voiced	Alveolar	Fricative
/ʃ/ as in ship	Voiceless	Postalveolar	Fricative
/ʒ/ as in pleasure	Voiced	Postalveolar	Fricative
/tʃ/ as in cherub	Voiceless	Postalveolar	Affricate
/dʒ/ as in June	Voiced	Postalveolar	Affricate
/m/ as in mail	Voiced	Bilabial	Nasal
/n/ as in nail	Voiced	Alveolar	Nasal
/ŋ/ as in sang	Voiced	Velar	Nasal
/l/ as in lull	Voiced	Alveolar	Lateral approximant
/r/ as in red	Voiced	Postalveolar	Approximant
/j/ as in yogurt	Voiced	Palatal	Approximant
/w/ as in went	Voiced	Labial-velar	Approximant
[ʋ]	Voiced	Labiodental	Approximant
[ʔ]	Voiceless	Glottal	Plosive

APPENDIX 3
LIST OF DIACRITICS FOR ALLOPHONIC TRANSCRIPTION OF SSBE

Voice

Devoicing of obstruents	[̊]	next to silence or voiceless sounds	g̊əʊld̥
Devoicing of approximants	[̊]	in a cluster after /ptk/ at the start of a stressed syllable	kl̥eɪ
Aspiration of /ptk/	[ʰ]	in the onset of a stressed syllable	tʰæŋk
Unaspiration of /ptk/	[⁼]	following /s/ in the onset of a stressed syllable	st⁼ænd
Voicing of /h/	[ɦ]	in between vowels	bɪɦeɪv

Place (primary)

Retraction of velars	[̠]	before back vowels	g̠us
Advancement of velars	[̟]	before front vowels	g̟is
Retraction of alveolars	[̠]	before postalveolars	t̠ɹæm
Dental realisations of alveolars	[̪]	before dentals	tɛn̪θ
Labiodental realisations of bilabials	[̪]	before labiodentals	lip̪fɹɒg

Place (secondary)

Velarisation	[ˠ]	for /l/ in coda or syllabic position, and any consonant preceding the /l/	bitˠlˠ
Labialisation of consonants	[ʷ]	before rounded vowels and /w/	tʷul
Palatalisation of non-velar consonants	[ʲ]	before front vowels and /j/	pʲjupə

Manner

Nasalisation of approximants	[˜]	up to two segments before and one segment after a nasal (as long as no obstruent intervenes)	pl̃ænəz
Nasal approach/ release of plosives	[^{n}]	before (release) or after (approach) a homorganic nasal	bʌt^{n}n æn^{n}t
Lateral approach/ release of /t/ and /d/	[^{l}]	before (release) or after (approach) /l/	wɪt^{l}l wɪl^{l}t
Ejective release of v-plosives	[’]	optionally before a pause	kwɪk’
Narrow release of plosives	[$^{s\ z\ θ\ ð}$] etc.	before a homorganic fricative	bɛt^{s}s
Inaudible release of plosives	[˺]	1. optionally before a pause 2. before a heterorganic plosive 3. before a heterorganic fricative	kwɪk˺ kwɪk˺ taɪm kwɪk˺ stɛp
Unreleased plosives	[˚]	before a homorganic plosive (optional unless the same POA has resulted from assimilation)	gʊd˚deɪ

Vowels

Nasalisation of vowels	[˜]	up to two segments before and one segment after a nasal (as long as no obstruent intervenes)	plæ̃nə̃z
Pre-fortis clipping of vowels	[˘]	before a voiceless obstruent in the same syllable	pəlɪ̆s

FLASH CARDS TO COPY AND COMPLETE

The following pages give flash cards for the SSBE consonants and vowels.

It is recommended that you photocopy them onto card, and then complete the backs of the cards with the following information.

Consonants

Example word/s:
Voice
Place
Manner

Vowels

Example word/s
Monophthong – height, frontness, rounding
Diphthong – closing, centring

p	b
t	d
k	g

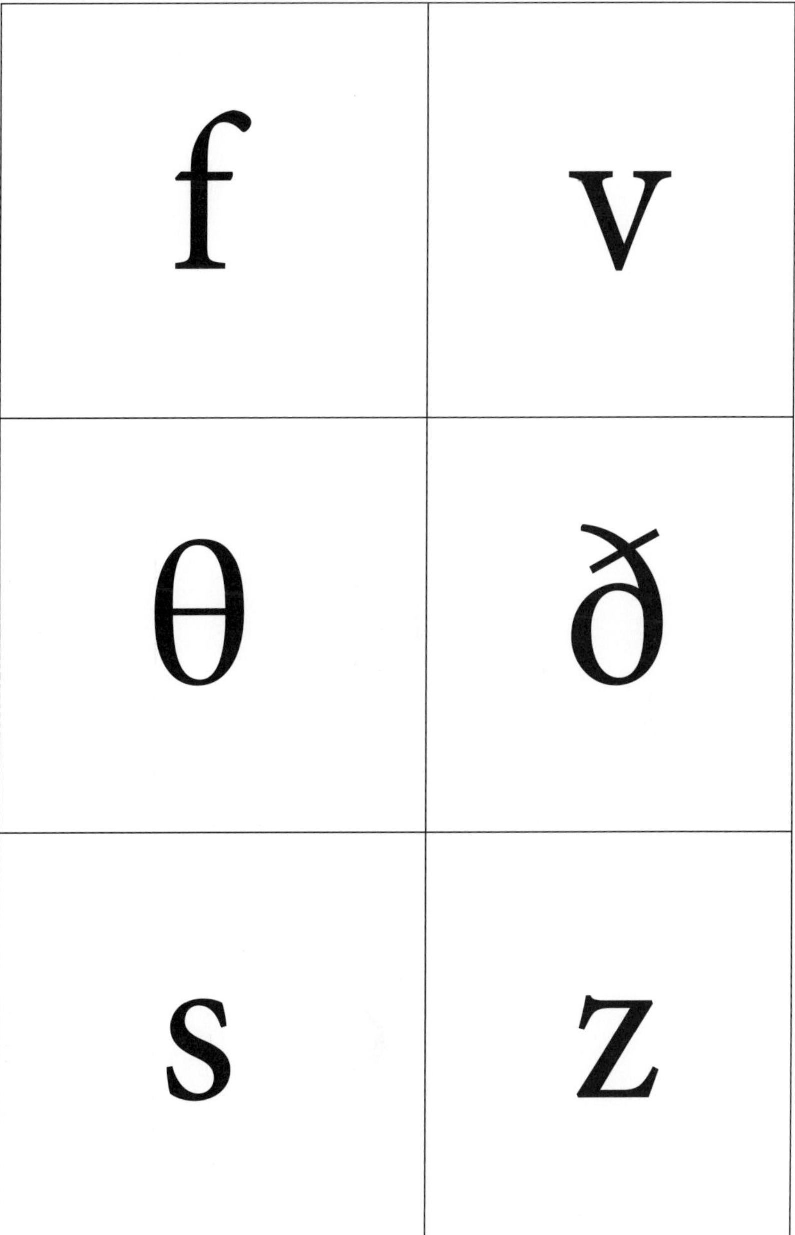
f
v
θ
ð
s
z

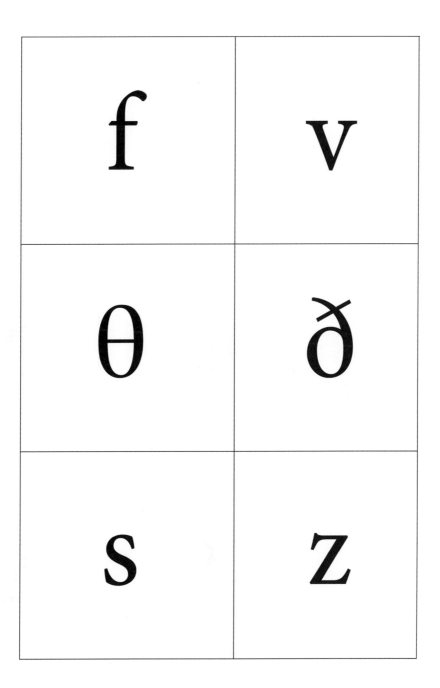

ʃ	ʒ
tʃ	dʒ
m	n

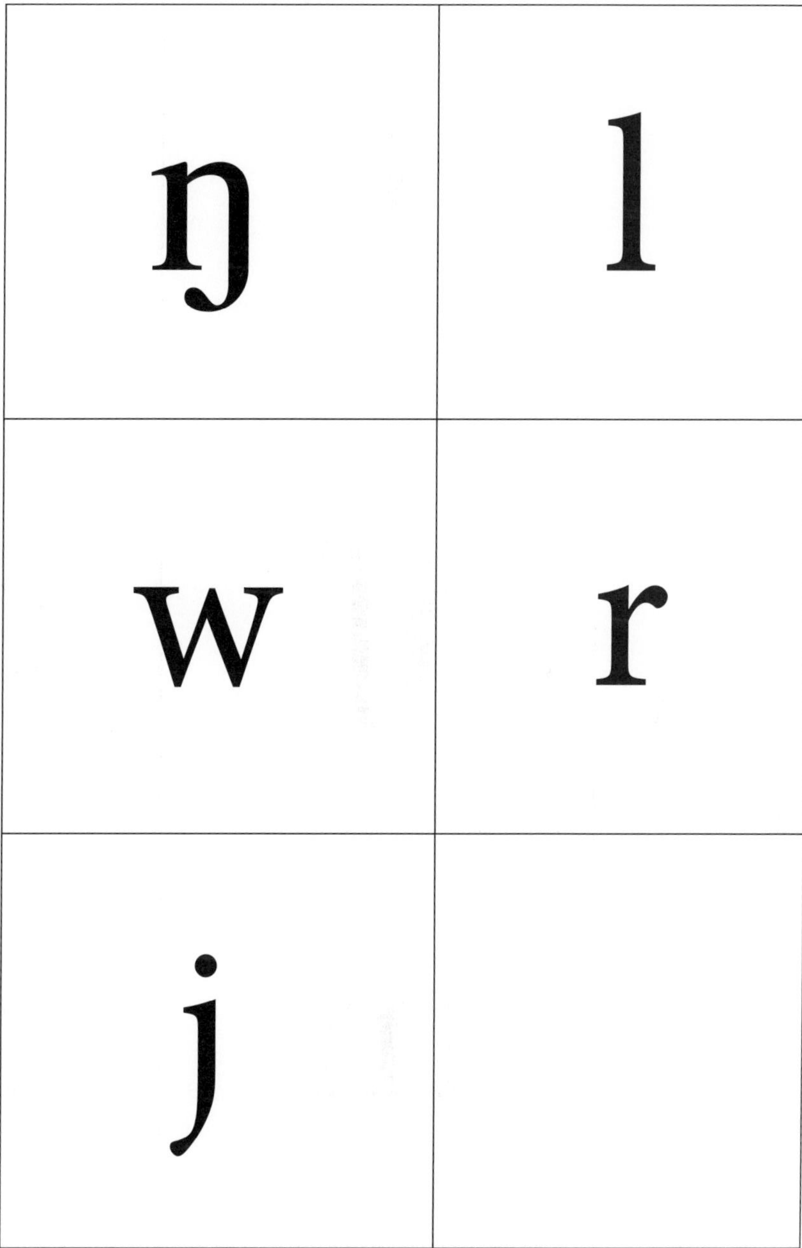
ŋ
l
w
r
j

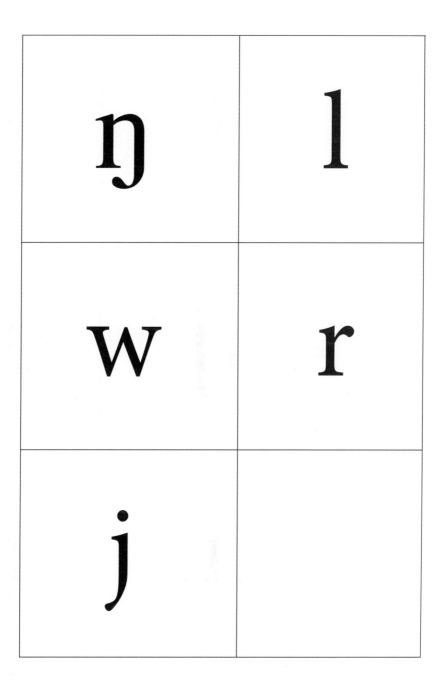

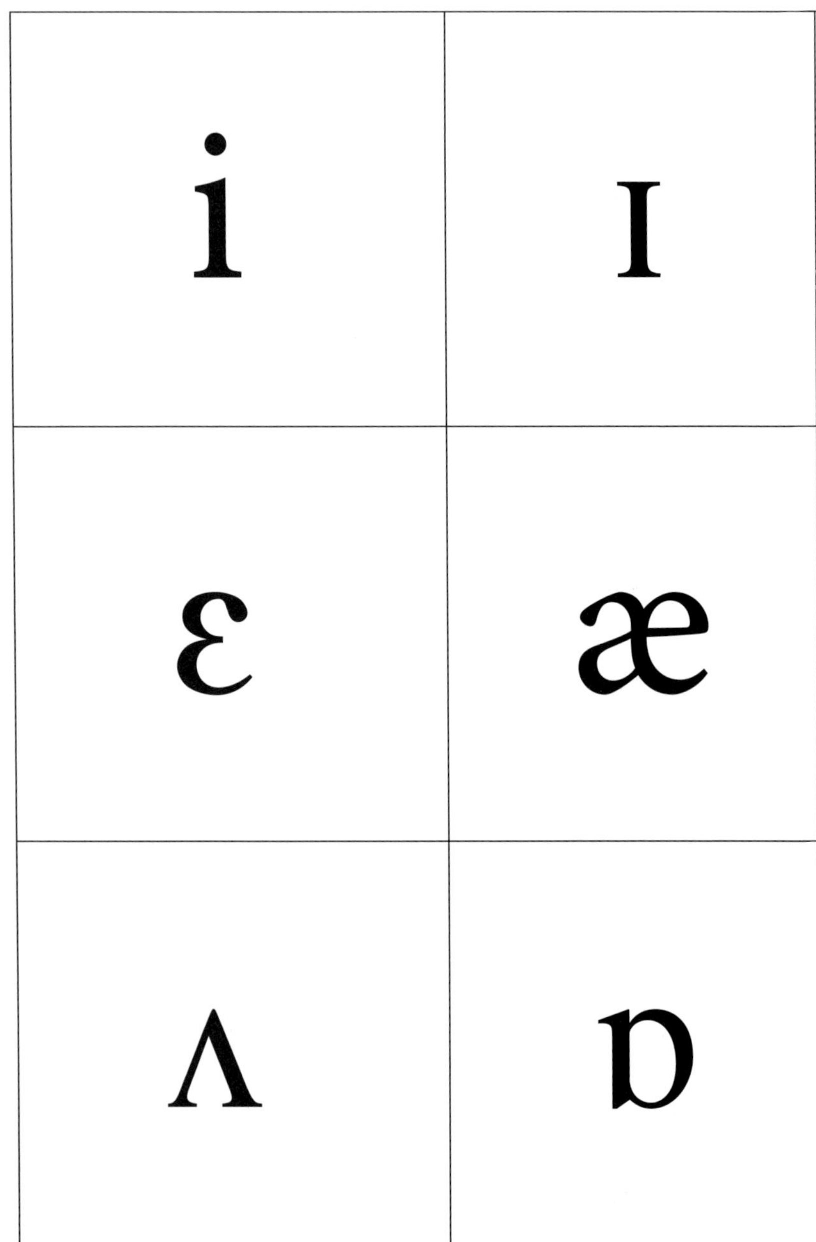
i
ɪ
ɛ
æ
ʌ
ɒ

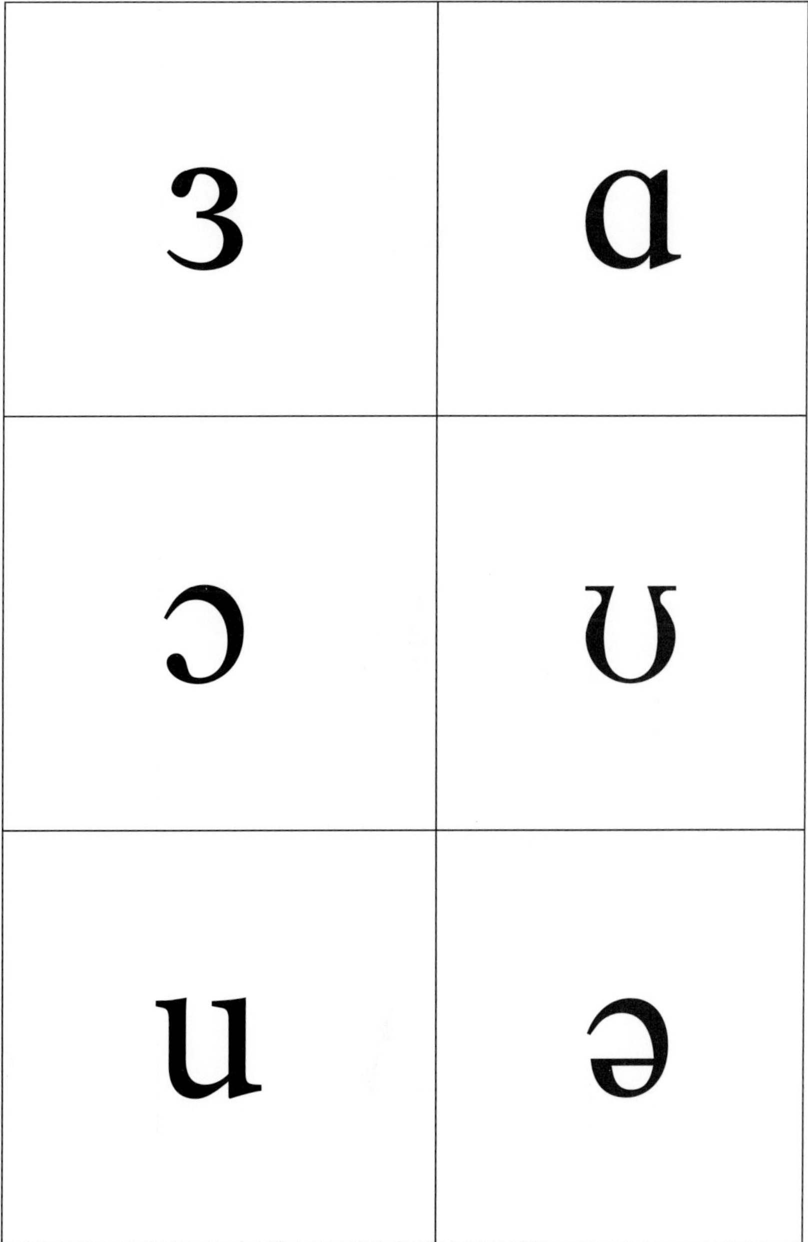
ɜ
ɑ
ɔ
ʊ
u
ə

eɪ	aʊ
əʊ	ʊə
ɛə	aɪ

ɔɪ	ɪə
	ʊ
ɹ	ʔ

INDEX

Page numbers in bold type indicate places in the text where definitions of terms are given.